homemade in a hurry

homemade in a hurry

MORE THAN 300 SHORTCUT RECIPES FOR DELICIOUS HOME-COOKED MEALS

BY ANDREW SCHLOSS

CHRONICLE BOOKS

SAN FRANCISCO

Library of Congress Cataloging-in-Publication Data available.

ISBN-10: 0-8118-4899-X
ISBN-13: 978-0-8118-4899-2

Manufactured in Canada

Designed by NOON
Typesetting by NOON
Illustrations by NOON
Photo styling by Sandra Cook
Photo assistance by Sara Johnson Loehmann

Distributed in Canada by
RAINCOAST BOOKS
9050 Shaughnessy Street
Vancouver, British Columbia V6P 6E5

10 9 8 7 6 5 4 3 2 1

CHRONICLE BOOKS LLC
85 Second Street
San Francisco, California 94105

www.chroniclebooks.com

acknowledgments

Birthing a book is usually a complex labor, but this one has come to life with such joy and ease I can only attribute it to the skill and professionalism of all who helped to nurse it along. Lisa Ekus, Bill LeBlond, Amy Treadwell, Marilyn Anthony, Tara Mataraza Desmond, Aya Akazawa, Yolanda Accinelli, Doug Ogan, and my family and friends who consumed with equal grace and helpful criticism both the triumphs and disasters that emerged from my kitchen as these pages were conceived.

table of contents

introduction

the changing face of homemade

When was the last time you made soup from scratch, or salad dressing, or cake? There's no need to apologize; "homemade" has changed. Today, the everyday home cook needs a few shortcuts, and I'm not just talking about sauces made from condensed soup and packets of dried onion dip. They've been usurped by jars of bruschetta, pesto, and tapenade. They've been elevated by demi-glace concentrate and fig balsamic glaze, and internationalized with cans of coconut milk, Thai peanut paste, and curry cooking sauce.

This new crop of prepared ingredients is not just a way to get food on the table; rather, they provide an opportunity for home cooks to rediscover the joy of cooking.

Let the naysayers decry the demise of homemade food. I say the future of home cooking is bright, for though we have less and less time to cook, we have more and more options. The tedious has become fun, the complicated has been demystified, and what used to take hours to prepare is now ready in minutes.

In these pages you will find more than three hundred inventive recipes that will jump-start the way you cook. With the help of carefully selected flavor-packed products combined with fresh ingredients, you will learn to create the kind of food you never would have thought you could make at home. Smoked Salmon Carpaccio (page 46), Dulce de Leche Banana Pie (page 304), and Pork Chops with Chipotle Cherry Demi-Glace (page 112) become effortless when you take advantage of the revolution that has transformed the food market into your own personal prep kitchen.

This phenomenon is not confined to individual ingredients—it's a new way to cook that streamlines the way we prepare everything, from soup to dessert. Our opportunities continue to expand. Salsas are being sweetened with fruit, and jams are being spiked with spices and herbs. Canned tomatoes and broths are

preseasoned to make Mexican, Mediterranean, or Asian cuisines more accessible. There are whole-grain baking mixes, whole-wheat couscous, and quick-cooking brown rice.

We have seen the birth of all-natural and organic prepared sauces, condiments, and marinades. Major food manufacturers are marketing organic salsa, ketchup, and juice. There are organic brownie mixes, spice blends, and condensed soups. The phenomenon is twofold, illustrating on one hand how organics have tipped into the mainstream, but also showing us that cooking shortcuts are being embraced by all segments of the population. Even all-natural devotees, who at one time saw themselves as definitive from-scratch cooks, are now taking advantage of products that meet their standards for purity and also simplify the way they cook.

Home cooking is constantly evolving toward ease and speed. A century ago the availability of commercially cleaned chickens made the need for home cooks to pluck and gut their own poultry obsolete. Now the notion of cutting a chicken into pieces or skinning and boning a breast seems hopelessly old-fashioned. Twenty years ago the 60-minute meal was promoted as fast; since then the notion of speed has devolved from 30 minutes to 20 to 15 to instantaneous.

In the modern world there are countless ways to get dinner on the table, and just a few of them involve cooking, which means that the only reason to cook is if you want to. It is my hope that once you start cooking with shortcut recipes, the number of times you choose to cook will multiply. And the more you taste the exciting results and experience how little effort they take, the more cooking at home will become an everyday pleasure that you won't want to miss.

what's your hurry?

We cook in a world where speed is confused with ease, but for each of us what is easy to cook changes depending on the occasion, who we're cooking for, and what else is going on in our lives. Sometimes having dinner on the table in the next 20 minutes is the only thing that matters, while on another day having something that can sit in the oven for a few hours without losing quality is just what is needed.

When I say "Homemade in a Hurry" I am not just speaking about time alone, but how you can prepare high-quality, spectacular-tasting food as efficiently as possible. To that end I never ask you to chop, or roll, or simmer an ingredient that you can purchase prepared, providing that what you buy is of similar or better quality than what you would cook yourself. I have made sure that when I ask you to do something elaborate, like create a special pastry, or idiosyncratic, like bake a cheesecake overnight, the results are worth your effort and time.

In all of the recipes contained in these pages, I have taken care that the combination of fresh and prepared ingredients always gives you meals that taste as though they were made from scratch by you in your kitchen, even though some of the heavy lifting has been accomplished elsewhere by food manufacturers.

This couldn't be accomplished without a thorough understanding of the trove of high-quality prepared ingredients inhabiting your grocers' shelves.

the ingredients

Most of the new generation of products falls into one of two broad groups:

- Bulk ingredients that have been processed to be easier to use (bags of washed and cut lettuce leaves, precooked meats, sliced mushrooms, and already mashed potatoes)

- Exotic or complex preparations that have been made more readily available (curry sauce, pesto, bruschetta, jerk, and satay sauce)

With regard to the first group, you probably already purchase the same ingredient in a less prepared state (whole unwashed heads of lettuce, fresh meat, and unpeeled whole potatoes), and you might notice that the processed products seem much more expensive. For example, a 3-ounce package of ready-to-serve precooked bacon costs the same as a whole pound of raw bacon. But once you realize that bacon shrinks to 20 percent of its original weight during cooking, the two products end up having nearly identical use costs, and the ready-to-serve product doesn't require cooking, which saves you time, mess, and the nuisance of getting splattered with grease.

The second group of ingredients is a different matter. Not only is buying a jar of peanut sauce cheaper than buying the ingredients you would need to make it, but you are unlikely to ever prepare peanut sauce, or tapenade, or curry sauce, or demi-glace outside of a specific recipe. When you have an arsenal of fully prepared sauces and condiments in your pantry, the next time you grill a chicken breast, instead of topping it with salt and pepper, you can reach for that jar of basil pesto, or stir-fry sauce, or tomato bruschetta. Just having these ingredients on hand will revolutionize the way you cook.

organic and all-natural ingredients

The fastest-growing segment in packaged food is products labeled "organic" or "all-natural." From precut produce to canned goods, frozen dinners, processed meats, and flavored dairy products, there is hardly a product in the supermarket that does not have an organic or all-natural counterpart sidling up to it on the shelf.

One of the most surprising aspects of this growth is the emergence of large manufacturers in the organic market. Although organic food pioneers may cringe at the notion of multinationals infiltrating their market-place, there is a potential benefit that is yet to be realized. As companies like General Mills and Frito-Lay begin to market more organic products, their potential need for organic ingredients will quickly outstrip current production, which means that more farmland will have to be devoted to organic crops, with the eventual result that organic products will become more the norm than the exception.

Until then, you may have to look a little harder for organic and all-natural renditions of the products in this book. Two that I strongly suggest you seek out are lemon and lime juice and chopped garlic. Most nonorganic versions of these products have an unpleasant aftertaste that makes them unsuitable substitutes for their fresh counter-parts. Fortunately, there are high-quality organic alternatives. They may not be exactly the same as fresh, but they are much better than what was previously available. I have found Santa Cruz natural lemon and lime juices and Christopher Ranch garlic products to be very close to fresh. Once opened, they will retain their quality for about a month in the refrigerator. If you'll be storing them longer, I suggest freezing them in ice cube trays.

setting up a pantry

Before you can start cooking any cuisine, you must first set up a pantry. Although in the pages that follow I have used a vast array of packaged ingredients, there is a core group of items that are helpful to have on hand. With them in your pantry, you will be able to prepare many recipes in this book by adding one or two fresh ingredients, like a chicken breast or some chopped vegetables. To help you build your pantry reasonably, I have divided the list into two parts—a basic all-purpose pantry and helpful additions.

BASICS

- Marinated artichoke hearts
- Tomato bruschetta
- Canned beans, white and/or black
- Shredded Cheddar cheese
- Chicken broth
- Coconut milk
- Chopped or minced garlic
- Minced ginger
- Organic lemon and/or lime juice
- Marinara sauce
- Spicy brown mustard
- No-stick spray oil (regular and/or olive)
- Extra-virgin olive oil
- Olive salad or muffaletta
- Grated imported Parmesan cheese
- Selection of dried pasta
- Basil pesto
- Roasted red peppers

- Quick-cooking brown rice
- Vinaigrette salad dressing and/or Caesar dressing
- Chunky salsa (any heat level)
- Curry sauce
- Soy sauce
- Hot pepper sauce
- Sun-dried tomato pesto or puree
- Tapenade (black olive puree)
- Teriyaki sauce or stir-fry sauce
- Canned diced tomato
- Canned fire-roasted tomatoes
- Tomato paste in a tube
- Balsamic vinegar
- Cider vinegar
- Red or white wine vinegar
- V8 vegetable juice
- Red wine and/or white wine

HELPFUL ADDITIONS

- Refrigerated guacamole
- Applesauce
- No-stick baking spray with flour, such as Baker's Joy
- Barbecue sauce or steak sauce
- Instant bean powder, such as black bean or powdered hummus
- Bean dip
- Bouillon cubes, fish and/or vegetable
- Capers
- Cornbread baking mix
- Couscous (preferably whole wheat)
- Chinese chili paste with garlic
- Mango chutney, or other fruit chutney
- Garlic and herb cream cheese
- Curry paste, red and/or green
- Fruit preserves
- Hoisin sauce

- Honey
- Horseradish
- Pickled ginger for sushi
- Mole paste (such as La Costeña or Goya brands)
- Dried wild mushrooms, such as porcini or shiitake
- Asian toasted sesame oil
- Instant potato flakes
- Peanut butter
- Creamy salad dressing
- Alternative salsas (such as fruit, pepper, verde, and/or corn and black bean)
- Demi-glace sauce concentrate (such as Aromont or More Than Gourmet brands)
- Frozen shelled and cleaned shrimp
- Wasabi in a tube

using the recipes

Throughout these pages you will find boxes and sidebars that explain how the various packaged ingredients called for in the recipes are manufactured. I have done this because it is my belief that once you understand that canned pears are the same thing as poached pears, and that a jar of salsa is nothing more than a mixture of tomatoes, onions, and peppers, you will be freed to use those products in ways that their manufacturers never envisioned. You will see that if you are making a curry that contains tomatoes, onions, and peppers, salsa gives you a head start, for there is nothing innately Mexican about the ingredients in a jar of salsa other than the context in which we place them. By seeing packaged foods for what they are, rather than what manufacturers tell us to do with them, we give ourselves the opportunity to make more elaborate, exciting dishes in less time and with less effort.

In general, I avoid the mention of specific brands. Each recipe in this book was tested with several brands of the specified ingredients, and though I almost always found some differences in flavor and consistency between brands, most of the time the disparity was not great. Usually all of the results were acceptable, and brand preferences were more a matter of taste than quality. In the cases where brand did make a difference, either positively or negatively, I have made a suggestion of a brand that worked well.

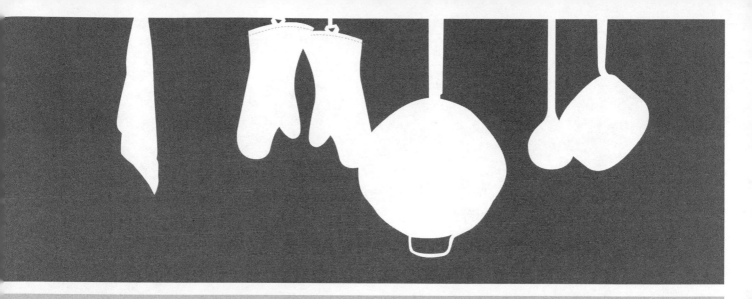

If you do find, when you are making one of the recipes, that a sauce is too thick or the flavor isn't spiced to your liking, feel free to make adjustments. It could be that you are using a brand that was unavailable to me, or that your preferences differ from mine. In either case, common sense is your best guide, but to help you out I offer the following tips:

- **Baking mixes**—Baking mixes, whether they are an all-purpose blend, like Bisquick or Jiffy brands, or designed to produce a particular kind of cake, muffin, cookie, or brownie, all contain the same basic elements: flour, flavoring, leavening, and fat. The ratio of these elements varies widely, but the main thing that differentiates one from another is what the consumer adds, such as the number of eggs, the amount of oil, and the amount of liquid.

Whenever a recipe in this book calls for a baking mix, it has been tested with all of the major brands—Duncan Hines, Betty Crocker, Pillsbury, Krusteaz—and with as many smaller organic and all-natural brands as were available in my area supermarkets. Their package directions frequently call for slightly different amounts of added ingredients, and therefore the recipes reflect a compromise that has been tested and works as far as our testing went.

If you have a brand that calls for a radically different amount of liquid (more than ¼ cup up or down), or oil (more than 2 tablespoons up or down), or eggs (more than 1 egg up or down), start with the lesser amount and see what the batter looks like. If it is overly thick or dry, add more of the ingredient in question until it is the texture described in the recipe. Note that this advice applies only if the mix is being used as the manufacturer intended. For instance, if you are making biscotti from a brownie mix, the amount of eggs, liquid, and oil in the recipe will have no connection to the amount recommended on the box for making brownies.

- **Canned beans**—The quality of canned beans varies greatly by brand. If you live on the East Coast, Goya is a high-quality brand, and nationally Bush's are far superior to other standard brands. Whole Foods markets beautiful cooked beans in jars under their 365 brand, although the pack size is larger than for canned beans, so you will have some left over if you use them in a recipe that gives amounts in cans.

- **Coconut milk**—Light coconut milk has been skimmed of most of its fat and coconut solids. It has a very different texture and flavor than regular coconut milk, and I don't recommend that you substitute one for the other.

- **Curry cooking sauce** (also called curry simmer sauce, masala sauce, or curry sauce)—These Indian convenience foods simplify complex curry recipes down to browning a few ingredients and adding the sauce. There are several brands; the two that you will find most frequently are Patak and Raj, but there is also Curry King, and Trader Joe's has several curry cooking sauces. Because there are many curries in

Indian cooking, you will find curry sauces that are interchangeable for shortcut recipes sold under several different names, such as tikka masala (an aromatic golden curry flavored with coriander and lemon), korma (rich with coconut, garlic, coriander, and ginger), Madras (spicy with cumin and chiles), and vindaloo (very spicy, made with tomatoes and lots of chiles). Don't confuse curry cooking sauce, which is fully prepared, with curry paste, which needs to be diluted to become a sauce. If you can't find curry sauce, you can make it by diluting a few spoonfuls of curry paste according to the directions on the jar or can.

• **Broths, stocks, and concentrates**— These products are all interchangeable. Although there is a distinct difference in classic terms between a stock and a broth, when it comes to manufactured products they are the same — they are all broth. Stock is made mostly from bones; broth is made mostly from meat, which means that broth has more flavor than stock, although stock has a rich, gelatinous consistency. Some companies call their product "stock" because they feel it lends a professional restaurant aura, but this has no bearing on the quality of the product.

Broth and stock concentrates vary greatly in quality and price. The best (and most expensive) are sold as paste or frozen. These products are made from stock that has been concentrated to about one sixteenth of its original volume (1 tablespoon of the concentrate makes 1 cup of stock). On the other end of the quality spectrum are bouillon powders, which tend to be salty and artificial tasting. Between these extremes are bouillon cubes, of which some are better than others. Knorr makes a fairly high-quality cube.

- **Minced garlic and ginger**—Although I shy away from recommending specific brands, I have to recommend that you use Christopher Ranch minced garlic and ginger products. They simply taste better than any other brand I have experienced.

- **Pumpkin**—Libby's canned pumpkin puree gives better results with less work than cooking pumpkin from scratch. This is partially because the canning process helps to break down tough fibers and concentrates the flavors of pumpkin more completely than simmering would, but it's also because Libby's pumpkin is made from a special variety of pumpkin that is unavailable to you and me. I'm not sure why the other brands, regardless of price, can't compare.

- **Quick-cooking brown rice**—For anyone in a hurry who is at all interested in cooking with whole grains, quick-cooking or instant brown rice is essential. It trims cooking time from 45 minutes to 5 or 10 minutes, depending on the brand. Unlike instant white rice, the results are quite good—not as chewy or aromatic as long-cooking brown rice but very acceptable, considering the time difference. For testing the recipes in this book I used a product that cooked in 5 minutes. If you have the 10-minute variety, you should follow the cooking directions for that product.

An alternative to quick-cooking products is fully cooked brown rice in a vacuum-sealed bag. These products are generally heated in a microwave and also take about 5 minutes to prepare. I found that they had a slightly better flavor than the quick-cooking rice, but a mushy texture. They are also much more expensive.

- **Salsa**—Standard tomato-based salsas differ in heat level, the size of the vegetable pieces, and the thickness of the sauce. In most recipes, heat is not the main attraction. Mild or medium heat levels are the most versatile, for you can always add hot sauce to taste. But if you like your food incendiary, and all you ever buy is hot salsa, feel free to use it. More important than heat level is thickness. The consistency of a salsa depends on the amount of tomato solids used in its production. Look at the label; if tomato puree (or paste) is the first ingredient, the salsa will tend to be thick; if it's crushed tomatoes the liquid will be medium-thick; and if tomatoes or water is the first or second ingredient, it indicates a thin salsa. I usually use salsas in the middle range. If you are preparing a recipe that has a large amount of salsa in it, and the finished product seems thick, add a little water. If it is too thin, add a bit of tomato paste or puree to the recipe.

- **Tomato pasta sauce**—There are two styles of tomato pasta sauce: ragù, which is made with meat and is long simmered until the meat breaks down and integrates into the sauce, and marinara, which is a fresh vegetable sauce that cooks briefly just until the tomato is soft. In general, ragùs are thick and marinaras are light, although there are many jarred meatless pasta sauces that have been loaded with tomato paste until they resemble thick ragùs. These are designed to cling to pasta, but they are too thick to cook with, which is why I recommend that you look for a jarred marinara sauce that is thin enough to move freely in the jar. Even though these may appear thin when you pour them into a pan, they will thicken as they cook. If all you have is a thick marinara, thin it with water or broth before you start cooking with it.

1 hors d'oeuvres, snacks & other small plates

I would much rather snack than eat. Not for a love of junk food or a penchant for eating on the run, but simply for the taste of it. Snacks are all sensation. They're too tiny to be nutritional, they're too casual to be taken too seriously, and their portions are so flexible that the only reason for ever getting jaded or overstuffed is one's own gluttony.

This chapter includes recipes for appetizers (tiny portions of palate-titillating foods to fuel the imagination without filling you up), hors d'oeuvres (tidbits to eat with drinks), snacks (anything you eat that's not a meal), and small plates (little sandwiches, breakfast bars, quesadillas, and other teeny tiny foods that don't fit neatly into another chapter).

- 1 can (about 15 ounces) navy beans, drained and rinsed
- 2 teaspoons chopped garlic, fresh or jarred organic
- 1 teaspoon hot pepper sauce
- 3 tablespoons avocado oil
- 1 tablespoon extra-virgin olive oil
- ¼ cup lime juice, fresh or bottled organic
- 1 teaspoon kosher salt

white guacamole

This culinary hybrid has all of the sensuality of a creamy guacamole with the nutritional pedigree of bean dip. The secret is avocado oil. Avocados are rich in monounsaturated fat, which makes avocado oil creamier than olive oil but not higher in calories or saturated fat. It is sold in the specialty oil section of your supermarket, usually beside the extra-virgin olive oils.

DIRECTIONS

Puree everything in a food processor until smooth. Serve as a dip with raw vegetables, cooked shrimp, chips, or crackers.

- 1 can (about 6 ounces) tuna in olive oil
- ⅓ cup baba ghanouj, purchased or homemade (page 348)
- 1 tablespoon lemon juice, fresh or bottled organic
- 1 teaspoon chopped garlic, fresh or jarred organic
- ½ teaspoon salt
- ¼ teaspoon ground black pepper
  Pinch crushed red pepper flakes
- 1 tablespoon finely chopped Italian (flat-leaf) parsley

tuna ghanouj

Tuna fish doesn't have to mean mayonnaise. There are many more flavorful mixtures that can turn a can of tuna into a spread with no more effort and a lot less fat. In this recipe the tuna is dressed with baba ghanouj, a classic Arab vegetable dip redolent with roasted eggplant, garlic, and lemon, which will transform your tuna salad from Ameri-bland to internationally intriguing.

DIRECTIONS

Break the tuna into large flakes in a medium bowl. Add the remaining ingredients and mix to combine. Use as a dip, a bruschetta topping, or a sandwich spread.

MAKES 6 SERVINGS,
1½ CUPS

1   can (about 10 ounces)
    enchilada sauce

6–8 large blue corn tortilla chips,
    crumbled

1   cup drained and rinsed canned
    black beans

1   clove garlic

6–8 sprigs cilantro

1   tablespoon olive oil

warm refried black and blue bean dip

Canned refried beans are a pale imitation of the real thing. Sure, they contain all of the ingredients you would use if you were making refried beans from scratch, but because they're steamed in the can rather than sautéed, they tend to taste bland and starchy. This recipe remedies all of that. Barely more difficult than warming a can of beans, the resulting dip is redolent with chiles, garlic, tomatoes, and tortillas. And because it uses olive oil instead of lard, it is very low in saturated fat.

DIRECTIONS

Combine the enchilada sauce and tortilla chips in a skillet and simmer over medium-high heat until the chips are soft, 2 to 3 minutes.

Combine the enchilada sauce mixture, black beans, garlic, and cilantro in the work bowl of a food processor and process until the ingredients form a coarse puree; scrape the sides of the work bowl as needed.

Wipe out the skillet and add the oil; heat until sizzling. Add the bean mixture and stir to combine with the oil. Cook until the beans are lightly thickened. Serve with vegetables, strips of chicken, and/or warm tortillas.

honey hot pepper pecans

MAKES 4 SERVINGS

7   ounces (about 2 cups)
     pecan halves

¼   cup honey

1   teaspoon ground cinnamon

1   teaspoon kosher salt

1   tablespoon hot pepper sauce

I know you already have a recipe for candied nuts. Throw it away! Replace it with this simple formula for slightly sticky, lip-stinging, caramelized morsels. Be sure to cook the honey until it is richly browned and clinging to the pecans; otherwise the glaze will not set as it cools.

DIRECTIONS

Place a large, nonstick skillet over high heat for 1 minute. Add the pecans and reduce the heat to medium. Stir until the nuts toast lightly, about 4 minutes. Add the honey and keep stirring until the honey browns and the nuts are shiny, 2 to 3 minutes. Turn off the heat; add the cinnamon, salt, and hot sauce and toss quickly to coat.

Immediately scrape onto a sheet pan and spread into a single layer. Wait for about 5 minutes, until the nuts are just cool enough to touch, and break them into individual pieces. Cool completely and store in an airtight container. Serve as an hors d'oeuvre or a snack.

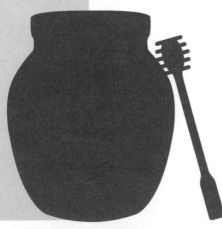

1½ pounds onions, cut into chunks

1 tablespoon olive oil

2 tablespoons fig preserves,
such as Adriatic Fig Spread

¼ teaspoon kosher salt

roasted onion and fig jam

Onions are full of sugar, and it just takes a little heat to quell their natural pungency and bring the sweetness out. This blend of oven-caramelized onions and a small amount of fig preserves is equally delicious served with cheese, plopped atop a grilled chicken breast, or used to garnish a roast. If you can't find fig preserves at your local food store, you can substitute a mixture of 1 tablespoon honey blended with two finely chopped dried figs.

DIRECTIONS

Heat the oven to 450°F. Toss the onions and oil in a roasting pan until the onions are thoroughly coated. Roast until the onions are caramelized, about 30 minutes, tossing them halfway through. Scrape up any brown bits clinging to the bottom of the pan.

Chop the onions in a food processor, using the steel blade until they become cohesive and sticky but not smooth. Mix with the fig preserves and salt. Serve with cheese or roasted strips of chicken, or as a condiment with grilled or roasted meats.

WHAT MAKES AN ONION SWEET?

Raw onion contains more natural sugars than the same weight of strawberries, and the best onions to use for roasting are those with the most sugar. Onions sold as "sweet onions," contrary to their name, have less sugar than ordinary yellow onions. Vidalia onions, a common brand of sweet onion, have 5.8 grams of sugar for ½ cup diced, and ordinary yellow onions have 7.5 grams of sugar for ½ cup diced. Their "sweet" name refers to their lack of pungency, which makes them easier to eat raw but also makes them bland when cooked. So when picking onions for roasting, walk right by the ones hyped as "sweet." You will get much fuller-tasting results (and probably save a little money) from a bag of humble yellow onions.

1½ cups (about 8 ounces) frozen shelled edamame, thawed

2 cloves garlic, peeled and halved

⅓ cup avocado oil or olive oil

2 tablespoons fresh lemon juice

1 teaspoon salt

½ teaspoon hot pepper sauce

⅓ cup water

¾ cup unsweetened shredded coconut

1 bag (about 6 ounces) sweet potato (or other vegetable) chips

1 can (about 15 ounces) Cuban black beans or refried black beans

1 jar (about 8 ounces) mango salsa

edamole

Moles (pronounced MOE-laze) are elaborate Mexican sauces, ranging from mole poblano, a complex stew of turkey, ground chiles, nuts, dried fruit, and chocolate, to the simplicity of a guacamole. This concoction is a takeoff on the latter. Replacing avocado with edamame (green soybeans) increases the protein and reduces the fat, while leaving the vibrant green of the original unaltered.

DIRECTIONS

Puree everything in a food processor until smooth. Serve as a dip with raw vegetables, cooked shrimp, chips, or crackers.

tropical nachos

These Caribbean-inspired nachos have little to do with their Mexican brethren: the chips are sweet potato, the salsa is mango, the beans are Cuban, and shredded coconut takes the place of shredded cheese.

DIRECTIONS

Spread the coconut in a single layer in a microwave-safe pie plate and microwave at full power for 3 minutes; it will have spots of brown. Toss and continue to microwave in 1-minute intervals, tossing as needed until uniformly toasted.

Spread half the chips on a microwave-safe serving plate. Place small spoonfuls of two-thirds of the beans and half of the salsa over the chips. Scatter half of the coconut over the top. Mound the remaining chips in the center. Top with small spoonfuls of the remaining beans and salsa. Cook in a microwave at full power until heated through, 2 to 3 minutes. Sprinkle the remaining coconut over the top. Serve immediately.

1   sheet (half a package) frozen
    puff pastry, such as Pepperidge
    Farm, thawed

⅓   cup muffaletta olive mixture,
    jarred or homemade (page 339)

olive empanadas

Preparing these minuscule firecrackers of flavor wouldn't be worth
the trouble if it were not for two high-quality readily available
packaged ingredients–frozen puff pastry and jarred muffaletta.
Not only are these two products easy to use, but their quality is
equal to or better than you could make from scratch.

DIRECTIONS

Heat the oven to 400°F.

Place the puff pastry sheet on a clean cutting board and push
gently until it forms a square. Cut into a 4-by-4 grid, forming 16
even squares. Place a teaspoon of the muffaletta in the center of
each square, and brush the edges with a thin film of cold water.
Fold each square in half diagonally, forming a triangle. Press the
edges together to seal, and make a small slit in the top of each
pastry. Place on a baking sheet, leaving as much space between
the empanadas as possible. Bake until golden brown and puffed,
about 15 minutes. Cool for 10 minutes before serving.

1   large fennel bulb, trimmed of
    stems and leaves

1   large apple

3   tablespoons rosemary-flavored oil

6   ounces (about 1¼ cups)
    crumbled Gorgonzola cheese

1   tablespoon garlic-flavored oil

⅓   cup milk, any type

3   tablespoons sour cream

    Ground black pepper to taste

fennel and apples with rosemary gorgonzola dip

Instead of crudités, try lightly grilled, broiled, or roasted produce surrounding a dip. In this recipe I've used slices of fennel and apple with a Gorgonzola dip enriched with rosemary and garlic oils.

DIRECTIONS

Heat a broiler and set the rack at a medium distance from the heat. Slice the fennel; it will fall into crescents. Remove the core and stem from the apple and slice into thin wedges. Toss the fennel and apple with 1 tablespoon of the rosemary oil and arrange in a single layer on a broiler pan. Broil until brown on both sides but still crisp, about 3 minutes per side.

Meanwhile mash the Gorgonzola with the back of a fork in a small bowl and mix in the remaining 2 tablespoons rosemary oil, garlic oil, milk, sour cream, and black pepper. Serve the broiled fennel and apple surrounding a small bowl of the dip.

FLAVORED OILS

All flavors besides sour, salt, sweet, and bitter (which is almost everything) are perceived through your nose, not your mouth. And in order for any aromatic ingredient, such as herbs, spices, fruits, vegetables, and flavorings (like vanilla), to be received by your olfactory receptors, they have to be suspended in oil.

All flavorful foods contain flavorful oils. Some have a lot, like olives, avocados, and nuts. These ingredients can be squeezed or pressed to extract their oils, but other ingredients, like herbs and spices, don't contain enough oil to extract through pressing. To get the fragrant, flavorful oils out of these foods, you must steep them in neutral-tasting oil until the neutral oil becomes infused with the fragrant oil of the herb or spice.

Good-quality flavored oils are made by bruising a large quantity of ingredient (usually an equal volume to the amount of oil being used) in order to break the cellular structure of the ingredient and allow the neutral oil to penetrate. Then the oil is heated to kill any bacteria and assist penetration into the tissue. As soon as the ingredients are combined, the mixture is cooled to avoid changing any delicate flavors, and then it is allowed to rest until the oil absorbs all that the ingredient has to give. This can take anywhere from an hour for very aromatic substances, like flowers, to several weeks for tough, hard spices.

1   bag (about 10 ounces) blue corn
    tortilla chips

1   can (about 15 ounces) black
    beans, drained and rinsed

2   canned chipotle peppers en adobo,
    seeded, stemmed, and chopped

6   ounces port wine Cheddar
    cheese or porter Cheddar
    cheese, shredded

1   cup salsa, any heat level

2   tablespoons chopped cilantro

nachos negros

In the fashion universe the little black dress may be a classic, but in the culinary world the little black appetizer will always be far out. Very few foods are black; squid ink and black pepper come to mind, but even foods that are billed as *black* aren't really. Black beans are dark brown and black bread is dyed. Here is a striking snack that takes its blackness with a grain of salt.

DIRECTIONS

Place half of the tortilla chips on a large, microwavable platter in an even layer. Scatter half of the beans, all of the chipotle peppers, and one third of the cheese over the top. Mound the remaining chips in the center, and top with the remaining black beans and cheese. Cook in a microwave at full power until the cheese melts, about 3 minutes. Top with the salsa and cilantro. Serve immediately.

CHILES—TOO HOT TO HANDLE

Chile peppers burn. It doesn't matter where they touch—the lips, the gullet, or the fingers—capsicum oils that are released whenever chiles are chopped or cooked are going to cause irritation on contact. On the tongue, at the right strength, capsicum titillates, but on the skin or in the eyes (if touched by chile-tainted fingers) any amount is disastrous. For that reason you should always wear gloves (disposable latex ones are perfect) when working with chiles, especially when cleaning out seeds or the internal white membranes.

2   ripe red tomatoes, cored, ends removed, and cut into 8 slices each

1   ripe yellow tomato, cored and cut into 8 slices

    Kosher salt and coarsely ground black pepper to taste

1   cup White Guacamole (page 24)

8   ounces (1 cup) refrigerated prepared avocado guacamole

2   tablespoons extra-virgin olive oil

8   large basil leaves, thinly sliced

tomato and guacamole towers

When tomatoes are perfectly ripe, the best thing to do with them is as little as possible. This garden-fresh appetizer does the next best thing by highlighting the vivid color and sweet-tart luxury of red and gold tomatoes by stacking them with contrasting layers of guacamole and white beans. The component elements can be prepared ahead, but don't let the assembled towers sit after assembly; juice from the tomatoes can cause the guacamole to become runny.

DIRECTIONS

Season the tomatoes with salt and pepper.

For each portion, layer a red tomato slice, 2 tablespoons white guacamole, a slice of yellow tomato, 2 tablespoons avocado guacamole, and another slice of red tomato in a stack on a small plate. Season with more salt and pepper, and top with some of the olive oil and a small pile of basil. Serve immediately.

1   tablespoon unsalted butter

1   tablespoon olive oil

8   ounces large mushrooms, cleaned and stems removed

Salt and ground black pepper to taste

1   package (12 ounces) Stouffer's frozen spinach soufflé

2   tablespoons grated Parmesan cheese

2   tablespoons seasoned breadcrumbs

mushrooms stuffed with spinach soufflé

This recipe is a classic–similar concoctions are in countless recipe files. But I couldn't resist. The preparation is so easy and the results are so impressive that I wanted to get it into your recipe file too.

DIRECTIONS

Heat the butter and oil in a nonstick skillet over medium heat. Add the mushroom caps, season with salt and pepper, and cook until brown on both sides and slightly soft, about 5 minutes total cooking time.

Meanwhile, remove the film from the tray of soufflé and cook in a microwave at full power for 5 minutes; stir.

Place the mushroom caps in a single layer, flat-side up, in a microwave-safe baking dish. Sprinkle with half of the cheese. Fill each mushroom cap with soufflé. Mix the breadcrumbs and remaining cheese and sprinkle on top of each soufflé-filled mushroom cap. Cook in a microwave at full power until the soufflé is puffed and set, 3 to 4 minutes. Let rest for 2 minutes before serving.

2 1/2 cups water

1   teaspoon salt

1   cup instant polenta, such as
    Bellino or Favero

7–8 ounces thinly sliced prosciutto,
    at least 14 slices

1/2 cup basil pesto, jarred or
    homemade (page 339)

2   roasted red peppers, jarred,
    frozen, or homemade (page
    337), each cut into 16 strips

2   ounces imported Parmesan
    cheese

INSTANT POLENTA

Instant polenta is made by precooking unseasoned cornmeal until it is soft, dehydrating it until it is crisp, and grinding the resulting shards into meal. All that is required to cook it at home is to rehydrate it with boiling water. Instant polenta is fairly new in the States but is frequently used in Italy. It makes polenta that is not as silken or creamy as a traditional recipe, which is simmered slowly for an hour or more, but for ease of preparation, and because you probably wouldn't make polenta at all if it wasn't for a product like this, instant polenta is a welcome pantry staple.

polenta sushi

There is something wonderfully perverse about this cross-cultural mongrel. The ingredients are purely Italian and the format is traditional Japanese, but this beautiful gem of an hors d'oeuvre owes its inception to neither culture. Rather it sprang from my demented culinary imagination; may the purists forgive me.

DIRECTIONS

Heat the water to boiling in a medium saucepan over medium-high heat. Add the salt and the polenta and stir until the mixture is smooth and thick, about 2 minutes. Cool to room temperature.

When the polenta is cool enough to handle, place 2 slices of prosciutto on a sheet of plastic wrap so that the slices overlap lengthwise by at least 1 inch, forming a rectangle measuring roughly 6 by 8 inches. Spread 1/4 cup of polenta into a 3-by-8 inch rectangle on the part of the prosciutto closest to you. Spread 1 tablespoon of pesto over the polenta, and place 4 strips of pepper along the edge of the polenta closest to you.

Using the plastic wrap for support, roll up the prosciutto and its contents, starting with the side closest to you; do not roll the plastic wrap into the roll. The finished roll should look like a big polenta cigar encased in a skin of prosciutto. Wrap it in its plastic wrap and squeeze gently to compact the roll. Repeat, forming rolls with the remaining ingredients. Do *not* refrigerate.

To serve, remove the plastic and slice each roll into 8 pieces; arrange cut-side up on a platter, as one would serve sushi. Shave the Parmesan with a vegetable peeler and serve in a little pile for topping the sushi, in the same style used for presenting pickled ginger with traditional sushi.

1 cup mashed potato flakes

½ teaspoon garlic salt

¼ teaspoon ground black pepper

1 pound sea scallops

Vegetable oil for frying

1 lemon, cut into wedges (optional)

potato-crusted scallop frisbees

Potato-crusted fish and chops are all the rage in trendy restaurants. The technique seems alien to a home kitchen until you realize that the essential ingredient has been in many pantries all along– instant mashed potato flakes. In this easy, elegant, totally surprising appetizer, potato flakes are pulverized with spices and dusted onto pounded sea scallops. The resulting discuses are quickly crisped in oil, enameling each scallop in a fried potato lacquer.

DIRECTIONS

Pulverize the potato flakes in a food processor, mini-chopper, or blender. Add the garlic salt and pepper, and process for a few seconds to blend. Place on a length of plastic wrap or wax paper, or on a plate.

Place the scallops, a few at a time, between sheets of plastic wrap and flatten with a flat-sided meat pounder, using firm but moderate force, until the scallops are about ¼ inch thick and 3 inches across. Remove the pounded scallops from the plastic and dredge in the potato-flake mixture until thoroughly coated.

Heat ¼ inch of oil in a large skillet over medium-high heat to about 375°F (until a small cube of bread browns in about 30 seconds). Fry the scallop fritters a few at a time, until golden brown on both sides, about 45 seconds per side. Transfer to paper towels to drain, and serve 3 or 4 per person with 2 lemon wedges each, if desired.

bacon, cheddar, and potato chip nachos

MAKES 4 SERVINGS

- 1 bag (about 5 ounces) Yukon Gold (or other thick-sliced) potato chips
- 3/4 cup (about 3 ounces) shredded sharp Cheddar cheese
- 3 strips ready-to-serve precooked bacon, finely chopped
- 2/3 cup chipotle salsa

"Nacho" is not just a flavor; it's a snack food blueprint—chips underneath, beans, beef, and whatever on top, and then enough cheese to hold the structure in place. This recipe follows the plan but abandons the traditional Mexican flavor palate for something far more Anglo—think Nachos Britannica.

DIRECTIONS

Pile the chips on a microwave-safe dish, and scatter the cheese and bacon over the top. Microwave at full power until the cheese is melted, about 1 minute. Spoon the salsa over the chips so that each bite will have a portion of cheese, bacon, and salsa. Serve immediately.

tangy potato nachos with onion relish

MAKES 4 SERVINGS

- 1 bag (about 5 ounces) salt and vinegar potato chips (or sour cream and chive)
- 3/4 cup (about 3 ounces) shredded sharp Cheddar cheese
- 1/4 cup jarred Vidalia sweet onion relish

The Brits down their grilled cheese accompanied by pickled onions and chips. These nachos employ the same flavors but turn everything inside out: the vinegar is in the chips, the cheese is on top, and a sweet and tangy Vidalia relish counters every bite—Blimey!

DIRECTIONS

Pile the chips on a microwave-safe dish, and scatter the cheese over the top. Microwave at full power until the cheese is melted, about 1 minute. Spoon the relish over the chips so that each bite will have a portion of cheese and relish. Serve immediately.

1 ounce (about ¼ cup) finely diced prosciutto

1 package (about 16 ounces) frozen shrimp or pork pot sticker dumplings (gyoza)

2 tablespoons fruity red wine, such as merlot or Chianti

¼ cup teriyaki sauce

¼ cup water

2 scallions, trimmed and thinly sliced

red wine teriyaki pot stickers

We tend toward bigotry when it comes to ingredients; prosciutto and Chianti are prototypically Italian, teriyaki and pot stickers are definitively Chinese. But if you think about what these foods taste like and the roles they can play in a recipe, it is not so far-fetched to throw them in a pot together. In this recipe for Chinese-style pot stickers, the prosciutto takes the place of red-cooked pork, and merlot stands in for Shaoxing. The results: mahogany-lacquered dumplings that are so full of flavor they don't require a dipping sauce.

DIRECTIONS

Cook the prosciutto in a large, nonstick skillet over medium heat until the bottom of the skillet is coated with a thin film of fat and the lean parts of the prosciutto are crisp. Remove and reserve the prosciutto.

Place the dumplings in the pan, flat-side down, and cook over medium-high heat until the bottoms are browned.

Meanwhile, combine the wine, teriyaki sauce, and water in a small bowl. Add to the skillet, shaking once to distribute the liquid evenly. Cover and steam the dumplings until they are tender and the liquid has reduced to a glaze. Add the scallions and reserved prosciutto; shake to coat the dumplings with glaze. Transfer to a platter and serve immediately.

2 tablespoons extra-virgin olive oil

1 cup chopped onion, fresh
   or frozen

1 teaspoon chopped garlic, fresh or
   jarred organic

1 can (about 14 ounces) artichoke
   hearts, drained and quartered

   Salt and ground black pepper
   to taste

1 cup tomato bruschetta, jarred
   or fresh

2 teaspoons red wine vinegar

1 tablespoon chopped Italian
   (flat-leaf) parsley

artichokes in bruschetta vinaigrette

Canned food is nothing more than steamed food, which is why artichoke hearts take so well to the can, as does anything that needs to be boiled or steamed for a long time. The one thing they lack is flavor; like most steamed ingredients they tend to be bland. Enter bruschetta, a chunky jarred tomato sauce/condiment that is redolent with olive oil, garlic, and herbs. In this recipe it is turned into a vinaigrette that infuses its flavor into seared canned artichokes. Don't overcook the artichokes. Canned ingredients are cooked already; all you need to do is add flavor.

DIRECTIONS

Heat half of the oil in a large skillet over medium-high heat. Add the onion and sauté until just tender. Add the garlic and sauté for another 30 seconds. Add the artichoke hearts, season with salt and pepper, and sauté until the artichoke hearts brown lightly, about 5 minutes.

Add the bruschetta, vinegar, and remaining olive oil; heat to simmering. Stir in the parsley, and serve warm with slices of crusty bread and a hard grating cheese, such as Asiago, if desired.

WHAT IS BRUSCHETTA?

In Italy, bruschetta (pronounced broo-SKEH-tah) is toast topped with something flavorful, such as roasted fennel, grilled eggplant, olives, or cheese. By far the most casual and ubiquitous of bruschetta is toast topped with freshly chopped tomatoes and garlic dressed with a little olive oil and herbs. About a decade ago, Italian restaurants in America started offering tomato-topped bruschetta with a vengeance, not only putting them on the menu but handing them out gratis with cocktails. Soon the topping started to appear in other parts of the menu—tossed with pasta, baked with eggplant, sautéed with prawns—and it wasn't long before the word "bruschetta" began to mean the topping rather than the toast. Which is why you can now purchase jars of chunky fresh-tasting high-quality tomato sauce labeled "bruschetta."

1   cup flour

4   tablespoons unsalted butter, cut
    into 4 to 6 pieces

4   ounces (about 1 cup)
    diced prosciutto

½   teaspoon garlic salt

½   teaspoon onion powder

50 small herb leaves: parsley, sage,
    thyme, basil, etc.

prosciutto shortbread

The fascinating thing about recipes with very few ingredients isn't their ease (they aren't always easy), it's their ability to do a lot with very little. That's why I like making shortbread. Nothing more than an amalgam of flour, fat, and flavoring, shortbread is simple and straightforward, but that doesn't mean you can't be creative with it. This recipe blows the shortbread formula wide open by substituting prosciutto for some of the butter, giving each melt-in-the-mouth morsel a Tuscan flair that goes perfectly with fresh fruit and a glass of Chianti.

DIRECTIONS

Heat the oven to 350°F.

Combine the flour, butter, prosciutto, garlic salt, and onion powder in the work bowl of a food processor and process until the prosciutto and butter have completely incorporated with the flour. The mixture will appear slightly moist and will adhere to itself when pressed into a ball.

Roll out to a ¼-inch thickness on a lightly floured surface; cut into rounds with a small (1¼-inch) biscuit cutter. Place slightly apart on a large sheet pan and place an herb leaf in the center of each shortbread. Bake until browned on the bottom, about 15 minutes. Cool on a rack. Serve immediately, or store at room temperature for up to 3 days.

2   large onions, quartered
    and sliced

1   large apple, peeled, cored, and
    cut into thin wedges

2   tablespoons olive oil

    Salt and ground black pepper
    to taste

1½ cups flour

1   stick (¼ pound) unsalted
    butter, cut into small pieces

4   ounces (about 1 cup) crumbled
    blue cheese

¼   cup cold milk

3   tablespoons grated imported
    Parmesan cheese

caramelized onion and apple tart with blue cheese pastry

As in the recipe for Prosciutto Shortbread (facing page), the traditional fat in this pie crust has been replaced by something far more flavorful–blue cheese. The results could change the way you bake. Why not goat cheese pastry, Cheddar pastry, or one flavored with Brie? In this recipe the blue cheese crust is filled with caramelized onions and apples. Take a bite; I dare you not to swoon.

DIRECTIONS

Heat the oven to 400°F. Toss the onions, apple, and all but 1 teaspoon of the oil on a large, rimmed sheet pan. Season with salt and pepper and bake for 30 minutes, until lightly browned and soft.

Meanwhile, make the pastry by combining the flour, butter, blue cheese, and a pinch of black pepper in the work bowl of a food processor. Process in pulses until the butter and cheese are uniformly cut into the flour. Add the milk and keep processing until the mixture is moist and climbs the side of the bowl. Remove from the processor and pat together into a flat disk. Roll out on a lightly floured board into a rough disk about ¼ inch thick and about 14 inches across.

Brush a sheet pan with the remaining teaspoon of oil. Place the pastry on the oiled pan and sprinkle with half of the Parmesan cheese. Mound the apple and onions in the center of the pastry and flatten into a 10-inch circle. Fold the edges over the filling; some of the filling will remain exposed. Dust with the remaining Parmesan. Bake until browned and crisp, 25 to 35 minutes. Cool for at least 15 minutes before serving. Cut into wedges before serving.

1   can (about 14 ounces) artichoke
    hearts, drained and halved

3   tablespoons extra-virgin olive oil

    Salt and ground black pepper
    to taste

1   tablespoon pine nuts

1   tablespoon fresh lemon juice

2   teaspoons chopped mint
    or parsley

roasted artichoke hearts with lemon drizzle

This simple, elegant hors d'oeuvre or appetizer can also be served as a side dish with a roast. The preparation is quick, and the cooking method is essential. Never underestimate the power of roasting—it concentrates an ingredient's flavor and, in this dish, creates contrasting textures as the edges of the artichoke hearts crisp and caramelize. Sometimes a cooking method is the most important ingredient in a recipe.

DIRECTIONS

Heat the oven to 375°F. Toss the artichoke hearts and 1 tablespoon of the olive oil in a roasting pan; season with salt and pepper and turn the artichoke halves cut-side down. Roast for 15 minutes; add the pine nuts and roast for another 5 minutes.

Meanwhile, mix the remaining 2 tablespoons olive oil and the lemon juice; season with salt and pepper. Place the roasted artichokes in a small serving bowl and drizzle with the lemon mixture; top with the chopped mint. Serve warm.

8 ounces smoked salmon

3 scallions, trimmed

1 tablespoon drained capers

1 tablespoon ponzu sauce

smoked salmon tartare

If the raw facts of tartare make you blanch, then I've got a version for you. Not only is this rendition as sophisticated as its steak progenitor, but it's easier to prepare, keeps longer, and best of all, nothing in it is raw.

DIRECTIONS

Finely chop the salmon, scallions, and capers and mix in a medium bowl with the ponzu sauce. Refrigerate for up to 24 hours. Serve with crackers or toast.

PONZU

Ponzu is a Japanese dipping sauce made from citrus juice, soy sauce, rice vinegar, and rice wine, flavored with bonito flakes (dried fish that is the flavoring in dashi, a classic Japanese soup broth) and seaweed. Although ponzu is easy to make yourself, it is increasingly available where Asian ingredients are sold. Ponzu is less pungent than soy sauce, less salty, and lighter in color. It is traditionally served with fish. If you can't find ponzu and want to make it, just combine ½ cup lemon juice, ⅓ cup rice vinegar, ½ cup tamari soy sauce, 1 tablespoon rice wine, 1 square inch kelp, and a small handful of bonito flakes; set aside for 24 hours, and then strain. Refrigerate for up to 1 year.

No-stick spray oil

1   tablespoon black olive tapenade, jarred or homemade (page 347)

2   tablespoons extra-virgin olive oil

4   sheets frozen phyllo dough, thawed and covered

¼   cup finely ground almonds (almond meal or flour)

tapenade phyllo brittle

If it were not for the fragrance of good olive oil and the lingering pungency of black olive tapenade, these diaphanous sheets would be almost like eating air. They disappear across the palate on contact, but the essence of olives remains, making them a perfect light snack with drinks (great with martinis) and cheese.

DIRECTIONS

Heat the oven to 400°F. Spray a large sheet pan with oil.

Mix the tapenade and olive oil. Place 1 sheet of phyllo on the prepared pan; brush with a thin layer of the tapenade oil. Top with another phyllo sheet and another layer of the oil, and sprinkle with half of the almonds. Bake until browned and crisp, 3 to 4 minutes. Transfer to a cooling rack with a long spatula.

While the phyllo is baking, prepare another batch with the remaining ingredients. Bake on the same sheet in the same way. Serve the whole sheets with cheese and fresh fruit; break off pieces to eat.

2   pita breads, halved

1   can (about 6 ounces) tuna in
    olive oil

2   tablespoons olive tapenade,
    jarred or homemade (page 347)

1   teaspoon lemon juice, fresh or
    bottled organic

1   tablespoon chopped Italian
    (flat-leaf) parsley

    Salt and ground black pepper
    to taste

2   tablespoons mayonnaise

2   teaspoons basil pesto, jarred
    or homemade (page 339)

2   teaspoons jarred sun-dried
    tomato pesto

12 spinach leaves, stems removed

niçoise tuna pockets

These Provençal-inspired stuffed pitas are no harder to prepare than any tuna fish sandwich, yet that is where the comparison ends. The recipe calls for tuna packed in olive oil. If you have had only tuna in water, I urge you to take the leap; the flavor upgrade is well worth the calorie jump.

DIRECTIONS

Warm the bread in a toaster oven or standard oven at 350°F.

Meanwhile, drain the tuna, reserving 1 tablespoon of the oil. Mix the tuna, reserved oil, tapenade, lemon juice, and parsley; season with salt and pepper. Mix the mayonnaise, basil pesto, and sun-dried tomato pesto in a separate bowl until well blended. Chop the spinach leaves coarsely.

Spread the interior of each pita bread with some of the mayonnaise. Fill with the chopped spinach and the tuna mixture and serve.

smoked salmon carpaccio

Juice of 1 lemon

2 tablespoons nonpareil (small) capers, drained

1 tablespoon spicy brown mustard

½ cup chopped Italian (flat-leaf) parsley

2 teaspoons garlic-flavored oil

2 tablespoons olive oil

Kosher salt and coarsely ground black pepper to taste

12 ounces thinly sliced smoked salmon

Like the Niçoise pockets in the preceding recipe, this version of carpaccio replaces raw beef with sheets of smoked salmon. Carpaccio differs from tartare only in format (slices versus chopped) and because the flavorful elements, such as capers, are blended into a sauce that is drizzled over the meat rather than mixed into it. You can mix the sauce days ahead and store it in the refrigerator.

DIRECTIONS

Mix the lemon juice, capers, mustard, parsley, garlic oil, and olive oil in a small bowl; season with salt and pepper. If you want a chunky sauce, just whisk the ingredients together. If you want a smooth sauce, puree them in a mini food processor.

To serve, arrange the slices of salmon on a platter or on individual plates. Drizzle the sauce over the top (about 1 tablespoon per serving).

- 2 ounces (about ⅓ cup) finely chopped walnuts

- 1 can (about 16 ounces) vegetarian refried black beans

- 1 cup chipotle salsa

- 1 teaspoon ground cumin

- 2 teaspoons five-spice powder

- ¼ cup finely chopped cilantro leaves, or 2 tablespoons cilantro pesto

- Salt and ground black pepper to taste

- ⅓ cup sour cream

- 1 tablespoon orange juice

- 1 scallion, trimmed and thinly sliced

chipotle black bean pâté

Beans and nuts are fairly nutritious by themselves, but put them together and the assets of one overcome the deficiencies of the other, creating a protein that is twice as potent as the two ingredients eaten separately. Complementing proteins is just one of the assets of this vegetarian pâté. Think of it as pumped-up hummus, heartier, spicier, and (for want of a better term) meatier. The spiciness can be adjusted by the heat level of the salsa you choose.

DIRECTIONS

Toast the walnuts in a microwave on a microwave-safe plate at full power for 2 to 3 minutes; set aside (see page 340).

Mix the beans, salsa, cumin, five-spice powder, and half of the cilantro in a medium bowl. Season liberally with salt and pepper. Mound on a serving plate and top with the walnuts.

Mix the sour cream, orange juice, and remaining cilantro. Top with the scallion and serve with the pâté, along with crackers or toast.

REFRIED BEANS

Frijoles refritos are Mexican soul food, and as with all entrenched forms of home cooking, variation is the rule. At their most basic, refried beans are made from boiled pinto beans that are mashed and sautéed in lard with onion, salt, and mild chiles. Some recipes add garlic or cream, or increase the heat of the chile pepper, but the crucial flavor element in refried beans comes from the fat. It has become more commonplace to increase the health benefits of refried beans by sautéing them in oil rather than lard. Labeled "vegetarian," these products are dismissed by purists, but for most people the reduced fat and calories are worth the flavor trade-off.

Commercially made refried beans are sold canned or powdered. The canned product is better known and therefore more popular, but dehydrated powdered refried beans shouldn't be overlooked. Made by cooking *refritos* from scratch and then freeze-drying the finished products, they go through less cooking than the canned products and give surprisingly fresh-tasting results, especially if you sauté them briefly after hydrating them. Use them for thickening a soup or stew.

6 ounces liver pâté, such as pâté de foie gras

24 wonton skins, thawed if frozen

1/3 cup water

1/2 cup jarred sweet and sour sauce

1 tablespoon orange juice

1/2 teaspoon ground sumac, or 1 teaspoon lemon juice

fried foie wontons

Plush pillows of pâté, encased in slender steamed wonton skins, dipped in a sweet and pungent orange sauce—so simple, so decadent.

DIRECTIONS

Place a teaspoon of liver pâté in the center of each wonton skin, and brush the edges with a thin film of water. Fold the wonton skins diagonally over the filling and press the edges to seal. Wet the two corners at either end of the folded side and bring them together; press to seal. If not cooking immediately, cover tightly and refrigerate for up to 6 hours.

Bring the 1/3 cup water to a boil in a large, nonstick skillet; add the wontons, puffy-side down, cover, and cook until the water has evaporated and the wonton skins are tender, about 5 minutes.

While the wontons are cooking, combine the sweet and sour sauce, orange juice, and sumac in a small microwave-safe bowl. Cover and microwave at full power until heated through, about 30 seconds.

Serve the steamed wontons on a platter, surrounding the dip. Provide chopsticks, small forks, or skewers for eating.

1   bag (6 ounces) micro-ready
    baby spinach

½   cup tartar sauce, preferably
    Hellmann's or Best Foods

1   tablespoon sour cream, regular
    or light

2   teaspoons chopped garlic, fresh
    or jarred organic

3   tablespoons grated imported
    Parmesan cheese

½   teaspoon salt

¼   teaspoon ground black pepper

1   pound jumbo (26–30 count)
    cooked shrimp, peeled and
    cleaned, thawed if frozen, cold

½   cup curry cooking (or simmer)
    sauce, jarred or homemade
    (page 349)

½   cup almond butter, preferably
    organic

1   teaspoon minced garlic,
    preferably fresh

½–1 teaspoon hot pepper sauce

1   tablespoon kosher salt

2   tablespoons toasted sesame
    seeds (page 340)

1   pound jumbo (26–30 count)
    cooked shrimp, peeled and
    cleaned, thawed if frozen, cold

shrimp cocktail florentine

In this shrimp 'n' dip appetizer, cocktail sauce is replaced with a warm, sour-creamy spinach dip reminiscent of bygone buffets. It has been updated by using prewashed baby spinach in a bag, which cooks in a fraction of the time of frozen spinach and gives you a fresher vegetable flavor.

DIRECTIONS

Punch several holes in the bag of spinach with a small knife. Cook in a microwave at full power until wilted, about 3 minutes. Remove the spinach from the bag; drain briefly. Puree in a food processor with the tartar sauce, sour cream, garlic, cheese, salt, and pepper. Serve in a small bowl surrounded by the shrimp.

satay shrimp cocktail with sesame salt

This easy shrimp satay explodes with flavor. Steamed shrimp are skewered and surround two competitive toppings: an almond satay sauce and a mixture of coarse salt and sesame seeds. To eat it, you dip a shrimp in the satay and sprinkle on some salt. Gustatory mayhem ensues.

DIRECTIONS

Mix the curry sauce, almond butter, garlic, and hot pepper sauce until smooth in a small bowl. Mix the salt and sesame seeds in a separate small bowl.

Skewer each shrimp with a bamboo skewer or sturdy toothpick. Serve the shrimp on a platter, surrounding the bowls of sauce and sesame salt. To eat, dip the shrimp into the sauce and sprinkle with some salt.

½ cup ketchup

2 teaspoons horseradish

1 tablespoon lemon juice, fresh or bottled organic

12 ounces cooked and peeled tiny shrimp

1 tablespoon minced cilantro

Salt and ground black pepper to taste

¼ cup mayonnaise

2 tablespoons white wine

1 box (10 ounces) Pepperidge Farm Puff Pastry Shells, baked according to package directions

shrimp cocktail tartlets

Frozen puff pastry shells make these savory pastries a snap. The pastry can be baked and kept at room temperature for up to 2 days, and the components for the filling will store equally well in the refrigerator. Assemble them while the oven preheats, and 10 minutes later you have a sophisticated shrimp cocktail. The tartlets look best made with tiny shrimp (70 or more per pound). If you have only bigger shrimp, cut them into ¼-inch pieces.

DIRECTIONS

Heat the oven to 350°F.

Mix the ketchup, horseradish, and lemon juice in a medium bowl. Stir in the shrimp and cilantro and season with salt and pepper. Mix the mayonnaise and wine together in a separate bowl.

Remove the centers from the baked pastry shells, and arrange the hollowed shells on a sheet pan. Spoon the shrimp mixture into the shells, filling them barely to the brim. Spoon 2 teaspoons of the mayonnaise-wine mixture into each shell, and shake each shell gently to help the sauce settle. Bake until the sauce has dried on the surface and the shrimp is heated through, about 10 minutes. Serve immediately.

PUFF PASTRY

Puff pastry dough is notoriously tricky to make by hand. Doing it well takes practice, and for those who don't practice, my recommendation is to purchase. You will find that frozen puff pastry sheets are of such high quality and so easy to use that only a culinary masochist would choose to make them from scratch. The most widely available brand of frozen puff pastry is Pepperidge Farms.

1   box (32 ounces) chai tea latte
    concentrate, such as Oregon Chai

1   cup half-and-half, cream, or milk

3   eggs, large or extra-large

    Pinch of salt

1   tablespoon unsalted butter

8   slices premium bread, such
    as challah

chai french toast

Chai is a sweetened tea latte infused with honey and spices. Made from scratch, it is a sweet and pungent beverage, but not strong enough to lend its flavor to a recipe. However, the ready availability of chai concentrate changes all that. A packaged beverage designed to mix with milk and serve warm or chilled, it is perfect for flavoring a sorbet, a cake, or in this case, French toast.

DIRECTIONS

Pour 2½ cups of the chai into a small saucepan and boil for about 10 minutes, until it has reduced to a syrup, about ¾ cup. Keep warm.

Mix the remaining 1½ cups chai, the half-and-half, eggs, and salt in a shallow bowl. Heat the butter in a large, nonstick skillet over medium heat. Meanwhile, dip each slice of bread in the egg mixture and moisten thoroughly. Add to the skillet and brown on both sides. You will need to dip and cook the French toast in batches; keep the cooked pieces warm in a low oven while you prepare the rest. Serve 2 slices per person, topped with some of the chai syrup.

2   tablespoons unsalted butter, melted

1/2   cup (about 4 ounces) cream cheese

3   tablespoons light brown sugar

1   egg, large or extra-large

1   teaspoon baking powder

1   teaspoon ground cinnamon

1   teaspoon vanilla extract

1 1/2   cups granola

1/2   cup pecan pieces

1/2   cup dried tart cherries, coarsely chopped

pecan cherry breakfast cookies

The addition of cream cheese helps to refine the crunchy granola persona of this wholesome breakfast pastry. Decidedly lower in fat and calories than a mega-muffin or a brace of doughnuts, these cookies are loaded with fruit and nuts, perfect for breakfast on the run. Make sure you use tart dried cherries; the sweet variety will taste flat in comparison.

DIRECTIONS

Heat the oven to 350°F. Grease a sheet pan or line with a sheet of parchment or a Silpat mat.

Mix the butter, cream cheese, and sugar until smooth in a medium bowl. Beat in the egg, baking powder, cinnamon, and vanilla. Stir in the granola, pecans, and cherries until everything is moistened. Scoop onto the prepared pan, using a standard ice cream scoop (2 ounces, 1/4 cup) and placing the cookies about 2 inches apart. Wet your hands and flatten each cookie slightly. Bake until browned and set, about 15 minutes. Cool on the pan for 5 minutes before transferring to a rack to cool all of the way. Wrap individually and store at room temperature for up to 5 days.

2 tablespoons unsalted
butter, melted

1/2 cup peanut butter, preferably
chunky

3 tablespoons brown sugar, light
or dark

1 egg, large or extra-large

1 teaspoon baking powder

1/2 teaspoon vanilla extract

1 1/2 cups granola

1/2 cup raisins

peanut butter breakfast cookies

I have never understood why granola bars are a legitimate breakfast food while a good, wholesome cookie is not. This recipe is designed to remedy the inequity. A cross between peanut butter and oatmeal cookies, the batter mixes up in minutes and the finished cookies will stay fresh at room temperature for several days. Warning: These are large cookies; one of them is a meal.

DIRECTIONS

Heat the oven to 350°F. Grease a sheet pan or line with a sheet of parchment or a Silpat mat.

Mix the butter, peanut butter, and sugar until smooth in a medium bowl. Beat in the egg, baking powder, and vanilla. Stir in the granola and raisins until everything is moistened. Scoop onto the prepared pan, using a standard ice cream scoop (2 ounces, ¼ cup) and placing the cookies about 2 inches apart. Wet your hands and flatten each cookie slightly. Bake until browned and set, about 15 minutes. Cool on the pan for 5 minutes before transferring to a rack to cool all of the way. Wrap individually and store at room temperature for up to 5 days.

No-stick flour and oil baking spray

1¼ cups (about 5 ounces) grated imported Parmesan cheese

1 can (about 15 ounces) pure pumpkin

1 teaspoon minced garlic, fresh or jarred organic

½ teaspoon salt

¼ teaspoon ground black pepper

⅛ teaspoon grated nutmeg

1 cup milk or half-and-half

3 eggs, large or extra-large

pumpkin parmesan flan

The combination of pumpkin and cheese is unusual to most Americans who are used to their pumpkin prepared with sugar and spice. But in Italy, where pumpkin is cooked more like a vegetable, pumpkin and cheese meet frequently in soups, stews, as a pasta stuffing, or as a side dish. This savory custard finds its inspiration there.

DIRECTIONS

Heat the oven to 350°F. Spray a 12-cup muffin tin with flour and oil spray; place in a roasting pan and pour enough water into the roasting pan to come at least 1 inch up the side of the muffin tin. Set ¼ cup of the Parmesan cheese aside for garnish.

Mix the remaining ingredients with a whisk until smooth. Spoon into the prepared muffin tin and bake until a tester inserted into one of the center flans comes out clean, about 30 minutes. Remove the muffin tin from the pan of water and allow the pan to cool for at least 15 minutes.

Run a knife around the edge of each flan; cover the pan with a cutting board and invert. Shake the muffin tin to ensure that all of the flans release; remove the tin. Serve the flans on individual plates, dusted with the reserved Parmesan cheese.

1   tablespoon olive oil

$1/4$ cup seasoned breadcrumbs

1   onion, diced

4   ounces prosciutto or other ham,
    finely chopped

2   packages (about 4 ounces each)
    herbed cream cheese, such
    as Boursin

1   package (8 ounces) cream
    cheese

$1/2$ cup sour cream

$1/4$ cup bottled garlic herb salad
    dressing

$1/2$ teaspoon salt

$1/2$ teaspoon ground black pepper

3   eggs, large or extra-large

ham and cheese cake

Where is it written that cheesecake has to be sweet? When you turn the tables on flavor, all kinds of savory possibilities unfold, and a food that was once confined to dessert gets a new life. This appetizer cheesecake can be served as an hors d'oeuvre with toast, or as an appetizer with fruit. Think of it as a cheese ball for the new millennium.

DIRECTIONS

Heat the oven to 325°F. Grease an 8-by-2-inch round cake pan with 1 teaspoon of the oil. Dust the interior with the breadcrumbs; set aside.

Heat the remaining 2 teaspoons oil in a large skillet over medium heat; add the onion and sauté until soft, stirring often; do not brown. Stir in the prosciutto or ham.

Meanwhile, beat the herbed cream cheese, cream cheese, sour cream, salad dressing, salt, and pepper in a large bowl until smooth and completely blended, scraping the sides of the bowl as needed. Beat in the eggs just until incorporated. Fold in the onion mixture, and scrape the batter into the prepared pan. Bake until a tester inserted in the center comes out almost clean, about 1 hour and 20 minutes.

Cool on a rack until the pan is cool enough to handle. Cover with plastic wrap and invert onto a platter; remove the pan. Refrigerate until chilled through, at least 3 hours. Serve with crackers or toast.

1 cup applesauce, not chunky

1/3 cup fig preserves such as
    Adriatic Fig Spread, large pieces
    finely chopped

2 cups drained ricotta cheese

6 eggs, separated

1/4 cup sugar

6 tablespoons flour

1/2 teaspoon vanilla extract

    Pinch of salt

    No-stick spray oil

sweet ricotta blini with figgy applesauce

These puffy pillows of ricotta cheese disappear in the mouth like bites of air. They are served with applesauce that is sweetened with preserves. Although fig is my favorite, you can substitute cherry, raspberry, orange, or plum preserves, depending on what you have on hand. You can also use cottage cheese in place of ricotta; the consistency is a little different but just as good. Serve for a weekend breakfast or a quick supper.

DIRECTIONS

Mix the applesauce and fig preserves; warm in a saucepan or microwave, if desired.

Mix the ricotta, egg yolks, sugar, flour, and vanilla in a large bowl. Beat the egg whites and salt to soft peaks, and fold into the ricotta mixture.

Heat a griddle or large, heavy skillet over medium-high heat and spray with oil. Make small 2- to 3-inch pancakes, browning them on both sides, about 2 minutes per side. Serve immediately with some of the applesauce.

1   cup half-and-half

2   eggs, large or extra-large

2   teaspoons granulated sugar

½   teaspoon rum extract

2   tablespoons unsalted butter,
    softened

12 slices premium bread, such
    as challah

2   tablespoons light brown sugar

3   bananas, peeled, halved, and
    cut lengthwise into ¼-inch slices

    Banana Rum Sauce
    (recipe follows)

5   tablespoons unsalted butter

⅓   cup light brown sugar

1   banana, peeled and thinly sliced

3   tablespoons water

3   tablespoons rum

1   teaspoon vanilla extract

banana foster french toast

These custard-drenched sugar-coated rum-glazed baked banana sandwiches make the most decadent brunch imaginable. Because they are baked rather than sautéed, they free you up to be with your guests, rather than needing to be at the stove.

DIRECTIONS

Mix the half-and-half, eggs, granulated sugar, and rum extract in a shallow bowl. Spread butter on half of the bread slices and sprinkle the buttered surfaces with brown sugar. Top with banana slices and the remaining bread slices. Dip each sandwich in the egg mixture and place on an oiled baking sheet. Bake for 20 minutes, turning once halfway through. Serve each "sandwich" topped with warm Banana Rum Sauce.

banana rum sauce

Serve this sauce with the previous recipe for Banana Foster French Toast or over ice cream, or with pound cake, or spooned around baked custard, or layered with pudding for a parfait. Better yet, drink it right out of the pan.

DIRECTIONS

Melt the butter in a large skillet over medium heat. Add the sugar and mix until dissolved. Add the banana and cook until heated through, about 2 minutes. Remove from the heat and stir in the water, rum, and vanilla. Serve warm.

1 tablespoon basil pesto, jarred
   or homemade (page 339)

1 tablespoon jarred sun-dried
   tomato pesto or chopped
   marinated sun-dried tomatoes

2 cups (3 ounces) cleaned baby
   spinach leaves

1 tablespoon bottled Italian
   dressing

4 8-inch flour tortillas

1   tablespoon extra-virgin olive oil

4 ounces (about 1 cup)
   shredded Mozzarella cheese

provençal quesadillas

Here I go, morphing cultures again. The basil-tomato-garlic–olive oil palate of Provence swallows up the quesadilla, and what comes out is a kind of stuffed pissaladière (Provençal pizza). They can be assembled and refrigerated ahead and cooked off as the need or the mood hits.

DIRECTIONS

Mix the two pestos; set aside. Toss the spinach and vinaigrette in a separate bowl; set aside.

Brush one side of each tortilla with oil. Heat a large iron skillet over medium-high heat until very hot. Cook the tortillas, oil-side down, until blistered, about 1 minute per tortilla. Brush the pesto mixture on the cooked side of each tortilla; top with the cheese. Cook the tortillas, one at a time, cheese-side up, until the cheese starts to melt, about 40 seconds. Place a mound of the spinach salad in the center and fold in half. Flip back and forth until both sides are blistered and crispy and the cheese is fully melted. Cook the remaining tortillas in the same way. Cut each quesadilla into 3 wedges before serving.

12 dinner rolls, split

2 tablespoons olive oil

1 onion, peeled, quartered, and sliced

3/4 cup chipotle salsa

8 ounces sandwich steak (thinly sliced round steak)

Salt and ground black pepper to taste

3/4 cup (3 ounces) shredded Monterey Jack cheese

chipotle steak sandwiches with jack cheese

These mini Philly-style cheesesteak sandwiches are seasoned with smoked jalapeño pepper, which gives them a spicy Mexicali BBQ personality. It is important to sauté the onions until they are browned. In my testing this happened in about 3 minutes, but if it takes longer on your stove, spend the time; it makes a difference.

DIRECTIONS

Toast the rolls in a toaster oven or under a broiler. Meanwhile, heat half the oil in a large skillet over medium-high heat. Add the onion and cook until browned, 3 to 4 minutes. Add the salsa and heat through; transfer to a bowl and keep warm.

Add the remaining tablespoon of oil to the skillet. Season the steak with salt and pepper and sear on both sides, shredding and chopping it with a sharp metal spatula into large, bite-size chunks. Divide the steak into 12 piles, and top each pile with 1 tablespoon cheese. Reduce the heat to medium, cover the skillet, and cook until the cheese melts, about 1 minute. Place a portion of cheesesteak in each of the rolls and top with some of the chipotle onion mixture.

2 soups & light stews

Once upon a time, a long list of ingredients was a soup's best feature. Soups were the way home cooks accounted for the constant buildup of vegetable and meat trimmings, discarded carcasses and herb ends that were the natural by-products of daily meal-making. But now that fewer meals are made from scratch at home, that ongoing inventory of itinerant ingredients has practically disappeared, and the art of soup-making has dried up along with it.

Today more people get their soup from a can than from a pot, but that doesn't mean that what the ladle holds can't be inventive, delicious, and brimming with all the ingenuity that was the essence of soups when they were concocted from a larder full of nothing-to-eat.

BBQ pork posole

MAKES 8 SERVINGS

1 tablespoon vegetable oil

½ cup diced onion, fresh or frozen

1 container (about 18 ounces) refrigerated barbecued pulled pork

1 cup chunky salsa, medium or hot

1 container (about 32 ounces) chicken broth

1 can (about 30 ounces) posole (whole hominy)

3 tablespoons lime juice, fresh or bottled organic

¼ cup chopped cilantro, or 2 tablespoons jarred cilantro pesto

Salt and ground black pepper to taste

The proliferation of refrigerated fully cooked meats sealed in their own microwave-to-table warming coffins is disheartening to anyone who appreciates the flavors of an authentic roast. I would never serve them as the centerpiece of a meal, but they sure make great, hearty soups that taste as if they had cooked for hours, even though they take little more than 15 minutes from package to dinner.

DIRECTIONS

Heat the oil in a large saucepan over medium-high heat. Add the onion and sauté until soft. Add the pork, salsa, broth, and posole. Simmer for 10 minutes. Add the lime juice, cilantro, salt, and pepper and simmer for 5 minutes more; serve.

- 1 jar (about 11 ounces) black bean salsa such as Southwest salsa, mild or medium heat level
- 1 1/2 cups corn kernels, canned or frozen
- 1 can (about 14 ounces) chicken broth
- 1/2 teaspoon dried Italian seasoning
- 12 ounces peeled and cleaned shrimp (any size), thawed if frozen

  Salt and ground black pepper to taste

shrimp, black bean, and corn chowder

Shrimp and black beans are the new surf 'n' turf. No one will guess that this beautiful soup, techni-colorful in the bowl and bursting with tongue-teasing textures and provocative flavors, came together in less than 5 minutes.

DIRECTIONS

Combine the salsa, corn, broth, and seasoning in a saucepan, and heat to a simmer over medium heat. If the shrimp are large, cut them into bite-size pieces; add to the pan and simmer for a minute more, until the shrimp are firm. Season with salt and pepper, and serve.

- 1 can (about 16 ounces) candied yams, drained
- 1 cup curry cooking (or simmer) sauce, jarred or homemade (page 349)
- 1/2 cup salsa, preferably medium-hot
- 1 cup chicken broth
- 1 tablespoon chopped cilantro
- 1/8 teaspoon ground allspice
- 1 cup light coconut milk

  Salt and ground black pepper to taste

- 2 scallions, trimmed and thinly sliced

caribbean sweet potato soup

I try not to use too many packaged ingredients in any one recipe, lest I begin to feel like a dump-and-heat dummy. But this recipe worked out that way and I couldn't have made it better if I had chopped and sweated all day. The flavors are exotic and intense. You can adjust the level of heat by using milder or hotter salsa.

DIRECTIONS

Mash the yams in a large saucepan. Add the curry sauce, salsa, broth, cilantro, allspice, coconut milk, season with salt and pepper, and heat to simmering. Simmer for 2 to 3 minutes, stir in the scallions, and serve.

1   tablespoon olive oil

2   cups diced onion, fresh or frozen

1   carrot, peeled and diced

1   rib celery, diced

1   bag (about 16 ounces) frozen
    or fresh cauliflower florets,
    coarsely chopped

1   tablespoon chopped garlic, fresh
    or jarred organic

1   teaspoon dried marjoram

¼   cup red wine

2   tablespoons paprika

1   tablespoon hot paprika

1   can (about 14 ounces) diced
    tomatoes with bell peppers
    and onions

1   can (about 14 ounces)
    chicken broth

¾   cup sour cream

cauliflower paprikash

Paprika has been dissed by ubiquity. Condemned to life as a garnish, its flavor is belittled and its culinary role unrecognized. Paprika is a ground dried pepper. Sweet paprika is made by removing the seeds and veins from the pepper before grinding. Since these parts contain most of the capsaicin (hot pepper compound), they are retained when hot paprika is ground. This classic paprikash plays with the affinity that you find frequently in Spanish and Indian cooking between paprika and cauliflower.

DIRECTIONS

Heat the oil in a large saucepan over medium heat. Add the onion, carrot, and celery and sauté until almost tender. Stir in the cauliflower, garlic, and marjoram; add the wine and heat to boiling. Stir in the paprikas, tomatoes (undrained), and broth. Simmer for 20 minutes, remove from the heat, stir in the sour cream, and serve.

kale and white bean caldo

Caldo, the nourishing, brothy soup of Spain and Portugal, is the heart of home cooking. This one, chock-full of greens and beans, is a mainstream example, although I've streamlined the timing by using precut carrots, washed and chopped kale, canned beans, and jarred marinated sun-dried tomatoes. The soup is vegetarian except for the bacon. If you want the smoky flavor but don't want the meat, you can replace the bacon with 1 tablespoon olive oil and add 2 strips of soy bacon, added to the recipe along with the beans.

DIRECTIONS

Cook the bacon in a large saucepan over medium heat until the fat has been rendered from it. Add the onion, carrots, and potato, and sauté until the onions are browned, about 10 minutes.

Add the garlic, broth, oregano, and bay leaves and heat to simmering. Add the kale and season liberally with salt and pepper. Cover and simmer until the kale is tender, about 10 minutes.

Add the beans and sun-dried tomatoes; cook for another 5 minutes. Remove the bay leaves and stir in the olive oil. Serve with freshly grated Parmesan cheese, if desired.

2   strips bacon, chopped

½   cup diced onion, fresh or frozen

8   ounces (about 1½ cups) baby carrots

1   red potato, diced

1   teaspoon chopped garlic, fresh or jarred organic

1   container (about 32 ounces) vegetable broth

½   teaspoon dried oregano

2   bay leaves

1   bag (about 16 ounces) chopped washed kale

    Salt and ground black pepper to taste

1   can (about 10 ounces) white kidney beans, drained and rinsed

⅓   cup marinated sun-dried tomato strips

1   tablespoon extra-virgin olive oil

    Grated imported Parmesan cheese, for serving (optional)

BABY CARROTS

Baby vegetables are dwarves, purposely cultivated to be diminutive, tender, and mildly flavored. Many full-size vegetables have baby counterparts, including carrots, but be aware: Most baby carrots are not the real thing. If you look at the label on a bag of baby carrots you will see that it reads something like "baby-cut carrots." In other words, what were once full-sized, fully mature carrots have been whittled down to look like babies. They are perfectly fine, but don't expect the delicate sweetness and tenderness one would expect from a baby vegetable.

curried pumpkin soup

1 can (about 15 ounces) Libby's 100% pure pumpkin

1 can (about 14 ounces) vegetable broth

1 can (about 13 ounces) coconut milk

1 jar (about 16 ounces) curry cooking (or simmer) sauce, or 2 cups homemade (page 349)

1 cup apple juice

   Salt and ground black pepper to taste

1 tablespoon chopped cilantro

The laborious part of making an authentic curry comes from the need to toast and blend and grind the spices, and then cook them into a fragrant base, a process that throwing in a tablespoon of curry powder cannot match. In this recipe a jar of curry sauce takes care of all that, delivering a long-simmered curry flavor instantly.

DIRECTIONS

Combine the pumpkin, vegetable broth, coconut milk, curry sauce, apple juice, salt, and pepper in a large saucepan and heat until simmering; simmer for 5 minutes. Stir in the cilantro, and serve.

CANNED PUMPKIN IS BETTER THAN FRESH

In the debate among pumpkin fanciers on the merits of canned versus fresh pumpkin puree, I come down on the canned side. This is partially because the canning process helps to break down tough fibers and concentrates the flavors of pumpkin more completely than simmering would, but it's also because the most popular brand of canned pumpkin, Libby's, is made from a special type of pumpkin that is designed for puree and is unavailable to you and me. I usually shy away from recommending a specific brand, but this is one instance where there is a significant difference in quality. If you can't find Libby's 100% Pumpkin (and you don't want to move to another state), any brand of canned product will be better than a homemade puree made from a carving pumpkin. However, if you insist on making your puree fresh, a butternut, acorn, or buttercup squash will give you the best results. Fresh pumpkin puree is watery and fibrous and never develops a rich flavor no matter how long you cook it.

One note: When a recipe calls for pumpkin puree, make sure you don't use pumpkin pie filling by mistake; it is sweetened and spiced and will not give you the same results.

- 1 tablespoon vegetable oil
- 1 rib celery, sliced
- 1 onion, diced
- 1 red or gold potato, peeled and finely diced
- 1/2 teaspoon dried thyme
- 1/2 teaspoon dried dill
- 1/4 teaspoon ground black pepper
- 2 cans (about 14 ounces each) vegetable broth
- 1 cup corn kernels, fresh, frozen, or canned
- 1 cup frozen shelled edamame (green soybeans)
- 2 ounces smoked salmon, finely chopped
- 1/4 cup instant mashed potato flakes
- 1/2 cup heavy cream

smoked salmon and edamame chowder

This New Age chowder is not as radical as it sounds. Smoked pork, beans, and potatoes are traditional chowder ingredients; here they appear with a twist. The smoked flavor comes from the salmon, and the beans are fresh green soy. Instead of relying on long simmering to thicken the soup, you add a small amount of potato flakes at the end of cooking, which gives the chowder a silken texture instantly.

DIRECTIONS

Heat the oil in a large saucepan over medium heat. Add the celery, onion, and potatoes and sauté until the vegetables are just beginning to get tender, about 5 minutes. Add the thyme, dill, pepper, and broth. Bring to a boil and simmer, uncovered, for 5 minutes. Add the corn, edamame, smoked salmon, and potato flakes, stirring until the potato flakes dissolve. Simmer for 5 minutes, until the edamame are tender and the broth is lightly thickened. Add the cream, heat through, and serve.

1 tablespoon olive oil

½ cup diced onion, fresh or frozen

½ teaspoon minced garlic, fresh or jarred organic

1 can (about 19 ounces) lentil soup

1 can (about 14 ounces) chicken broth

1 cup fresh or canned diced tomatoes, drained

½ teaspoon crushed dried rosemary leaves

   Salt and ground black pepper to taste

1 bag (about 7 ounces) baby spinach leaves

⅓ cup tabbouleh (bulgur wheat)

   Plain yogurt for serving (optional)

lentil soup with bulgur and spinach

This instantaneous soup is a meal. Greens, beans, grains, and herbs meld together in a matter of minutes into a fragrant, hearty stew, and it all starts with a humble can of lentil soup. If you want to make it vegetarian, just switch to vegetable broth. The results, although not quite as rich, are delicious nonetheless.

DIRECTIONS

Heat the olive oil in a large saucepan over medium heat; add the onion and sauté until tender. Stir in the garlic, lentil soup, chicken broth, tomatoes, rosemary, and season with salt and pepper; simmer for 5 minutes.

Add the spinach and tabbouleh and simmer for another 10 minutes, until the tabbouleh is tender. Serve with plain yogurt, if desired.

1   jar (about 16 ounces) salsa verde

1   can (about 13 ounces)
    coconut milk

1   teaspoon dried ground
    lemongrass, such as Thai Kitchen

2   cups water

1   large (about 9 grams) fish-flavored
    bouillon cube, such as Knorr

1   package (about 6 or 7 ounces)
    pink salmon, flaked and drained

1   can (about 6 ounces) lump
    crabmeat

8   ounces cooked shrimp, thawed if
    frozen, cut into bite-size pieces

thai seafood chowder

A catch of fresh seafood is a great excuse for putting on a pot of chowder, but what about when fresh isn't available? Fortunately, canned, pouched, and frozen fish are remarkably similar to fresh when cooked in a soup. And why wouldn't they be? Canned seafood has been simmered just as it would be in a soup pot. All you have to do is heat it through.

DIRECTIONS

Combine the salsa, coconut milk, lemongrass, and water in a saucepan, and bring to a boil over medium heat. Add the bouillon cube and stir to dissolve. Stir in the salmon, crab, and shrimp and heat through, about 2 minutes. Serve hot.

THE ALLURE OF POUCHED FISH

When it comes to packaged fish, the can is rapidly being replaced by the pouch. Made from high-grade poly-nylon plastic lined with foil, pouches are vacuum sealed and cooked under pressure in water and steam. The results are fresher because the fish is processed for less time, and pouches don't require draining because they are packed without adding extra water. As pouch packaging catches on, more products are becoming available; shrimp, crab, clams, mussels, oysters, eel, and sardines have joined a wide variety of tuna and salmon products, including steaks and preseasoned products.

2   bags (about 7 ounces each)
    spinach, coarsely chopped

1   jar (about 16 ounces) curry
    cooking (or simmer) sauce, or

2   cups homemade (page 349)

1   container (about 32 ounces)
    vegetable broth

1   package (about 16 ounces)
    prepared mashed potatoes,
    refrigerated or frozen and thawed

    Dash of grated nutmeg

    Ground black pepper to taste (you
    probably won't need more salt)

curried spinach soup

The combination of spinach, potato, and curry is at the heart of
northern Indian cooking. Several years ago it would have taken
a long list of ingredients and a longer stretch of time behind the
stove to get this simple, hearty soup on the table. Now, with the
ready availability of high-quality prewashed spinach, jarred curry
sauce, and premashed potatoes, what once took hours takes only
minutes.

DIRECTIONS

Combine the spinach, curry sauce, and broth in a large saucepan.
Add the potatoes, nutmeg, and pepper, and bring to a simmer,
stirring often. Serve hot.

1   container (about 32 ounces) chicken broth

1   teaspoon soy sauce

3   scallions, trimmed and sliced

1   teaspoon minced garlic, fresh or jarred organic

1   teaspoon minced ginger, fresh or jarred

8   frozen chicken wontons, or other Asian-style dumpling

1   package (about 3.5 ounces) ramen noodles (discard flavor packet)

wonton noodle noodle soup

Asian dumplings abound. Refrigerated and frozen, folded into wontons, crimped into shiu mai, or pleated as pot stickers, they are ready to transform a box of broth and a few vegetables into a delicious soup hearty enough for a light dinner or an elaborate lunch. Any style of Asian dumpling will work in this soup.

DIRECTIONS

Combine broth, soy sauce, scallions, garlic, and ginger in a large saucepan; heat to boiling over medium-high heat. Add the wontons and noodles; reduce the heat and simmer, covered, until the wontons and noodles are tender, 3 to 5 minutes. Serve hot.

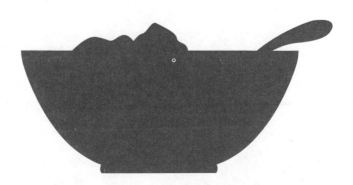

fire-roasted tomato soup

2 tablespoons chopped roasted garlic, homemade (page 338) or jarred organic

1/2 cup chopped roasted caramelized onions (page 336)

1 can (about 14 ounces) diced fire-roasted tomatoes

1 can (about 14 ounces) crushed fire-roasted tomatoes

1 can (about 14 ounces) vegetable broth

1/4 teaspoon ground chipotle pepper

1 tablespoon chopped cilantro

The advent of canned fire-roasted tomatoes has revolutionized the way I cook. Redolent with a whiff of wood fire, and speckled with natural bits of charred tomato, they transform a simple, straightforward soup such as this into a rustic, full-flavored dining experience.

DIRECTIONS

Combine everything in a saucepan and heat to simmering; simmer for 5 minutes. Serve hot.

tomato soup with fennel and prosciutto

1 tablespoon olive oil

2 ounces (about 1/2 cup) diced prosciutto

1 rib fennel, finely diced (about 1/2 cup)

2 containers (about 18 ounces each) prepared tomato soup

1/8 teaspoon (a pinch) five-spice powder

Sometimes a brand is so ingrained in our collective culinary unconscious that it becomes our gold standard without our even realizing it. Such is the case with Campbell's tomato soup. Here this icon of American food is transformed into something completely new and equally delicious with the addition of prosciutto and fennel. Prosciutto can be expensive, especially if it is the real stuff imported from Parma. Many stores chop the ends and reserve the scraps to be sold at a greatly reduced price. They are perfect for this soup.

DIRECTIONS

Heat the olive oil in a saucepan over medium-high heat. Add the prosciutto and the fennel and cook until the fennel is barely tender, about 4 minutes. Add the soup and five-spice powder and simmer for 5 minutes. Serve hot.

2   strips ready-to-serve precooked bacon, finely chopped

½   cup chopped onion, frozen or fresh

2   teaspoons chopped garlic, fresh or jarred organic

1   can (about 15 ounces) Libby's 100% pure pumpkin

1   container (about 32 ounces) chicken broth

    Salt and ground black pepper to taste

1   cup cream or half-and-half

2   ounces smoked Gouda cheese or other smoked cheese, shredded

1   tablespoon chopped Italian (flat-leaf) parsley

pumpkin bisque with bacon and smoked gouda

If you think pumpkin belongs only in pies, cakes, or muffins, or in soups scented with cinnamon and fruit, get ready to change your mind. Here's a silken, caramel-colored pumpkin bisque speckled with bacon, laced with cream, and fragrant with garlic and a whiff of smoked cheese.

DIRECTIONS

Render the fat from the bacon in a large saucepan; add the onion and sauté until tender. Add the garlic and sauté a few seconds more. Add the pumpkin and chicken broth; season with salt and pepper. Stir to combine, and simmer until the flavors meld and the soup thickens slightly, about 5 minutes. Stir in the cream and heat through. Remove from the heat and stir in the cheese and parsley, until the cheese melts. Serve immediately. Do not heat the soup after the cheese is added. Serve hot.

MELTING CHEESE

Cheese is a mixture of protein and fat. When it is heated, the protein becomes firm and the fat melts. Melting cheese is therefore a balancing act of getting the fat to melt without causing the protein to harden into an impenetrable lump. Fortunately, chemistry is on our side: the fat in cheese melts at about 100°F, while the protein doesn't start to seize until 140°F or so. The trick, therefore, is to keep the heat low and to shred or chop the cheese finely so that heat can penetrate it easily. I recommend heating the soup or sauce to a boil, turning off the heat, adding the cheese, and letting the residual warmth of the liquid melt the cheese as you stir the mixture until it is smooth. That way the cheese never becomes hot enough to form lumps.

1   tablespoon olive oil

½ cup diced onion, fresh or frozen

1   rib celery, finely chopped

1   carrot, peeled and finely chopped

1   teaspoon dried thyme

1   bay leaf

¼ teaspoon ground allspice

1   package (about 1 pound) peeled
    butternut squash cubes, cut into
    1-inch pieces

2   cups vegetable broth

1   cup V8 vegetable juice

½ cup orange juice

½ cup apple juice

harvest vegetable and orchard fruit bisque

This amalgam of vegetable and fruit flavors sounds strange, but I assure you, the results are perfectly delicious. The one ingredient that may be unusual to you is precut butternut squash. You will find it in the produce section of your food store alongside other prepared fresh vegetables. Some markets have cut-up squash only in the fall, when it is traditionally served, even though it is available year round. If you can't find it, you can substitute a medium-size butternut, acorn, or buttercup squash that has been peeled, cleaned of seeds and stem, and cut into rough 2-inch chunks.

DIRECTIONS

Heat the oil in a large saucepan over medium heat; add the onion, celery, and carrot and sauté until tender, about 5 minutes. Add the thyme, bay leaf, allspice, squash, and broth; cover and simmer until the squash is tender, about 15 minutes. Remove the bay leaf and puree the vegetables and broth in a blender or food processor until smooth.

Return the puree to the saucepan. Stir in the juices and heat until simmering; cook for 5 minutes. Serve hot.

DEFINING FRUIT

There are two definitions for fruit—botanical and culinary. Botanically, a fruit is the pulpy part of a plant that houses its seed. Under that definition the fruit category includes tomatoes, eggplants, chiles, squash, and corn, along with oranges, apples, and bananas. Confused? You're not alone. The problem comes from our cultural preference for defining fruit by how we use it, rather than by what it is. In the kitchen we use the word "fruit" only to connote botanical fruits that are high in sugar or that we prepare with sugar. Therefore, watermelon is a fruit, but cucumber is not (even though they are genetically related). There are numerous examples of botanical fruits that are known as vegetables, but there is only one botanical vegetable that we think of as fruit. Rhubarb, which is usually cooked in sugar to tame its tartness, is a not a fruit—it is a stem.

1 tablespoon vegetable oil

½ onion, chopped

1 carrot, peeled and sliced

1 rib celery, sliced

1 package (about 10 ounces) frozen squash puree, thawed

1 container (about 32 ounces) vegetable broth

⅓ cup apple juice

½ teaspoon dried thyme leaves

Salt and ground black pepper to taste

1 package (about 14 ounces) soft tofu

1 teaspoon ground cinnamon

2 tablespoons maple syrup

winter squash soup with cinnamon tofu cream

"Vegan" and "gourmet" are not frequently used in the same sentence, but this savory winter vegetable soup swirled with honey-sweet vegan cream may be an exception. Frozen winter squash puree is a great vegetable to keep on hand for spur-of-the-moment side dishes and soups, or for adding nutrients and improved consistency to a sauce or a pot of stew. It is usually made from butternut squash, although depending on the brand and the harvest, it could be acorn or hubbard squash.

DIRECTIONS

Heat the oil in a large saucepan over medium heat. Add the onion, carrot, and celery and sauté until barely tender, about 5 minutes. Add the squash puree, broth, apple juice, thyme, salt, and pepper, and simmer until the vegetables are tender, 10 to 15 minutes.

Meanwhile, combine the tofu, cinnamon, and maple syrup in a food processor and puree until completely smooth. Stir ½ cup of the tofu cream into the soup until blended. Serve, swirling a spoonful of the remaining tofu cream into each portion.

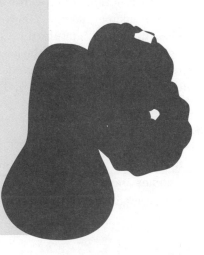

no-chicken noodle soup

MAKES 8 SERVINGS

2   containers (about 32 ounces each) vegetarian "chicken" broth, such as Imagine Organic No-Chicken broth

1   carrot, peeled and thinly sliced

1   rib celery, thinly sliced

6   ounces spaghetti, broken into thirds, regular or whole grain

1/4 teaspoon dried poultry seasoning

    Salt and ground black pepper to taste

8   ounces seitan, cut into 1/2-inch chunks

2   tablespoons chopped Italian (flat-leaf) parsley

A rich, slightly thick version of vegetable broth is sold as a replacement for all-purpose chicken broth, under the name "No-Chicken" or "Vegetarian Chicken." Although the flavor is not a perfect match, the color is similar, and the effect is satisfying. This recipe increases the resemblance by adding random chunks of seitan–an isolate of soy protein that (like so many other things) "tastes just like chicken."

DIRECTIONS

Heat the broth, carrot, and celery in a large saucepan until simmering; simmer for 5 minutes. Add the spaghetti, poultry seasoning, salt, and pepper and cook until the noodles and vegetables are tender, about 8 minutes. Stir in the seitan and parsley, heat through, and serve.

miso soup with soba and bean curd

MAKES 6 SERVINGS

1   container (about 32 ounces) vegetable broth

4   cups water

1   package (about 8 ounces) soba (buckwheat) noodles, broken in half

2   packets (0.3 ounce each) dried miso soup mix

1/2 cup finely diced tomato, fresh or canned

1   pound firm tofu, cut into 1/2-inch cubes

4   scallions, trimmed and thinly sliced

This Japanese-style noodle soup uses dried miso soup mix as its base. A commonplace convenience product in Japan, it is becoming increasingly available in American markets, piggybacking on the success of instant ramen soups. You will find it either in the Asian section of your supermarket or shelved with other dried soups. If you fail to find it, you can substitute 1 tablespoon red miso paste, although you will need to add the paste a little earlier (about 3 minutes into the cooking of the noodles). Simmer the soup for a few minutes after adding the miso, if you make that substitution.

DIRECTIONS

Heat the broth and water to boiling in a large saucepan. Add the soba noodles and cook until tender, about 5 minutes. Stir in the miso mix, tomato, tofu, and scallions, heat through, and serve.

hungarian vegetable borscht

1   tablespoon vegetable oil

1   cup diced onion, fresh or frozen

4   ounces (1 cup) sliced mushrooms

1   teaspoon chopped garlic, fresh or jarred organic

1   bag (16 ounces) refrigerated coleslaw mix (see Note)

1   teaspoon dried dill

½   cup red wine

1   tablespoon apple cider vinegar

1   can (about 14 ounces) diced tomatoes with bell peppers and onion

1   can (about 14 ounces) vegetable broth

2   cups V8 vegetable juice

1   cup apple juice

2   tablespoons soy sauce

Borscht is a hearty vegetable soup that has its roots in Eastern Europe. The most well-known borscht in America is summer borscht, which is made from beets and is served cold, but the bulk of borscht recipes are for winter borscht, which, as you might have guessed, is served hot. The main ingredient in winter borscht is cabbage. I've streamlined the traditional procedure by using coleslaw mix for the cabbage and V8 juice to supply other vegetable flavors.

DIRECTIONS

Heat the oil in a large saucepan over medium heat; add the onion and mushrooms and sauté until tender, about 5 minutes. Add the garlic and coleslaw mix and stir until the coleslaw is wilted.

Add the dill, red wine, vinegar, diced tomatoes, broth, V8, apple juice, and soy sauce. Simmer until the vegetables are uniformly tender, about 15 minutes.

Note: Some bags of coleslaw include dressing packets. Do not use the dressing in this recipe.

V8: A GARDEN IN A JAR

V8 was the first vegetable juice to gain popularity, and to my taste it is still the best. Although most people would characterize V8 as tasting like tomato juice, their perceptions are being skewed by its color and pulpiness. If you close your eyes and take a swig, you will notice that the dominant flavor is celery, modified by onion, bell pepper, and tomato. There are many varieties of V8. The most versatile one for cooking is the low-salt product (although in this recipe I use original V8).

2 tablespoons unsalted butter

1 cup diced onion, fresh or frozen

1 can (about 15 ounces) yams in syrup, drained

1/2 cup unsweetened applesauce

2 cups vegetable broth

1/2 teaspoon salt

1 teaspoon ground cinnamon

1 cup heavy cream or half-and-half

2 tablespoons chopped chives, fresh or dried

sweet potato and apple vichyssoise

This beautiful pale auburn soup is mildly sweet and like velvet on the palate. It is one of the only chilled soups I find rich enough to serve in cold weather. Although you might be tempted to heat it up, I would advise against it. The acidity of the apple can cause the cream to develop off-flavors, and if your cream isn't perfectly fresh it could curdle upon heating.

DIRECTIONS

Heat the butter in a large saucepan over medium heat; add the onion and sauté until lightly browned, about 8 minutes. Cool.

Puree the onion, yams, applesauce, and broth in a blender or food processor. Scrape into a serving bowl and stir in the salt, cinnamon, cream, and chives. Refrigerate until thoroughly chilled before serving.

MAKING SUBSTITUTIONS FOR CREAM

I am often asked if it is okay to substitute milk for cream in soups. The answer is "sometimes," and to help you figure out when "sometimes" is, you need to consider what the cream is doing in a particular soup recipe. Cream gives a soup dairy sweetness and a rich mouth-feel. Without it, the pulpiness of vegetables, like sweet potato, is a bit more obvious, and the spices and vegetable flavors are less blended. Milk provides sweetness, and will help to marry the disparate flavors in the soup, but milk does not contain enough fat to affect mouth-feel. In this recipe the sweet potato is providing some richness, which will make up for part of the difference between the cream and the milk. So in this soup substituting milk for cream could be a viable option.

goulash of quorn and onions

Goulash is onion stew that traditionally is loaded up with so much onion and cooked so slowly that the vegetable literally melts into a jelly that gently thickens the broth as its sweet, pungent flavor radiates through the soup. In this version I've sped everything up by chopping the vegetables finely in a food processor so that they break down quicker and release their flavors more easily. Goulash frequently has pieces of chicken in it. I've kept this soup vegetarian by using Quorn. A meat substitute that was developed in Europe but is making inroads in the States, it has a convincing meaty texture and is sold ground or formed into patties, nuggets, or tenders.

DIRECTIONS

Puree the onions, carrot, and celery in a food processor. Heat the butter and oil in a large saucepan over medium-low heat. Add the pureed vegetables, cover, and cook until very soft, at least 10 minutes. Add the mushrooms and poultry seasoning and cook, uncovered, stirring often, until the mushrooms are tender, about 5 minutes.

- -

Add the broth, Quorn, salt, and pepper and simmer until the soup is lightly thickened, 10 to 15 minutes. Stir in the parsley and sour cream, and serve.

3   onions, trimmed, peeled, and cut into chunks

1   carrot, trimmed, peeled, and cut into chunks

1   rib celery, trimmed and cut into chunks

1   tablespoon butter, salted or unsalted

1   tablespoon vegetable oil

4   ounces (1 cup) sliced mushrooms

2   teaspoons whole-leaf poultry seasoning, or 1 teaspoon ground poultry seasoning

1   container (about 32 ounces) vegetable broth

1   package (about 12 ounces) frozen Quorn tenders, defrosted

    Salt and ground black pepper to taste

2   tablespoons chopped Italian (flat leaf) parsley

¼   cup sour cream

③ salads & their dressings

Salad is a cook's salvation. With it, any meal is guaranteed to be one of genuine refreshment, and without it, even the most carefully composed menu is left longing for a lift.

Salads can be grilled or poached, chilled or warm, tossed into a jumble or meticulously constructed. When you add meat, fish, poultry, potatoes, pasta, or a grain, the ubiquitous mound of raw fresh greens, interrupted by a crouton, becomes fertile ground for imaginative combinations of ingredients and dressings.

One of the more intriguing ideas I have been working with in these recipes is the use of precooked ingredients, like canned beans, frozen spinach, or tomato puree, to thicken a salad dressing in place of most of the oil. Not only does it cut calories, but it also increases the amount of vegetables in the salad.

For the dressing:

1   can (about 15 ounces) cannellini beans, drained and rinsed

1   clove garlic, halved

¼   cup white wine vinegar

2   tablespoons extra-virgin olive oil

1   teaspoon kosher salt

1   teaspoon Tabasco hot pepper sauce

¼   cup hot water

For the salad:

1   pound escarole lettuce mix, including radicchio, escarole, frisée, chicory, and mâche

6   marinated sun-dried tomatoes, quartered

3   scallions, trimmed and sliced

2   ounces (about ⅓ cup) pitted black olives, quartered

escarole salad with warm white bean vinaigrette

This easy, healthful vinaigrette is thickened with a puree of white beans rather than a dram of oil. The role of oil in salad dressing is twofold: flavor (that's why there always has to be a little bit) and consistency. Heating the dressing boosts its seasoning, and its warmth helps it to wilt the escarole, allowing it to absorb more dressing and counteracting its natural bitterness.

DIRECTIONS

To make the dressing, puree the dressing ingredients in a blender or food processor until smooth. Transfer to a skillet.

To make the salad, toss the lettuces, sun-dried tomatoes, scallions, and olives in a large mixing bowl. Heat the dressing until simmering, stirring often; add more water if needed to keep it the texture of unbeaten cream. Toss the dressing with the salad ingredients, and mound on a large platter or individual plates.

For the dressing:

¹/₃   cup mayonnaise

3   tablespoons bottled French dressing

For the salad:

2   bags (about 8 ounces each) romaine lettuce salad mix

2   ripe medium tomatoes, each cut into 8 wedges

4   strips ready-to-serve precooked bacon, crisped and broken into small pieces

1¹/₂   cups (about 2 ounces) seasoned croutons

BLT salad

Imagine a classic BLT. Now deconstruct it into its basic elements—bacon, lettuce, tomato, mayo, toast. You got it? Good! Now turn the toast into croutons and toss it all together in a salad bowl. That's all there is to it.

DIRECTIONS

To make the dressing, mix the ingredients in a small bowl.

To make the salad, toss the ingredients with the dressing in a serving bowl.

READY-TO-SERVE PRECOOKED BACON

These all-natural bacon slices have been precooked and are ready to be eaten as is, crisped in a microwave, or rendered in a skillet. They are real bacon, their quality is good, and they cost the same to use as raw bacon. The price per pound is usually four to five times the price of raw bacon, but since bacon loses about 80 percent of its weight during cooking, the usage costs are almost identical. Precooked bacon can be found in your supermarket in the refrigerator, alongside other bacon and sausage products; it will last in the refrigerator for about 2 weeks after opening. Imitation bacon bits and strips, which are made from isolated, reformed, and flavored soy (or other vegetable) protein, are not an adequate substitute.

For the dressing:

1 can (about 15 ounces) pear halves or slices in juice

⅓ cup reserved juice from pears

⅓ cup white wine vinegar

¼ teaspoon vanilla extract

¾ teaspoon kosher salt

¼ teaspoon coarsely ground black pepper

Pinch cayenne pepper

For the salad:

1 small red onion, halved and thinly sliced

2 bags (about 8 ounces each) endive lettuce mix, including Belgian endive, radicchio, escarole, frisée, and chicory, or 2 pounds of the same vegetables in heads, cleaned of damaged leaves, cored, washed, and broken into bite-size pieces

1 cup chopped toasted walnuts, pretoasted or homemade (page 340)

mixed endive salad with vanilla pear vinaigrette

"Plain vanilla" is slang for insipid, ordinary, and bland. But taste vanilla out of context and its true character blossoms. Vanilla is the fruit of a tropical orchid, and that's the exotic flower you perceive in this tangy, fruity, slightly spicy dressing and salad.

DIRECTIONS

To make the dressing, puree the dressing ingredients in a blender or food processor until smooth.

To make the salad, soak the onion slices in ice water for at least 10 minutes; drain. Toss the lettuce and onions with the dressing in a serving bowl. Garnish with the toasted walnuts.

ENDIVES

Chicory, curly endive, Belgian endive, radicchio, and escarole are related botanically and can almost be used interchangeably in recipes. They all share a bitter aftertaste, which gives them a limited following, but when doused with a strong vinaigrette or an assertively spicy dressing their natural bitterness can be intriguing. Chicory and curly endive both have slim, pale stalks and darker frilly leaves. The darker the leaves, the more bitter the vegetable will taste. Escarole has a broader leaf and a stalk tinged with yellow. Radicchio is a deep, dark magenta.

For the dressing:

1   can (about 15 ounces) whole figs
    in syrup, drained

⅓   cup sherry wine vinegar (or a
    combination of equal parts
    balsamic and red wine vinegars)

1   clove garlic, halved

2   teaspoons crushed dried rosemary

2   teaspoons kosher salt

½   teaspoon ground black pepper

¼   cup orange juice

¼   cup grapeseed oil or other
    mild-flavored oil

For the salad:

3   ounces (about ¾ cup) chopped
    prosciutto

1   medium red onion, diced

1   large head romaine lettuce or
    3 romaine hearts, trimmed and
    torn into bite-size pieces

2   bags (about 7 ounces each)
    baby spinach

greens tossed with sherry fig vinaigrette

The magic pairing of fruit and prosciutto is the impetus behind this versatile salad that could be either a side dish or an entrée. The dressing is made from figs, rosemary, and orange juice, and crisp sautéed prosciutto is tossed separately with the greens to keep it from becoming soggy in the dressing.

DIRECTIONS

To make the dressing, puree the dressing ingredients in a blender or food processor until smooth.

To make the salad, sauté the prosciutto in a medium skillet over medium heat until its fat renders and some of the pieces get crisp at their edges. Add the onion and cook for a minute to soften slightly. Toss the romaine and spinach in a large salad bowl. Add the dressing, prosciutto, and onion; toss. Serve immediately.

For the dressing:

2   roasted red bell peppers, jarred or homemade (page 337)

1   large clove garlic

1   tablespoon apple cider vinegar

2   tablespoons extra-virgin olive oil

1   teaspoon kosher salt

½   teaspoon coarsely ground black pepper

    Juice of 1 lime

2   teaspoons sugar

2   tablespoons chopped cilantro

For the salad:

12 ounces boneless, skinless roasted turkey breast, cut into ½-inch pieces

2   ribs celery, peeled and thinly sliced

1   can (about 15 ounces) white posole (whole hominy), drained

3   scallions, trimmed and sliced

1   roasted red bell pepper, jarred or homemade (page 337)

¼   cup toasted pine nuts, pretoasted or homemade (page 340)

turkey posole salad with roasted pepper vinaigrette

This easy (just whirl everything together in a blender), vibrant (nothing is quite so red as the enflamed glow of a roasted red pepper), and flavor-packed dressing (peppers and garlic and lime, oh my!) turns a run-of-the-turkey salad into an extraordinary meal.

DIRECTIONS

To make the dressing, puree the dressing ingredients in a blender or food processor until smooth.

- -

To make the salad, combine the turkey, celery, posole, scallions, and roasted pepper in a serving bowl. Toss with the dressing and garnish with the pine nuts.

For the dressing:

1	can (about 20 ounces) crushed pineapple in juice, undrained
2	tablespoons chopped ginger, jarred or fresh
1½–2	teaspoons kosher salt, to taste
6	tablespoons rice wine vinegar
2	teaspoons toasted sesame oil

For the salad:

1	can (about 8 ounces) sliced water chestnuts, drained
2	bags (about 16 ounces each) refrigerated coleslaw mix
2	cups (about 4 ounces) shredded carrots
2	ounces (7 to 8 slices) candied ginger, finely diced

savoy slaw with ginger pineapple dressing

The Asian flavors in this easy fruit-based dressing take coleslaw to a whole other continent.

DIRECTIONS

To make the dressing, puree the dressing ingredients in a blender or food processor until smooth. Cut the water chestnut slices into thin strips.

To make the salad, toss the coleslaw mix, water chestnuts, carrots, half of the candied ginger, and the dressing in a serving bowl. Allow to rest for 20 minutes before serving. Serve garnished with the remaining candied ginger.

PRECUT PRODUCE

The bags of trimmed carrots, chopped greens, and snapped beans may be convenient, but that doesn't mean they are anything but 100 percent natural produce. Read the ingredients: all that's in those bags are vegetables. And don't be deterred by the price. A 10-ounce bag of washed and torn romaine leaves sells for the same price as an unwashed head of romaine that weighs twice as much. However, after you wash the head of romaine, discard its core, its larger ribs, and any damaged leaves, you are left with about 12 ounces of servable lettuce. Not much of a price differential after all.

For the dressing:

½ cup canned crushed tomatoes

2 tablespoons extra-virgin olive oil

2 tablespoons red wine vinegar

1 teaspoon minced garlic, fresh or jarred organic

Salt and ground black pepper to taste

For the salad:

8 ounces fresh mozzarella, cut into 12 thin slices

4 ounces fresh goat cheese, cut into 10 slices

12 large basil leaves

Kosher salt and coarsely ground black pepper to taste

mozzarella and goat cheese with tomato vinaigrette

Fresh cheese, fresh basil, and perfectly ripened tomatoes are a ménage made in culinary heaven. But because of the short tomato season, it is a treat confined to a few weeks at the end of summer. Canned tomatoes, which are picked ripe and preserved, are not usually appropriate as a replacement for fresh, but the problem is largely textural. Puree them into a vinaigrette and the flavor of summer arrives.

DIRECTIONS

To make the dressing, mix the dressing ingredients with a whisk in a bowl.

To make the salad, fan the slices of cheese on a serving plate, alternating the cheeses and placing the basil leaves between the slices. Season with salt and pepper and spoon the dressing over the top.

For the dressing:

²/₃ cup canned fire-roasted crushed tomatoes

2 tablespoons extra-virgin olive oil

¼ cup red wine vinegar

1 teaspoon minced garlic, fresh or jarred organic

2 tablespoons chopped fresh basil

½ teaspoon chipotle hot sauce

1 teaspoon kosher salt

¼ teaspoon coarsely ground black pepper

For the salad:

1 pound mixed field greens or other European lettuce blend

1 cup (about 3 ounces) sliced mushrooms

1 roasted red bell pepper, jarred or homemade (page 337), diced

½ small red onion, halved top to bottom and thinly sliced

2 ounces fresh goat cheese log, cut into small pieces

¼ cup toasted pine nuts, pretoasted or homemade (page 340)

chèvre, field greens, and fire-roasted tomato vinaigrette

Tomatoes must be peeled before they are canned, lest they be riddled with flecks of skin. Traditionally, skinning is done by plunging the raw fruit into rapidly boiling water, causing the skin to blister away from the flesh. In desert-dwelling Native American cooking, and in other cuisines that developed where water was scarce, it is done by exposing the tomato to direct flame until the skin burns and blisters. The skin comes off either way, but when fire roasted, the tomato develops a pronounced smokiness.

DIRECTIONS

To make the dressing, puree the dressing ingredients in a blender or food processor until smooth.

To make the salad, combine the lettuces, mushrooms, roasted pepper, and red onion in a large bowl. Toss with the dressing and top with the goat cheese and pine nuts.

MAKES 4 SERVINGS
(about 1 cup dressing)

For the dressing:

1 tablespoon lemon juice, fresh or bottled organic

¾ cup orange juice

2 teaspoons toasted sesame oil

2 teaspoons soy sauce

1 teaspoon kosher salt

For the salad:

1 package (about 8 ounces) shredded carrots

1 red bell pepper, cut into thin strips

¼ cup chopped cilantro

2 tablespoons sesame seeds

carrot cilantro slaw

The juxtaposition of red pepper and carrot is not only beautiful, it is also bursting with flavor and texture. In this simple slaw the two are complemented by the fragrance of cilantro and a delicate Asian-inspired dressing.

DIRECTIONS

To make the dressing, mix the ingredients with a whisk in a small bowl until combined.

To make the salad, toss the carrots, red pepper, and cilantro in a serving bowl. Add the dressing and toss to coat; let rest for 30 minutes and garnish with the sesame seeds. Serve immediately, or refrigerate for up to 24 hours.

½ large sweet onion (such as Vidalia), cut into wedges

2 large cucumbers, peeled, sliced in half lengthwise, and seeded

1 rib celery, peeled

1 tablespoon kosher salt

¼ cup bottled ranch dressing

1 tablespoon sweet orange marmalade

1 teaspoon apple cider vinegar

1 cup finely diced watermelon

cucumber watermelon slaw

Cucumbers and watermelons are botanical cousins, and their similarities far outweigh their differences. Both are crisp, moist, and refreshing, and they have similar flavor compounds. The main difference is that we tend to want our cucumbers underripe and watermelons very ripe, so that the subtle cucumberlike flavors in watermelon are overshadowed by a pronounced sweetness. Taste the similarities and the differences for yourself in this very beautiful and refreshing slaw.

DIRECTIONS

Cut the onion, cucumbers, and celery into very thin slices. Toss with the salt in a bowl and set aside for 10 to 15 minutes.

Meanwhile, mix the ranch dressing, marmalade, and vinegar in a serving bowl and set aside.

Drain the vegetables and rinse. Dump into a clean kitchen towel; wring out any excess liquid. Add the vegetables and watermelon to the dressing and toss well to coat. Chill, if desired, before serving.

SALTING TO COOK, NOT JUST FOR FLAVOR

Salt is dynamic; it increases our perception of flavor, cures salmon, and causes home-churned ice cream to freeze. When tossed with raw vegetables like cucumbers, eggplants, or cabbage, it breaks down chemical bonds within the cell walls of the vegetables, causing them to soften and release some of their water. For eggplants this phenomenon rids the vegetable of some of its bitter liquid and prepares it for cooking, but salting cucumbers and cabbage is usually done when the vegetables will be eaten raw. If you don't presalt these vegetables, the salt in a dressing will cause them to weep liquid into a salad, making the finished dish watery. Getting rid of some of their moisture ahead of time makes the finished slaw more flavorful, and its dressing will remain creamy.

For the dressing:

⅓ cup extra-virgin olive oil

¼ cup red wine vinegar

1 teaspoon minced garlic, fresh or jarred organic

Salt and ground black pepper to taste

For the salad:

1 bag (about 2 pounds) frozen potato wedges

2 tablespoons garlic-flavored oil

1 teaspoon kosher salt

1 small onion, halved top to bottom and thinly sliced

1 roasted red bell pepper, jarred or homemade (page 337), sliced into strips

1 bag (about 7 ounces) baby spinach

roasted potato and spinach salad

In the escarole salad recipe on page 82, I proclaimed the sensual glory of wilted salad and showed you the method of tossing greens with hot dressing until they soften. Here's another way that works well with a vinaigrette-style dressing, which would tend to break down when heated. Season potato wedges and roast them; then, right from the oven, toss them with greens and the dressing. The greens will soften immediately, and the hot potatoes will sop up any extra dressing.

DIRECTIONS

Heat the oven to 450°F.

To make the dressing, mix the dressing ingredients in a small bowl.

To make the salad, toss the potatoes, oil, and salt on a rimmed sheet pan, spread in a single, even layer, and roast until browned and tender, about 30 minutes. While the potatoes are still hot, toss them with the remaining salad ingredients and the dressing. Adjust the seasoning with more salt and pepper, if needed, before serving.

MAKES 4 SERVINGS

1   pound frozen shelled edamame

    Juice of 1½ lemons

1   teaspoon Chinese chili paste
    with garlic

1   teaspoon toasted sesame oil

½   cup vegetable oil

1   teaspoon kosher salt

½   red onion, finely diced

1   cup garlic croutons, crushed

edamame salad

Edamame, green soybeans, are touted for their health benefits, but I recommend them for their flavor. Tossed with a spicy sesame lemon dressing, they redefine the notion of bean salad.

DIRECTIONS

Place the edamame in a small saucepan and cover with water. Heat to boiling and boil until tender, about 4 minutes. Drain.

Meanwhile, mix the lemon juice, chili paste, sesame oil, vegetable oil, salt, and onion in a serving bowl. Toss the hot edamame with the dressing; cool to room temperature. Top with the crushed croutons just before serving.

MAKES 4 SERVINGS

1   small cucumber, peeled, seeded,
    and finely chopped

1   medium tomato, finely chopped

½   cup chopped mixed olive,
    chopped muffaletta, or chopped
    olive salad, jarred or homemade
    (page 339)

4   ounces cooked salmon, leftover
    or canned, crumbled

1   tablespoon extra-virgin olive oil

4   slices French bread, toasted

¼   cup ranch dressing

1   tablespoon tomato paste or
    tomato pesto

1   bag (about 7 ounces)
    baby spinach

salmon bruschetta on spinach salad with tomato ranch dressing

This elaborate-looking salad couldn't be easier. The bruschetta topping is made with canned salmon that has been inundated with garden vegetables and a balm of olive oil. The toasts are simply perched atop a spinach salad dressed with garlicky ranch dressing that has been sweetened with tomato paste.

DIRECTIONS

Combine the cucumber, tomato, olive, salmon, and oil in a bowl. Mound a portion of the salmon mixture on each slice of toast. Mix the ranch dressing and tomato paste. Toss the spinach with the dressing mixture in a bowl and mound on 4 small plates. Place a salmon bruschetta on top of each salad and serve.

For the dressing:

1   cup sliced pickled beets, half drained

2   teaspoons dried dill

½   teaspoon chopped garlic, preferably fresh

3   tablespoons apple cider vinegar

2   tablespoons sugar

1½ teaspoons kosher salt

¼   teaspoon ground black pepper

For the salad:

1   pound baby potatoes, red or yellow

½   cup toasted walnut pieces, pre toasted or homemade (page 340)

2   ribs celery, peeled and thinly sliced

2   scallions, trimmed and sliced

2   tablespoons sweet pickle relish

¼   cup chopped Italian (flat-leaf) parsley

pickled pink potato salad

This magenta potato salad is shocking. The color is outrageous and the flavor combinations raucous. It is sweet and tart, creamy and crunchy, pickled and fresh. If you are looking for a dish to stand out at the community picnic, there is no need to turn the page.

DIRECTIONS

To make the dressing, puree the dressing ingredients in a blender or food processor until smooth.

To make the salad, cook the potatoes in a pot of lightly salted water just until tender, about 15 minutes; drain and set aside until cool enough to handle. Slip the peels off with your fingers, and cut the potatoes into bite-size pieces. Toss all of the salad ingredients and the dressing in a serving bowl. Serve at room temperature, or refrigerate until ready to serve.

For the dressing:

2 tablespoons Thai fish sauce (nam pla)

3 tablespoons light brown sugar

½ teaspoon chopped garlic, preferably fresh

½ teaspoon sriracha, Thai hot pepper sauce

¼ cup lime juice, fresh or bottled organic

For the salad:

2 mangoes, barely ripe, peeled

1 small cucumber, peeled, seeded, and finely diced

2 scallions, trimmed and thinly sliced

¼ cup finely chopped red onion

2 cups (about 6 ounces) mung bean sprouts

¼ cup dry-roasted peanuts, chopped

thai mango salad

Thai fish sauce (nam pla), which flavors this exotic meat salad, is an ancient and important flavoring in Southeast Asian dishes. If you are unfamiliar with it, don't get grossed out when you take your first whiff. It's quite intense, but like other fermented aromas (truffles, anchovies, blue cheese), it is tamed by the addition of other flavors. There are many brands of fish sauce and a range of quality. The one I use most often is called Tiparos, from Thailand. Serve this salad as a main course, or as a first course in an elaborate meal.

DIRECTIONS

To make the dressing, simmer the fish sauce, brown sugar, and garlic in a small saucepan, stirring, until the sugar dissolves. Stir in the hot pepper sauce and lime juice, and let cool.

To make the salad, shred the mangoes, rubbing the broad sides against the coarse teeth of a grater until you reach the pit. Turn and shred the other sides in the same way. Toss with the cucumber, scallion, red onion, and cooled dressing in a bowl. Make a bed of the sprouts on a plate and mound the salad on top. Garnish with the chopped peanuts.

SPROUTS: AN INSTANT SALAD

A sprout is the first appearance of a plant from its seed, and it contains much of the nutrition of that plant. Because sprouts are miniature plants, they do not require trimming or cutting; you can simply toss them into a salad or use them as the base for a slaw.

Different sprouts have different flavors. If a type of sprout is new to you, use your knowledge of the mature plant to understand what the sprout might taste like. For instance, radish sprouts are spicier than broccoli sprouts, which are stronger than clover or alfalfa sprouts. Look for sprouts that are brightly colored, firm, and crisp. Avoid those that are damp or matted or are starting to brown or shrivel. Keep sprouts refrigerated, and use them as soon as possible.

For the dressing:

1   tablespoon sesame tahini

1   tablespoon lime juice,
    preferably fresh

1   tablespoon soy sauce

½   cup plain yogurt

For the salad:

12 ounces cooked salmon, leftover
    or canned, crumbled

4   scallions, trimmed and sliced

1   tablespoon chopped parsley

4–5 radishes, trimmed and
    thinly sliced

    Toasted pita or pita
    chips (optional)

salmon tahini salad

This Arab-inspired salmon salad can be served as a dip or scooped into pita pockets and eaten as a sandwich. Tahini (sesame paste) is thick and flavorful. You don't need a lot to get a strong impact and a creamy texture.

DIRECTIONS

To make the dressing, mix the tahini, lime juice, soy sauce, and yogurt in a small bowl.

To make the salad, combine the salmon, scallions, parsley, and tahini dressing in a serving bowl. Garnish with the radish slices and serve with toasted pita.

1   can (about 16 ounces) chick-
    peas, drained and rinsed

2   teaspoons chopped garlic,
    preferably fresh

    Juice of 1½ lemons

2   tablespoons extra-virgin olive oil

2   tablespoons chopped mint
    leaves (about 30 leaves)

½   cup chopped Italian
    (flat-leaf) parsley

    Salt and ground black pepper
    to taste

chickpea tabbouleh

Think coarsely mashed chickpeas seasoned with lots of garlic and lemon juice and an avalanche of parsley. It's bean tabbouleh. Serve it as a salad or a chunky dip.

DIRECTIONS

Mash the chickpeas coarsely in a bowl. Add the remaining ingredients and mix to combine; serve.

For the dressing:

½ cup grapefruit juice, preferably fresh

2 tablespoons extra-virgin olive oil

⅛ teaspoon dried dill

¼ teaspoon minced garlic, preferably fresh

Salt and ground black pepper to taste

For the salad:

1 bag (about 5 ounces) cleaned watercress leaves (cresson)

1 grapefruit, peeled, sections removed from membranes

1 pound cooked shrimp, peeled and cleaned

¼ cup (about 1 ounce) crumbled blue cheese

¼ cup walnut pieces

shrimp and cress salad with grapefruit vinaigrette

Grapefruit can be overpowering eaten on its own, but when combined with other ingredients it is surprisingly delicate, much more subtle than other citrus. I especially like it in relationship with a bitter green, like watercress, where its aromatics and sweetness begin to emerge. In this salad the combination is complicated with bites of shrimp and pungent nuggets of blue cheese.

DIRECTIONS

To make the dressing, mix the ingredients with a whisk in a small bowl.

To make the salad, toss the watercress in a bowl with half the dressing, and mound on a serving platter. Toss the grapefruit sections and shrimp with the remaining dressing in the same bowl and arrange attractively on the watercress. Scatter the blue cheese over the top and garnish with the walnuts.

**MAKES 4 APPETIZER OR
2 ENTRÉE SERVINGS**

6   ounces skinless salmon fillet,
    preferably the tail end

4   ounces sea scallops, trimmed

¼   cup fresh lime juice

2   tablespoons rice wine vinegar

    Salt and ground black pepper
    to taste

1   teaspoon soy sauce

2   scallions, trimmed and
    thinly sliced

1   package (about 4 ounces)
    sprouts, preferably of greens,
    like alfalfa or clover

sprouted seviche

Seviche is the quintessence of freshness: just-caught seafood, sliced wafer-thin and quickly cured in citrus juice. Usually it is served as an appetizer, but here it garnishes a salad of sprouts, its fresher-than-fresh counterpart in the vegetable world. The recipe calls for sprouts from greens, like alfalfa, clover, or broccoli, as opposed to bean sprouts (mung, lentil, soy, etc.), which are stronger tasting and not as pretty when paired with fish.

DIRECTIONS

Cut the salmon and scallops into paper-thin slices. Toss in a bowl with the lime juice and vinegar; cover and refrigerate for at least 1 hour; drain. Add the salt and pepper, soy sauce, and scallions. Serve on a bed of sprouts.

COOKING WITHOUT HEAT

Curing is a way of cooking protein without using heat. When protein cooks, it becomes firm, opaque, and dry. For example, think of the difference between a raw, rare, medium-done, and well-done steak. As the meat progresses through the stages of doneness, it becomes firmer (a rare steak is soft, well-done is hard), its color changes from translucent red to opaque brown, and its moisture content reduces from juicy to dry. The same changes happen when a protein is soaked in acid or salt; it just happens more gradually.

Cured seafood, like seviche, gravlax, and pickled fish, has a fresh, barely cooked appearance and taste, and the process is almost effortless. All you do is mix up the cure, which can be either a combination of citrus juices, or other acidic fruit juices and vinegar. Cover the food with the cure and refrigerate until the food is "cooked" to your liking. This can take anywhere from a few hours for thinly sliced seafood to a day for whole scallops or shrimp. To serve, simply remove from the cure and you're done.

For the dressing:

¼ cup extra-virgin olive oil

2 tablespoons fresh lemon juice

1 tablespoon fresh lime juice

2 tablespoons basil pesto, jarred
   or homemade (page 339)

   Salt and ground black pepper
   to taste

For the salad:

1 lemon

1 lime

8 ounces skinned and boned
   salmon fillet, cut into ¼-inch cubes

¼ teaspoon crushed red
   pepper flakes

1 small cucumber, thinly sliced

salmon seviche with basil drizzle

Seviche is usually associated with tropical cuisine, but in this quick and refreshing recipe the technique of cooking fish in citrus is given a Mediterranean flair by seasoning the seviche with pesto and enriching it with olive oil.

DIRECTIONS

To make the dressing, mix the ingredients with a whisk in a small bowl.

To make the salad, grate the zest from the lemon and lime on a fine grater. Squeeze the juice from the lemon and lime and toss with the salmon and pepper flakes in a bowl; cover. Refrigerate for 45 to 60 minutes (until the salmon is barely flaky); drain. Mound the seviche on a plate and garnish with cucumber slices. Drizzle the dressing over the top.

roasted corn cobb salad with balsamic blueberry vinaigrette

For the dressing:

1   can (about 14 ounces) blueberries in water, drained

1   teaspoon sugar

1   teaspoon kosher salt

1   teaspoon dried tarragon

⅓   cup aged balsamic vinegar

2   teaspoons tarragon vinegar

2   tablespoons grapeseed oil or other mild-flavored oil

For the salad:

1   cup frozen corn kernels (preferably roasted), thawed

1   roasted red bell pepper, jarred or homemade (page 337), diced

1   large tomato, stem removed, cut into small dice

1   small cucumber, peeled, seeded, and cut into small dice

½   medium red onion, finely chopped

1   bag (about 5 ounces) washed and trimmed watercress or arugula

8   ounces roasted chicken breast, thinly sliced, rotisserie or freshly made

2   strips ready-to-serve precooked bacon, crisped and crumbled

1   avocado, peeled and diced, tossed with 1 teaspoon lemon juice

The bold graphic stripes of bacon, egg, poached chicken, tomato, and avocado that are the hallmark of a classic Cobb salad are the inspiration behind this Technicolor staging. The layout is the same, but the dressing brings in a new hue. A magenta stain of blueberry vinaigrette, drizzled over all, interrupts the orderliness with a tart, fruity, herbal provocation.

DIRECTIONS

To make the dressing, puree the dressing ingredients in a blender or food processor until smooth.

To make the salad, toss the corn and red pepper in a small bowl; set aside. Toss the tomato, cucumber, and red onion in a separate bowl.

Arrange a bed of the watercress or arugula on a large platter. Top one third of the greens with the corn mixture. Mound the tomato and cucumber mixture next to the corn, covering another third of the greens. Cover the remaining greens with the sliced chicken; top the chicken with crumbled bacon. Drizzle the dressing over the top, and scatter the avocado over all.

1   can (about 6 ounces) tuna packed in oil, drained

1   tablespoon extra-virgin olive oil

2   tablespoons black olive tapenade, jarred or homemade (page 347)

1   tablespoon drained capers, chopped

1   teaspoon basil pesto, jarred, refrigerated, or homemade (page 339)

For the dressing:

Juice of 1 lemon

2   tablespoons extra-virgin olive oil

1   teaspoon minced garlic

1   tablespoon finely chopped cilantro

Salt and ground black pepper to taste

For the salad:

1   can or pouch (6 or 7 ounces) white tuna, drained and broken into chunks

¾   cup salsa, medium or hot

2   cups thinly sliced romaine lettuce

8   ounces refrigerated prepared guacamole (about 1 cup)

4   ounces tortilla chips (about 28 chips)

extra-virgin tuna salad

In this Mediterranean-style tuna salad, mayonnaise is replaced with a combination of olives, olive oil, capers, and basil. If you want to make it heartier, toss in a can of rinsed and drained white beans.

DIRECTIONS

Combine all of the ingredients in a bowl. Serve as a salad or sandwich spread.

tunacamole

This mountain of shredded lettuce, guacamole, and vinaigrette-dressed tuna is drizzled with salsa so that it looks like an erupting volcano. Use the chips that surround it to scoop up the landscape.

DIRECTIONS

To make the dressing, mix the lemon juice, oil, garlic, and cilantro in a bowl with a whisk. Season with salt and pepper.

To make the salad, toss the tuna with the dressing. Puree the salsa in a blender or food processor.

Make a circular mound of lettuce on a serving plate. Top with the guacamole, spreading it loosely toward the edge of the lettuce. Mound the tuna in the center, and spoon the salsa over the top, like lava flowing down the cone of a volcano. Surround with the chips to use for scooping.

4 beef, pork, lamb & veal

At heart, we are carnivores. Even as vegetarianism makes its mark on our culinary consciousness, meat has remained central to the American diet. Moist, rich, toothsome, and tender, it has everything we applaud in a dinner, with none of the fuss.

The problem with meat cookery has never been how to cook it (what could be simpler than tossing something in a hot oven and giving it its privacy until it's done?) but how to make it more than . . . well . . . more than a slab of meat. That's what this chapter is all about: the sauces and glazes, spice pastes and pestos, marinades, vinaigrettes, and chimichurris that transform a plain piece of meat into a meal.

2   tablespoons olive oil

1   medium onion, thinly sliced

1   tablespoon minced garlic, fresh
    or jarred organic

1   cup diced tomato, fresh or
    drained canned

1   cup bottled Caesar dressing

1   pound sandwich steak (thinly
    sliced round steak)

    Salt and ground black pepper
    to taste

4   ounces (1 cup) crumbled
    blue cheese

4   6-inch sandwich rolls, split
    and toasted

blue cheesesteaks

Sandwiches are more about architecture than cooking, their success dependent on the integrity of each element stacked upon the next. In this far-flung rendition of a Philly cheesesteak, the sautéed onions (essential for a good cheesesteak) are refreshed with chopped tomato and a tang of Caesar dressing. The steaks are topped with blue cheese, and the elements are layered on a toasted roll.

DIRECTIONS

Heat half of the oil in a large skillet over medium-high heat. Add the onion and sauté until tender. Add the garlic and tomato and cook until the tomato softens, about 2 minutes. Stir in the dressing; transfer to a container and keep warm. Wipe out the skillet.

Heat the remaining oil in the skillet over high heat. Add the steak and sauté until browned and cooked through, about 1 minute per side; season with salt and pepper, and chop with the end of a spatula into large bite-size pieces as they cook. Separate the steak in the pan into 4 equal portions; top each portion with 1 ounce of the cheese. Cover the pan and cook until the cheese melts, about 1 minute.

To serve, place a portion of steak in each roll and top with some of the onion mixture.

1½ pounds ground beef, preferably 85% lean

Salt and ground black pepper to taste

¼ cup refrigerated barbecued beef, large pieces shredded

No-stick spray oil

4 kaiser rolls, split and toasted

½ cup refrigerated coleslaw mix (optional)

burgers molten with BBQ beef

Since rare burgers have been outlawed by the *E. coli* police, my search for a juicy burger has led me into uncharted regions. One of my best discoveries is this recipe. By stuffing the heart of the burger with a moist interior, you get the flavor of the filling, added moisture, and a thinner layer of burger meat that needs to cook through. Warning: Serve with extra napkins.

DIRECTIONS

Heat a grill to medium. Season the ground beef with salt and pepper; divide into eight 3-ounce flattened burgers. Place a tablespoon of the barbecued beef in the center of each of 4 of the burgers. Top with the remaining burgers and mold into 4 large burgers stuffed with barbecued beef. Spray liberally with oil.

Grill the burgers until the ground beef is cooked through and the barbecued beef interior is hot, 3 to 4 minutes per side on a covered grill, 5 to 6 minutes if the grill is open. Serve the burgers on toasted rolls; top each burger with coleslaw mix, if desired.

2　tablespoons olive oil

1　teaspoon dried Italian
　seasoning blend

1–1½　pounds boneless tenderloin,
　sirloin, or porterhouse steak

⅓　cup balsamic vinegar

1　tablespoon Worcestershire
　sauce

1　tablespoon spicy
　brown mustard

2　teaspoons ketchup

steaks with balsamic steak sauce

This recipe probably doesn't belong in this book. It takes a standard two-ingredient preparation, grilled steak served with bottled steak sauce, and ups the ante. I've included it for a noble reason—flavor. The sweet tangy spicy pulpy cacophony that is steak sauce is phenomenally easy to mix up. Made from just four ingredients, it keeps for months and will give you the prestige that only someone who makes his own sauce can possess.

DIRECTIONS

Combine the olive oil and the seasoning; rub into the surface of the steaks, and set aside for 10 to 20 minutes. Preheat a grill or broiler. Meanwhile, make the sauce by boiling the balsamic vinegar in a skillet for 1 minute. Stir in the Worcestershire sauce, mustard, and ketchup. Grill or broil the steak to the desired degree of doneness, about 5 to 7 minutes per side for medium, depending on thickness. Serve with the sauce.

CHOOSING MEAT

Meat from an older animal or an exercised muscle group is more flavorful, darker, and tougher, so when looking at the lean part of a meat, check out the color. The paler it is, the milder and more tender the meat will be.

Next, look at the texture. Large, tough muscle fibers make the surface of a piece of meat look rough. Small, undeveloped fibers are barely visible, giving tender meat a sleek, silken appearance. The thickness of the connective tissue surrounding the fibers, which also affects tenderness, magnifies these textural differences.

Fat is, by far, the most controversial element in meat. Cursed with a reputation for causing obesity and heart disease, fat is the skeleton in every meat producer's closet. But while they scramble to rid their product of the unmentionable, meat marketers fail to realize, and do nothing to help consumers understand, that fat is the principal element that makes meat taste good.

But it's important to note where the fat is. A thick layer of fat framing the exterior of a piece of meat doesn't do anybody any good. But marbling—the barely visible veins of fat webbed throughout the lean—makes meat more tender, more flavorful, and perceptibly moister. As a piece of meat cooks, the marbling melts into the fibers, spreading its flavor impact into every bite. In addition to being flavorful itself, fat is essential for the perception of all aromatic flavors, so marbling helps carry the impact of sauces and seasoning on the meat to the palate.

It is not necessary to have visible globs of fat striated through the lean, but neither should you seek out fat-free specimens. If fat is a dietary concern, limit the quantity of meat, but don't sacrifice the quality and succulence of the small amount that your diet allows.

¼ cup tamari soy sauce

3 tablespoons lime juice, fresh or bottled organic

¼ teaspoon crushed red pepper flakes

2 tablespoons sugar

1 teaspoon minced garlic, fresh or jarred organic

1 teaspoon minced ginger, fresh or jarred

2 pounds hanger steak

No-stick spray oil

grilled tamari and lime hanger steaks

Marinades are less effective than we want to believe. They can flavor the surface of meats and tenderize the outer crust, but they do not penetrate deeply. However, if subtle change is what you're after, the right marinade is a wonderful thing. Hanger steaks are rich and flavorful; they can be a little chewy, but they are relatively low in fat. This marinade does nothing to mask the qualities of the beef; rather, it provides a counterpoint to the richness with the clean sensation of citrus, soy, and hot pepper.

DIRECTIONS

Combine the tamari, lime juice, pepper flakes, sugar, garlic, and ginger in a gallon-size zipper plastic bag. Add the steak and massage the marinade into the meat. Refrigerate for at least 2 hours, or for as long as 6 hours.

Heat a grill to high. Remove the steak from the marinade and pat dry; discard the excess marinade. Spray the meat liberally with oil and grill for 5 minutes per side for medium. To serve, cut in thin slices against the grain.

HANGER STEAK

A popular bistro steak that is better known in Europe than America, hanger steak is the cut that used to be reserved for the butcher; hence its nickname, butcher's steak. Recently, chic chefs have become enamored with its intense flavor and casual presentation, so it has started to appear on restaurant menus and in specialty butcher shops. Similar in texture and flavor to skirt steak, a hanger is a small steak (about 1 pound) that is composed of two long muscles attached by an elastic membrane that should be removed by your butcher, yielding two 8-ounce strips; each strip is a portion.

4   bone-in rib pork chops, about
    6 ounces each

    Salt and ground black pepper
    to taste

1   tablespoon vegetable oil

1/2 teaspoon fennel seed or
    caraway seed

1   bag (about 10 ounces) shredded
    red cabbage

1   cup cranberry juice

1/2 cup chicken broth

1/3 cup dried cranberries

1   tablespoon chopped basil (optional)

pork chops with cranberries and red cabbage

Pork and cabbage are a classic combo that can take many forms, from paprikash to choucroute. Here, rouge is the theme: the cabbage is red, the cranberries are red, and the cooking liquid is cranberry juice. Not only are most of the ingredients tawny, but the acid in the cranberry juice helps to protect the red pigment in the cabbage so that it stays bright during cooking.

DIRECTIONS

Season the pork chops with salt and pepper. Heat the oil in a large skillet over medium-high heat, and brown the chops on both sides. Transfer to a plate. Add the fennel seed and cabbage to the pan and toss to coat with oil. Add the cranberry juice, chicken broth, and cranberries. Return the pork chops to the pan, cover, and simmer until the pork chops are tender, about 10 minutes. Transfer the pork chops to a platter. Stir the basil into the cabbage, if desired, and serve with the chops.

MAKES 4 SERVINGS

4   rib or loin pork chops, about
    6 ounces each

    Kosher salt and coarsely ground
    black pepper to taste

1   tablespoon vegetable oil

1   can (about 15 ounces) posole
    (whole hominy), drained

3/4 cup chunky salsa, medium-hot

1   can (about 14 ounces)
    chicken broth

2   tablespoons chopped cilantro

    Juice of 1 lime

pork chops braised with posole

Posole, or whole hominy, is corn that has been cooked with an alkali, like lime or lye, which softens the grain, plumps its innards, and gives it a unique mineral flavor and a chewy texture. Traditional recipes call for dry posole, which can take hours to cook; here we rely on heat-and-eat canned posole (a.k.a. hominy). Most hominy is made from white corn, although some Hispanic brands sell yellow hominy as well. Either color will work in this recipe.

DIRECTIONS

Season the pork chops on both sides with salt and pepper. Heat the oil in a large skillet over medium-high heat. Add the pork chops and brown on both sides; drain off the excess oil. Add the posole, salsa, and broth and simmer until the chops are springy to the touch, 3 to 5 minutes; do not overcook. Stir in the cilantro and lime juice and serve.

MAKES 4 SERVINGS

2   tablespoons olive oil

1   pound hot Italian sausage links

2   onions, halved and sliced

1   large tart apple, cored and cut
    into 12 wedges

1   teaspoon fennel seeds, crushed

16 ounces chopped kale or collards,
    fresh or frozen

1   cup chicken broth

    Salt and ground black pepper
    to taste

hot sausage braised with greens and apples

This simple dish of braised sausage and greens has it all: a balance of hot peppers, sweet-tart apple, and acrid bitter greens. Served with bread it is a one-pot meal, and any leftovers are great the next morning chopped into a frittata.

DIRECTIONS

Heat the oil in a large skillet over medium-high heat. Brown the sausages on all sides and remove. Add the onions and cook until brown; add the apple and brown. Add the fennel and kale and toss until the kale wilts, about 2 minutes. Add the broth and simmer for 5 minutes. Return the sausages to the pan and cook until the greens are tender, the sausage is cooked through, and the broth is mostly evaporated, another 3 to 4 minutes. Season with salt and pepper, and serve.

1/2 cup teriyaki sauce

2 1/2 pounds country-style pork ribs

12 (about 3 ounces) pitted dried plums (prunes)

1/2 cup boiling water

1 cup beef broth

1/8 teaspoon crushed red pepper flakes

teriyaki pork ribs braised with prunes

The inspired juxtaposition of salty, tangy teriyaki and sweet, plush prunes is glorious. You don't have to do anything except introduce the ingredients and give them time to meld. Here they are teamed with country pork ribs.

DIRECTIONS

Put the teriyaki sauce and the pork in a large zipper bag and massage to moisten all of the meat. Refrigerate for at least 15 minutes. Meanwhile, soak the plums in the boiling water until softened, about 10 minutes.

Heat a heavy skillet over high heat. Remove the pork from the zipper bag and brown on both sides, about 3 minutes per side. Add the used teriyaki marinade, the plums and their soaking liquid, and the broth and pepper flakes. Heat to boiling, reduce the heat to a simmer, and simmer until the pork is tender, about 20 minutes. Serve the pork with its cooking liquid.

4   thick loin pork chops, bone in

1   teaspoon dried Italian seasoning

1   tablespoon olive oil

1   can (about 14 ounces) reduced-sodium chicken broth (see Note)

1   canned chipotle pepper, finely chopped, or 1 teaspoon chipotle hot sauce

3   tablespoons whole-fruit cherry preserves

pork chops with chipotle cherry demi-glace

Chile peppers and fruit seem like odd flavor partners, but I've found that chipotle peppers (smoked jalapeños) have a distinct affinity for tart cherries (try the Chipotle Cherry Pie in the dessert chapter, page 305). There is something about the scent of smoke and the subtle afterburn of chipotle that finds its soulmate in the over-the-top sweet-tart fruit of sour cherry preserves. Titillating flavors and a mahogany sheen make this dish seem gourmet, but the preparation is almost effortless.

DIRECTIONS

Season the pork chops with the seasoning on both sides. Heat the oil in a large skillet over medium-high heat. Brown the pork chops on both sides and remove to a plate. Pour off the excess oil from the pan.

Add the broth to the pan and boil until it is reduced to about half of its volume. Reduce the heat so the broth simmers; return the pork chops to the pan and simmer, turning once or twice, until they feel resilient to the touch, about 3 minutes. Transfer the chops to a platter.

Add the chipotle pepper and cherry preserves to the pan; increase the heat to medium-high and boil until the pan liquid thickens slightly. Pour over the pork and serve.

Note: Because the broth is going to be reduced to make a sauce, it is important to use a reduced-sodium broth for this recipe. Otherwise, the amount of salt in the broth will become overpowering once it is concentrated through reduction.

4	boneless center-cut pork chops, each about 6 ounces and ¾ inch thick
1	teaspoon garlic spice blend
1	tablespoon olive oil
1¼	cups bottled Thai peanut sauce
½	cup water
1	tablespoon mesquite steak sauce, such as A-1
1	tablespoon chopped Italian (flat-leaf) parsley

smoky peanut pork chops

Thai peanut sauce comes fully prepared in a bottle, or as a dry mix (to which you have to add coconut milk). This recipe can use either type, but it is easiest made with the bottled sauce. The spicy-sweet flavor of the peanut sauce is heightened with a smoky hit of mesquite, a seemingly slight adjustment that makes all the eye-watering, sinus-clearing, lip-smacking difference in the world.

DIRECTIONS

Season the pork chops on both sides with the spice blend. Heat a large, nonstick skillet over medium-high heat, add the olive oil, and brown the pork on both sides. Add the peanut sauce and water, stir, cover, and simmer until the chops are not quite firm in the center, about 5 minutes. Transfer the pork to a serving plate. Stir the steak sauce and parsley into the sauce, bring to a boil, and pour over the pork and serve.

MESQUITE SAUCES

I tried lots of mesquite-flavored sauces while testing this recipe, and the one I liked best is A-1 Mesquite Steak Sauce. This is not to say that another of the many mesquite-infused marinades, grilling sauces, barbecue sauces, and hot sauces isn't perfectly fine. The A-1 product is a little peppery, so if the sauce you use has more of a sweet or tart profile, you might want to add a touch of hot sauce. On the other hand, if you want to substitute a mesquite-flavored hot pepper sauce for the steak sauce, use ½ teaspoon or so for the mesquite flavor, and cut it with a tablespoon of barbecue sauce, vinaigrette-style salad dressing, or ketchup.

2   cups apple cider

½   cup maple syrup

1   teaspoon mustard

1½   pounds pork tenderloin,
     2 medium sized

     Salt and ground black pepper
     to taste

maple-glazed pork tenderloins

The tenderloin is the muscle that allows a four-legged animal to arch its back, something that four-legged animals never do. Void of exercise, tenderloin muscles never develop. They stay small and tender and bland, which means they cook quickly but need some help in the flavor department. In this recipe, a sweet and tangy paste of apple cider syrup (made by boiling down apple cider to concentrate its flavor), maple sugar, and mustard is slathered over pork tenderloins as they cook. Pay attention once you start basting with sauce; the glaze can burn in an instant.

DIRECTIONS

Boil the cider in a skillet over medium heat until reduced to about ½ cup and lightly thickened. Stir in the maple syrup and mustard.

Heat a broiler to high, and set the rack as close to the flame as possible. Season the tenderloins with salt and pepper and place them on the broiler pan; brush each with a tablespoon of the maple glaze. Broil until lightly browned, 4 to 5 minutes. Baste with glaze and broil for 3 more minutes. Turn, baste with glaze, and broil until lightly browned and resilient to the touch (medium-done), 5 to 7 minutes more (12 to 15 minutes total cooking time). Let rest for 5 minutes before slicing. Slice and nap with the remaining glaze before serving.

2 pork tenderloins, about 12 ounces each

1 tablespoon extra-virgin olive oil

Juice of 2 limes

1 tablespoon Greek spice rub, or dried seasoning blend

¼ cup jarred chimichurri sauce

1 tablespoon minced garlic

Kosher salt and coarsely ground black pepper to taste

grilled pork tenderloins with lime chimichurri

Chimichurri, the tangy, herbaceous condiment found on every table in Argentina, is typically paired with beef. I've modified it a bit by sweetening jarred chimichurri with lime juice and garlic to make a spectacular grill sauce for white meats. Although it is used with pork in this recipe, it is equally good with chicken, turkey, and most seafood.

DIRECTIONS

Rub the tenderloins with the oil and half of the lime juice, then rub with the Greek spices. Heat a grill set up for direct grilling to high. While the grill is heating, mix the chimichurri, remaining lime juice, garlic, salt, and pepper in a bowl. Grill the tenderloins to 150°F, about 15 minutes, turning 2 or 3 times. Let rest for 5 minutes and slice on the diagonal. Spoon the chimichurri mixture over the top before serving.

CHIMICHURRI

Fresh red meat is so ubiquitous in Argentina (most families eat it every day) that the cuisine never developed elaborate preparations for it. There are two types of meat cookery in Argentina: *asado* is for cooking large cuts and is similar to Southwest barbecue; *parilla* (pronounced par-EE-yah) is straightforward grilling used for steaks, chops, and sausages, and these meats are always sauced and served with chimichurri. There are just four ingredients in a basic chimichurri: parsley, garlic, vinegar, and salt (although many recipes include hot peppers and oregano).

1   bag (about 12 ounces) micro-
    ready chopped and washed
    broccoli rabe

3   tablespoons extra-virgin olive oil

1   spicy sausage (about 3 ounces),
    any type, finely chopped

3   cloves garlic, chopped

1   pound frozen bread dough,
    thawed and risen according to
    package directions

1/4 cup (about 1 ounce) grated
    Romano cheese

sausage and rabe stromboli

Stromboli is a rolled-up pizza. If you work in a pizzeria, throwing one together is no big deal, but in a home kitchen, by the time you make the dough, cook the ingredients for the filling, assemble the stromboli, and bake it, you might as well have made Thanksgiving dinner. But by relying on two packaged products, microwavable precut, prewashed broccoli rabe and frozen bread dough, you can streamline the process down to 15 minutes of assembly and 20 minutes in the oven, You might even think about opening a pizzeria.

DIRECTIONS

Heat the oven to 400°F. Poke several holes in the bag of broccoli rabe and cook in a microwave for 4 minutes at full power.

- -

Heat 1 tablespoon of the oil in a large skillet over medium-high heat. Add the sausage and sauté until cooked through. Add the garlic and stir for a few seconds. Add the rabe and 1 tablespoon of the remaining oil; toss to combine, and cook until the mixture is almost dry.

- -

Spread the dough into a rough 12-inch square on a clean work surface. Sprinkle with the cheese and spread the rabe mixture over the surface, leaving 1 inch of dough uncovered along one edge. Roll the dough with the filling toward the uncovered edge, pinching the ends and open edge to seal in the filling. Rub the loaf with the remaining tablespoon of oil, and place seam-side down on a large sheet pan. Make a few slits on the surface with a sharp knife. Bake until puffed and brown, about 20 minutes. Let cool for a few minutes before serving.

FROZEN DOUGH

Making bread dough is a lengthy, multistage process that can't be rushed. On the other hand, it can be stalled. At several points during its assembly, not only is it possible to stop and rest, but it is essential, and the longer the dough rests the better the resulting bread will be, which means a dough can be frozen at any of the resting points and then reactivated after thawing without affecting the quality.

In the first stage of bread-making, yeast, water, and flour are mixed together into a mudlike dough called a sponge. Beating the sponge activates the protein in the flour, forming long elastic bands (gluten) that will give the bread texture. After the gluten is sufficiently developed, the sponge has to rest to give the yeast time to feed on the starch in the dough and produce carbon dioxide gas, which gets trapped in the bands of gluten, causing the dough to stretch and rise. If the sponge is frozen, the activity of the yeast will stop, allowing the baker to store the sponge for extended periods. After thawing, the yeast will resume its life, and the process can continue without any ill effect.

The next stage involves adding enough flour to make it semi-solid and kneading the mass of dough until it becomes bouncy. While this is going on, the yeast continues to feed and thrive and the gluten becomes stronger and stretchier. Again the dough must rest to help it rise and develop texture, after which it is ready to be formed into a loaf and baked. Commercial frozen bread dough is at this stage of development, so once you thaw it at home and let it rise briefly it is ready to go into the oven.

1 large container (about 16 ounces) garlic hummus (if you can't find garlic hummus, add 1 teaspoon minced garlic to a container of regular hummus)

¼ cup lemon juice, fresh or bottled organic

1 cup (about 8 ounces) plain yogurt

12 rib or loin lamb chops, about 2 pounds

Oil for grilling

garlic garbanzo lamb chops

The marinade for these grilled lamb chops is a tzatziki sauce that has been enriched with beans. The addition creates a delicious savory crust as the chops cook.

DIRECTIONS

Mix the hummus, lemon juice, and yogurt in a bowl. Reserve ⅓ cup and toss the rest with the lamb chops in a large zipper bag; refrigerate for at least 1 hour.

Prepare a grill for direct grilling and heat to high; rub the rack with oil. Remove the chops from the marinade and wipe off any excess. Grill for 3 to 4 minutes per side for medium-rare. Serve the chops topped with the reserved hummus mixture.

1   package (about ½ ounce) dried
     wild mushrooms, such as porcini

2   cups boiling water

4   lamb shoulder chops, about
     2 pounds

     No-stick flour and oil baking spray

     Salt and ground black pepper
     to taste

1   box (about 10 ounces) frozen
     pearl onions, thawed and drained

1   package (about 10 ounces)
     sliced portobello mushrooms,
     halved

½   teaspoon crushed dried
     rosemary

1½   tablespoons demi-glace
     concentrate

1   cup V8 vegetable juice

lamb shoulder braised with wild mushrooms

Dried wild mushrooms may seem extravagant if you just look at the price tag, but a little bit goes a long way. Here a half ounce is all it takes to inundate the recipe with mushroom flavor. Lamb shoulder is a budget cut that has great flavor but needs a little simmering time to reach full tenderness.

DIRECTIONS

Soak the dried mushrooms in the boiling water until softened, about 10 minutes. Drain, reserving the soaking liquid and the mushrooms separately.

Heat a large skillet over medium-high heat. Coat the chops on both sides with baking spray and season with salt and pepper; brown on both sides. Remove to a plate.

Add the onions, portobellos, and rosemary to the skillet and cook until the mushrooms lose their raw look. Add the soaked mushrooms and the soaking liquid, leaving behind any sediment; heat to boiling. Stir in the demi-glace concentrate until dissolved. Stir in the V8 juice and return the chops to the skillet; reduce the heat and simmer until the chops are cooked through, about 20 minutes.

Remove the chops to a serving platter. If the liquid in the pan is too thin, boil until it is lightly thickened. Pour over the chops before serving.

RESTAURANT-STYLE STOCK AND SAUCE CONCENTRATES

Meat stock and the classic sauces derived from it are the province of great restaurants, not home kitchens. First of all, the mass of vegetable trimmings and meat bones required to prepare stock are uncommon in a home kitchen, and second, no one could afford the time and attention it takes to make fine stocks and sauces if they weren't getting paid for it. Fortunately, several companies produce high-quality stock and sauce concentrates. These products are a bit pricey, but they are the real thing, made in the classic style—simmered for hours and reduced to a paste. All we need to do is add water for surprisingly professional results.

½ teaspoon ground coriander

¼ teaspoon ground black pepper

½ teaspoon salt

1½ pounds boneless leg of lamb, butterflied

2 tablespoons olive oil

2 teaspoons minced garlic, fresh or jarred organic

¼ cup white wine

½ cup chicken broth

½ cup canned diced tomatoes, preferably fire-roasted

Pinch of crushed red pepper flakes

1 can (about 15 ounces) white kidney beans, drained and rinsed

¼ cup minced cilantro

lamb braised with white beans and cilantro

I don't know why cilantro is not often paired with lamb. To my palate the slightly acrid, pungent perfume of cilantro is the perfect foil for lamb's musky gaminess. This recipe speeds up the cooking of a butterflied leg of lamb by simmering it briefly with white beans and chiles.

DIRECTIONS

Mix the coriander, pepper, and salt and rub all over the lamb. Heat the oil in a deep skillet over medium-high heat. Brown the lamb on both sides.

Add the garlic, wine, broth, tomatoes, crushed red pepper, and beans; stir briefly, reduce the heat to medium, cover, and cook until a thermometer inserted into the thickest part of the lamb registers 130°F for medium, 10 to 12 minutes. Remove the meat to a cutting board and cook the beans for another minute, until the liquid has reduced to a lightly thickened sauce. Stir in the cilantro. Slice the lamb and serve with the beans.

PRESERVATIVES IN JARRED GARLIC

If this book had been written several years ago, I would not have used jarred garlic in any recipe. Up until then, the amount of preservative used in processed garlic products gave them an unpleasant aftertaste that was overwhelming. The amount of preservative needed depends on how finely the garlic is chopped. Whole cloves need very little, but the smaller the pieces, the more perishable the garlic is.

The principal preservative in garlic processing is citric acid, which is vitamin C. It is not harmful, but it has a tart aftertaste that has to be balanced. Some of that balance can come from oil that is added during processing, and some can come from the strength of the garlic flavor itself. I recommend that you use organic jarred garlic because it has more garlic flavor and less citric acid. Christopher Ranch, which is the largest grower and packager of organic garlic, uses just enough citric acid in its chopped garlic to give it a pH slightly below 4.5, which is approximately the acidity of yogurt.

4   rib veal chops,
    about 8 ounces each

2   teaspoons dried Greek seasoning

    Kosher salt and coarsely ground
    black pepper

¼   cup extra-virgin olive oil

1   jar (about 12 ounces)
    tomato bruschetta

2   tablespoons red wine vinegar

1   tablespoon chopped Italian
    (flat-leaf) parsley

1   teaspoon lemon juice, fresh or
    organic bottled

veal chops with bruschetta vinaigrette

This simple, elegant dish of seared veal, chunky tomatoes, and a bright spark of red wine vinegar epitomizes the wisdom of short-cut cooking. By using high-quality fresh ingredients, teamed with prepared foods like jarred bruschetta, you get dishes that seem to contain many ingredients, and to have taken lots of time, with minimal effort and maximum effect.

DIRECTIONS

Season the veal on both sides with the Greek seasoning, salt, and pepper. Heat 2 tablespoons of the oil in a large skillet over high heat. Brown the chops on both sides in the hot oil; do not crowd the pan.

Add the bruschetta and vinegar; stir to combine. Reduce the heat to a simmer, cover, and simmer until the chops are cooked to the desired doneness, about 8 minutes for medium.

Remove the chops to a platter. Stir the remaining 2 tablespoons oil, parsley, and lemon juice into the pan and pour over the chops before serving.

2   tablespoons olive oil

4   pieces veal shank, about
    8 ounces each, cut for osso buco

    Kosher salt and coarsely ground
    black pepper

1   cup diced onion, fresh or frozen

2   teaspoons chopped garlic, fresh
    or jarred organic

1   teaspoon dried Italian seasoning

1   box or can (about 15 ounces)
    creamy butternut squash soup

1   can (about 14 ounces) diced
    fire-roasted tomatoes

2   canned chipotle peppers, chopped

2   cans (about 14 ounces each)
    chicken broth

½   cup golden raisins

¼   cup chopped cilantro

osso buco with chipotle chiles and golden raisins

This remarkable vegetable-laden, sweet-and-savory, subtly smoky, deceptively creamy rendition of osso buco is a revelation. A perusal of the ingredients list seems nonsensical until you realize that squash, tomatoes, chiles, and raisins all find a home in the moles of Mexico. The sauce is plentiful, so serve the dish with rice, bread, or tortillas to help sop up any excess.

DIRECTIONS

Heat the oil in a large Dutch oven over high heat. Season the veal shanks with salt and pepper and brown on all sides in the hot oil. Remove to a plate. Reduce the heat to medium, add the onion, and sauté until lightly browned. Stir in the garlic and season-ing and cook for about 1 minute. Add the soup, diced tomatoes, chipotle peppers, and broth; cover and simmer for 30 minutes.

Add the raisins, return the cover, and simmer for 30 minutes. Stir in the cilantro and serve.

TOUGH CUTS OF MEAT

Meat is muscle. If a muscle is exercised, two things happen: it increases in protein, which gives it more fla-vor, and it becomes harder, which makes it tough. Therefore, when a cut of meat is taken from an exercised muscle, like veal shanks, which come from the leg, it will be tough, but it will also have lots of flavor.

The main factor that has traditionally influenced the popularity of one cut of meat over another is tender-ness. It has made filet mignon sell for the same price per ounce that budget meats cost per pound. It is what makes veal chops more expensive than veal breast, and scaloppine costlier than shanks. These meats do not taste any better than cheaper cuts, but they can be sliced with a butter knife. And for that alone many diners are willing to blow the budget. So as long as meat prices are driven by tenderness, flavorful meats will stay affordable. Start buying meat for its flavor and your spending will go down.

1½ pounds veal stew meat

No-stick flour and oil baking spray

1 tablespoon olive oil

1 onion, cut into chunks

1 tablespoon chopped garlic, fresh or jarred organic

1 jar (about 12 ounces) marinated quartered artichoke hearts

1 cup chicken broth

1 teaspoon crushed dried rosemary

½ teaspoon dried thyme

1 can (about 14 ounces) diced tomatoes

1 can (about 10 ounces) chickpeas, drained and rinsed

2 tablespoons Italian (flat-leaf) parsley

stir-fried veal stew with artichokes

Stir-frying and stewing differ only in timing. Both techniques call for browning and simmering, but in stir-frying the ingredients are tender enough to cook in minutes, and stewing takes an hour or more. In this recipe we combine the two and split the difference. You get the seared surfaces of cooking in a wok and the complex melding of flavors of a stew, and you also get to cut the stewing time by 30 percent.

DIRECTIONS

Heat a large wok over high heat. Coat the veal with baking spray and brown in the wok in batches. Do not crowd the pan. Remove the veal and set aside.

Add the oil and onion to the wok and stir-fry until brown. Add the garlic and stir-fry for another 10 seconds. Return the veal to the wok and add the marinade from the artichoke hearts, the broth, rosemary, thyme, and diced tomatoes with their liquid. Cover and simmer for 20 minutes. Add the artichoke hearts and chickpeas and simmer until the veal is tender, about 20 minutes more. Stir in the parsley, and serve.

1 pound calf's liver, thinly sliced, membranes trimmed

1/2 teaspoon kosher salt

1 teaspoon cracked black pepper

2 tablespoons olive oil

2 teaspoons minced garlic, fresh or jarred organic

1/3 cup aged balsamic vinegar (at least 10 years; 15 years or more is preferable)

1 tablespoon unsalted butter

1 teaspoon basil pesto, jarred or homemade (page 339), or 1/4 teaspoon dried basil

calf's liver with garlic balsamic glaze

Cooking liver is tricky. The line between lush and mush is hairline, leading all but a privileged few to reject this most wonderful of meats with prejudice. So I realize I am talking to a meager minority when I tell you that this recipe is swoonably good. The only way you can screw it up is by overcooking the liver. Slice it thin and get it out of the pan while it is still slightly soft in the center, and you are in for a treat.

DIRECTIONS

Season the liver with the salt and pepper. Heat the oil in a large, nonstick skillet over medium-high heat until smoking. Add the liver and sear on both sides, 1 to 2 minutes per side for medium-rare. Transfer the liver to a platter and remove the pan from the heat. Add the garlic and vinegar and return to the heat; boil until reduced to a thin syrup, about 1 minute. Turn off the heat and stir in the butter and pesto. Pour over the liver, and serve.

1 pound ground beef, preferably 85 percent lean

½ cup black bean dip

2 tablespoons ketchup

Salt and ground black pepper to taste

No-stick spray oil

1 can (about 10 ounces) red enchilada sauce

½ cup (about 4 ounces) shredded Cheddar cheese

beef and black bean burgers with enchilada glaze

The secret to working with ground beef is in the filler. Once beef is ground, any moisture or textural quality it previously possessed is gone. Cooking it only manages to dry up what's left. To make it succulent you must refurbish its structure and replenish its moisture from the inside out by adding liquid and starch to absorb the moisture and hold it in the meat. In this recipe the liquid and starch, as well as added protein and great flavor, are delivered in a single ingredient—bean dip.

DIRECTIONS

Mix the beef, bean dip, ketchup, and salt and pepper in a bowl until well blended. Form into 4 burgers. Heat a large, heavy skillet (preferably iron) over high heat for several minutes. Spray the burgers with oil and brown on both sides.

Add the enchilada sauce, reduce the heat to a simmer, and simmer until the sauce reduces to a glaze, turning the burgers several times to glaze evenly and cook through. Top with the cheese; cover the pan and cook until the cheese melts, 1 to 2 minutes, before serving.

5 chicken, turkey & other

There are chickens in every pot and skillet and oven in this country almost every night. We have become a nation of chicken eaters and, from all accounts, happily so. But the glut has made us hungry for more than plain poultry. We crave recipes: quick, easy, delicious ways to turn our favorite birds into memorable meals.

In order to guarantee success, it's important to pair the cut of poultry you are preparing with the right cooking technique. The ubiquity of boneless, skinless chicken breasts has made us think that we can cook this lean, delicate piece of meat any way we choose—not so. It's great for sautéing, grilling, or stir-frying, but choose a heartier cut, protected by skin and reinforced with a skeleton, for roasting. Try boneless thighs in a stew, or whole legs for simmering in a sauce. And don't forget game hens or duck breast for a roast that is ready in a fraction of the time it would take to cook a whole chicken or turkey. The following collection gives you lots of options.

poultry

3   pounds skinless chicken thighs and/or drumsticks

Salt and ground black pepper to taste

1   tablespoon olive oil

1   container (about 14 ounces) creamy sweet corn soup

1   can (about 14 ounces) diced tomatoes with jalapeños

1   can (about 11 ounces) corn kernels, preferably no salt, drained

1   lime

2   scallions, trimmed and sliced

chicken legs braised with corn and tomato

The ubiquity of the boneless breast and the buffalo wing has created a perpetual discount on dark-meat chicken and caused butchers to find new ways to entice you to buy drumsticks and thighs. One of the most versatile of these is skinless and boneless chicken thighs, which taste richer and moister than white-meat chicken and cook in about the same amount of time. The vegetable-laden sauce in this recipe emerges magically as the flavors of caramelized chicken, sweet corn soup, tomato, and lime mingle.

DIRECTIONS

Season the chicken with salt and pepper. Heat the oil in a large skillet over medium-high heat. Add the chicken and brown on both sides, about 4 minutes per side. Add the soup, tomatoes, and corn; simmer until the chicken is cooked through and the soup mixture has thickened slightly, about 20 minutes.

Grate the zest from the lime, using a fine grater, or peel with a vegetable peeler and chop finely; cut the zested lime in half. When the chicken is ready, add the lime zest, lime juice, and scallions. Simmer for a few minutes and serve.

pan-roasted garlic chicken

1 cut-up chicken (about 4 pounds), 8-cut

Kosher salt and coarsely ground black pepper to taste

2 tablespoons garlic-flavored oil

20 cloves garlic, fresh or jarred organic

8 sprigs rosemary, thyme, or sage

It takes an hour to roast a 4-pound chicken, but cut that chicken into pieces and trade your oven for an iron skillet, and the whole process shrinks to half that time. The trick is in the pan. A heavy skillet (particularly one made of iron) with a tight-fitting lid heats high to create a crispy crust and then distributes the heat evenly. The results are darker and richer than roasting in an oven.

DIRECTIONS

Season the chicken liberally with salt and pepper. Heat the oil in a large, heavy skillet (preferably iron) over medium-high heat. Place the chicken pieces, skin-side down, in the hot oil and cook until browned, about 5 minutes. Turn and brown on the other side, about 3 minutes. Scatter the garlic cloves around the chicken pieces, and place an herb sprig on each chicken piece. Reduce the heat to medium-low, cover, and cook until the chicken is cooked through, 15 to 18 minutes. Rest for about 5 minutes, then carve and serve.

POTS AND PANS

Different materials have different properties, which means there is no line of cookware that will do all forms of cooking flawlessly. There are four criteria by which to judge a cooking vessel:

- How it takes on heat
- How it transfers heat
- How it holds heat
- How it interacts with its environment

The chart on the next spread describes the benefits and inefficiencies of the most common materials used in manufacturing cookware. Note that regardless of the material, the heavier its gauge the better it will manifest its properties.

know your pots and pans

MATERIAL	HEATING	HEAT TRANSFER	HEAT RETENTION
Copper lined with tin	Very quick and even	Very quick and even	Cools down very quickly
Copper lined with steel	Quick and even	Quick and even	Cools down quickly
Aluminum	Quick and even, depending on gauge of metal	Quick and even, depending on gauge of metal	Cools down quickly
Anodized aluminum	Quick and even, depending on gauge of metal	Quick and even, depending on gauge of metal	Cools down quickly
Nonstick aluminum	Heats up gradually	Does not transfer heat well	Holds heat moderately well
Stainless steel	Heats up slowly; better if thicker gauge	Does not transfer heat well	Holds heat moderately well
Stainless steel with copper or aluminum core	Quick and even	Quick and even	Cools down quickly
Copper-bottom stainless steel	Heats up slowly; better if copper is thicker gauge	Does not transfer heat well	Holds heat moderately well
Iron	Heats up slowly	Transfers heat slowly	Holds heat well
Enamel-coated iron	Heats up slowly	Transfers heat slowly	Holds heat well
Heat-resistant glass	Heats up slowly	Transfers heat slowly	Holds heat well
Ceramic	Heats up slowly	Transfers heat slowly	Holds heat well

TOXICITY	GOOD FOR	UPKEEP	COST
Toxic if not lined; must be relined occasionally	Sauté pans, skillets	Must be polished frequently; lining scratches easily	Expensive
Toxic if not lined; lining will not scratch easily	Sauté pans, skillets	Must be polished frequently	Expensive
If pan is scratched it can leach aluminum into the food; do not use with high-acid foods	Sauté pans, skillets, saucepans, stockpots, roasting pans	Wash and dry; food can stick	Moderate
Pan is scratch-resistant and will not interact with food	Sauté pans, skillets, saucepans	Wash and dry; food can stick	Expensive
Safe, although there is some evidence that the plastic lining can break down at very high temperatures	Omelet pans	Wash and dry	Inexpensive
Completely safe	Saucepans, stockpots	Wash and dry	Price depends on gauge of metal
Completely safe	Sauté pans, skillets, saucepans	Wash and dry; food can stick	Expensive
Completely safe	Saucepans, stockpots	Wash and dry	Price depends on gauge of metal
Safe; does leach iron into food	Dutch ovens, deep skillets, griddles	Must be seasoned; rinse; dry quickly; can rust	Inexpensive
Completely safe	Dutch ovens, deep skillets, casseroles	Wash and dry	Expensive
Completely safe	Baking dishes, casseroles	Wash and dry	Expensive
Completely safe	Baking dishes, casseroles	Wash and dry	Expensive

12   ounces chicken sausage, plain
      or with apple

½   cup chopped onion, frozen or
      fresh

1½   cups apple juice

1   cup stuffing mix

1   chicken, about 4 pounds

roasted chicken with apple sausage stuffing

The glory of a roast is in the stuffing, and although this five-ingredient recipe tastes as though it took time and talent, it couldn't be easier. If you can't find chicken sausage, any mild herb-scented sausage will work well.

DIRECTIONS

Heat the oven to 375°F. Chop the sausage into small pieces and cook in a dry skillet over medium-high heat until the bottom of the skillet is glazed with fat. Add the onion and sauté until the onion is tender and the sausage is cooked through. Stir in ¾ cup of the apple juice and the stuffing mix until blended.

Spoon the stuffing into the chicken and place on an oiled rack in a metal roasting pan. Roast for 1 hour. Brush ¼ cup of the remaining apple juice over the top and roast until a thermometer inserted into the thickest part of the thigh registers 165°F, another 15 to 20 minutes.

Remove the chicken to a cutting board. Spoon or pour off most of the fat from the pan drippings. Place the roasting pan over medium-high heat, add the remaining ½ cup apple juice to the pan, and combine with the drippings by scraping any bits stuck to the bottom of the pan into the juice.

Carve the chicken into serving pieces and spoon the stuffing into a serving bowl. Serve the chicken topped with pan juices and with stuffing on the side.

1   teaspoon kosher salt

½   teaspoon coarsely ground
    black pepper

1   teaspoon dried poultry seasoning

1   roasting chicken, about 6 pounds,
    washed and dried

1   tablespoon garlic-flavored oil

2   cans (about 15 ounces each) pear
    halves, drained

1   can (about 16 ounces) whole-
    berry cranberry sauce

1   teaspoon dried rosemary, crumbled

roasted chicken and pears with cranberry gravy

This extravagant roast mega-chicken is overcome with fruit. Canned pear halves are roasted along with the chicken. I know, I know . . . canned fruit? Have I lost my mind? Maybe, but not about this. Canned pears are poached pears. Think about it. To poach pears you cook them in a syrup until they are soft, which is exactly what happens in canning. The gravy is made by deglazing the pan drippings with cranberry sauce and rosemary.

DIRECTIONS

Heat the oven to 400°F. Mix the salt, pepper, and poultry seasoning and sprinkle in the interior cavity of the chicken. Rub the garlic oil all over the outside of the chicken and place the chicken breast-side down on a roasting rack set in a roasting pan. Roast for 1 hour. Place the pears in the bottom of the pan and roast until a thermometer inserted in the thickest part of a thigh registers 165°F, about 1 hour more.

Remove the chicken to a cutting board and surround with the pears. Remove the fat from the drippings. Measure the remaining drippings; you should have at least 1 cup. If you don't, add enough water to make 1 cup. Place the roasting pan over medium heat. Add the cranberry sauce, rosemary, and defatted drippings, and scrape any bits clinging to the bottom of the pan into the sauce.

Carve the chicken and serve with the pears and cranberry gravy.

4 chicken breast halves, bone-in

Kosher salt and coarsely ground black pepper to taste

1/4 cup basil pesto, jarred, in a tube, refrigerated, or homemade (page 339)

2 tablespoons extra-virgin olive oil

1/4 cup sun-dried tomato pesto, jarred or in a tube

1/4 teaspoon minced garlic, fresh or jarred organic

2 tablespoons red wine vinegar

basil-stuffed chicken with tomato vinaigrette

Boneless chicken breast is fast, it's easy, it's already trimmed, it can be flavored countless ways, it keeps you slim, and it doesn't clog your arteries. Too bad it's so bland. And the solution is easy—use a bone-in breast. Yes, it takes about twice as long to cook, but that's still only 20 minutes, and the flavor difference is exponential. One trick to ensure thorough cooking is to broil or grill it on its bone side until it is almost cooked through. That way the meaty side (the public side) can be cooked just until it's golden brown without fear of underdone chicken next to the bone.

DIRECTIONS

Heat the broiler to high, and position a rack about 6 inches from the burner.

Cut a pocket into each chicken breast. Season the outsides of the breasts with salt and pepper. Fill the pockets with pesto, and coat the surface of each breast with olive oil. Place bone-side up on a broiler pan and until the bone sides are deeply browned and the chicken is almost cooked through, about 15 minutes. Turn over and broil for 5 more minutes to brown the meaty sides.

While the chicken is broiling, mix the sun-dried tomato pesto, garlic, and vinegar in a bowl. Spoon over the broiled breasts and serve.

moroccan almond chicken

MAKES 4 SERVINGS

4–6 boneless, skinless chicken breast halves

Salt and ground black pepper to taste

2 tablespoons olive oil

1 cup chopped onion, fresh or frozen

1½ teaspoons minced garlic, fresh or jarred organic

1 tablespoon chopped jalapeño pepper, fresh or canned

½ cup almond meal or finely ground almonds

½ teaspoon ground cinnamon

½ teaspoon dried oregano

2 cups almond milk

1 teaspoon cilantro pesto, or 1 tablespoon chopped cilantro

This spicy sauté of garlic chicken, cinnamon, and almonds uses an ancient cooking method. Before the advent of flour- and starch-thickened sauces about 200 years ago, the main way to turn thin liquid into a clinging sauce was to add ground crumbled baked goods, cracked grains, or ground nuts. Not only did these ingredients fortify a sauce nutritionally, but they added greater flavor and more interesting textures. The recent emergence of nut meals (marketed for low-carbohydrate baking) has made it easy to recapture the richness of that exotic past.

DIRECTIONS

Season the chicken breasts with salt and pepper. Heat 1 tablespoon of the oil in a large, nonstick skillet over medium-high heat. Brown the chicken on both sides; remove to a plate. Add the remaining 1 tablespoon oil to the pan, reduce the heat to low, add the onion, and sauté until tender; do not brown.

Add the garlic, jalapeño, almond meal, cinnamon, and oregano and cook until the seasoning is aromatic, about 10 seconds. Add the almond milk and stir to distribute the almond mixture. Return the chicken to the pan, along with any juices that have collected on the plate. Simmer until the chicken is cooked through and the liquid has reduced to a lightly thickened sauce. Stir in the cilantro pesto, and serve.

FOOD IN A TUBE

Americans don't readily take to food in tubes. To our way of thinking, tubes are for ointments, lubricants, and toothpaste; they belong in the medicine cabinet, not in the kitchen. That's too bad, for Europeans and Asians caught on long ago that the tube is the perfect package for a squirt of tomato paste, basil pesto, pureed lemongrass, or prepared wasabi. Not only is dispensing easy, but storage problems are nil. Take tomato paste, for instance. How many times have you confronted a desiccated half-can of tomato paste lurking in the nether reaches of your refrigerator? Tomato paste in a tube never goes bad, because after you use what you want and replace the cap, air can't get into it, and if air can't get in, neither can molds, which would cause the contents to decay. More and more essential cooking ingredients are available in tubes. In my local supermarket I can buy cilantro, lemongrass, basil, hot peppers, tomato paste, sun-dried tomatoes, basil pesto, garlic, and anchovy paste in tubes.

Oil for coating the grill rack

3½ pounds chicken parts

2 teaspoons Southwest or
Mexican spice rub

1 cup barbecue sauce, bottled
or homemade

twenty-minute barbecued chicken

Barbecuing is different than grilling. In grilling the heat is high; in barbecuing, it's low. In grilling the meat is tender enough to cook through in the time it takes to brown. In barbecuing it needs moisture and time to soften tough fibers. To barbecue chicken properly takes about 40 minutes and constant attention, but by starting with a brief period of steaming in a microwave, before browning the chicken on the grill, you can cut the time in half. The skin is not quite as crisp and the flavor is not as concentrated, but the technique makes really good chicken in record time.

DIRECTIONS

Heat a grill for hot, direct cooking; coat the grill rack with oil.

While the grill is heating, sprinkle the chicken with the spice rub; place in a 9-by-13-inch glass baking dish and pour the barbecue sauce over the top. Roll the chicken around to coat thoroughly. Cover tightly with plastic wrap and microwave at full power for 10 minutes.

Remove the chicken from the sauce and grill, bone-side down, 7 minutes for breasts and 5 minutes for everything else. Turn and grill on the other side for 3 minutes for breasts and 5 minutes for everything else. The interior of the thickest pieces of chicken should register 165°F. Serve.

Oil for coating the grill rack

4 boneless, skinless chicken breast halves

2–3 tablespoons Southwest spice rub

No-stick spray oil

1 package (8 ounces) refrigerated guacamole, or half of a 1-pound box

6 scallions, trimmed and thinly sliced

½ teaspoon minced garlic, fresh or jarred organic

2 tablespoons white vinegar

Big pinch crunched red pepper flakes

1 lime, quartered

grilled chicken with guacamole relish

The longest task in this light, simple, colorful grilled chicken recipe is the time it takes to preheat the grill. The hero is refrigerated guacamole, which is 100 percent natural, has no preservatives, and tastes wonderfully fresh.

DIRECTIONS

Heat a grill for hot, direct cooking; coat the grill rack with oil.

Season the chicken with the spice rub and spray with oil; grill for 3 to 4 minutes per side, until cooked through, 155°F internal temperature.

While the chicken is grilling, combine the guacamole, scallions, garlic, vinegar, and pepper flakes in a bowl. Serve the chicken topped with some of the guacamole and garnished with lime.

REFRIGERATED GUACAMOLE

Just a few years ago the notion of fully prepared commercially available guacamole was unthinkable. Avocados are too perishable; they brown as soon as they are cut, and with that browning comes off-tasting metallic flavors. The only alternative was to load the guac with enough ascorbic acid to cure the common cold, and then the results were inedible. Enter high-pressure food preservation technology, which has revolutionized the way perishable fruit and vegetable preparations can be manufactured.

Here's how it works: food (in this case guacamole) is vacuum-packed in plastic and submerged in sealed tanks of cold water. More water is pumped in until the pressure reaches an astronomical 80,000 pounds per square inch. At that force, any bacteria, enzyme, or mold in the food is killed as its molecular structure collapses and its cell walls pop like balloons. Then the pressure is turned off and the food returns to its original volume and appearance.

High-pressure preservation eliminates the need for chemical preservatives and heat processing, which in the case of guacamole would be disastrous.

MAKES 4 SERVINGS

½ cup sweet and sour sauce

2 tablespoons soy sauce

1 teaspoon Chinese chili paste
or bottled hot sauce

½ cup chicken broth

1¼ pounds chicken tenders

2 tablespoons vegetable oil

1 tablespoon minced garlic,
fresh or jarred organic

1 tablespoon minced ginger,
fresh or jarred

1 bag (about 10 ounces)
broccoli slaw

1 cup candied pecans

stir-fried chicken with candied pecans

This recipe, a rip-off of the classic Chinese restaurant dish, fried shrimp with candied almonds, is simpler than its inspiration and lower in fat. Best of all, it's been streamlined by using commercially prepared candied pecans. A recent entry into the marketplace, candied nuts coated with different flavors are now being sold by several companies. Any of them will work well in this dish.

DIRECTIONS

Mix the sweet and sour sauce, soy sauce, chili paste, and chicken broth in a bowl; set aside. Remove the thick end of the tendon that runs through the chicken tenders, and cut each tender into 2 or 3 pieces.

Heat 1 tablespoon of the oil in a large wok or skillet over high heat. Add half the chicken and stir-fry until browned. Remove and reserve. Add the remaining tablespoon of oil, and stir-fry the rest of the chicken. Add to the first batch of chicken.

Add the garlic, ginger, and broccoli slaw to the pan and stir-fry until barely tender, about 2 minutes. Return the chicken to the pan, along with any juices that have collected around it. Add the sauce mixture and stir-fry until everything is coated with sauce. Serve topped with the candied pecans.

grilled red curry chicken

2   teaspoons Thai red curry paste

2   cups buttermilk

3/4 cup teriyaki sauce

2   tablespoons ketchup

2   teaspoons garlic salt

2   pounds boneless, skinless
    chicken breast halves
    and/or thighs

    Oil for coating grill rack

Real tandoori chicken is impossible to make in an American kitchen. For one thing, a large, spherical wood-fired ceramic oven and a practiced hand are required to make it correctly. This ersatz version is delicious nonetheless. It is a gorgeous red, and it radiates with curry spices, the tang of buttermilk, and a little sweetness.

DIRECTIONS

Dissolve the curry paste in a small amount of the buttermilk in a large bowl. Stir in the remaining buttermilk, teriyaki sauce, ketchup, and garlic salt. Add the chicken and turn to coat and submerge. Cover and refrigerate for 1 hour.

Heat a grill for hot direct grilling. Coat the rack with oil and set it about 3 inches from the fire. Remove the chicken from the marinade and grill until browned and cooked through, about 5 minutes per side; serve.

- 2 pounds boneless chicken thighs
- Salt and ground black pepper to taste
- 2 teaspoons vegetable oil
- ½ cup fruit salsa: mango, pineapple, or peach
- ¾ cup orange juice
- 2 teaspoons soy sauce
- 2 tablespoons honey
- 1 teaspoon chopped garlic, fresh or jarred organic

fruit-glazed chicken thighs

The fruit-infused lacquer that coats this stove-top barbecue materializes effortlessly as the subversive spice of fruit salsa, the perfume of honey, the tang of orange juice, and the salt in soy sauce concentrate and caramelize over the surface of simmering chicken thighs.

DIRECTIONS

Season the chicken with salt and pepper. Heat the oil in a large skillet; brown the chicken on both sides.

While the chicken is browning, puree the salsa, orange juice, soy sauce, and honey in a food processor or blender. Add the garlic to the skillet and cook for a few seconds. Pour the salsa mixture into the pan and boil until the chicken is cooked through and the salsa mixture has reduced to a glaze. It will be necessary to toss and stir the mixture frequently near the end of cooking to make sure that the chicken is coated and the glaze doesn't burn. Serve.

THE JOY OF SOY

Soy sauce is made by fermenting soybeans, wheat, and salt in two stages. In the first stage, molds are mixed with a mash of wheat and soy, which is kept warm, moist, and aerated for about two days, over which time spores from the mold multiply, producing enzymes that break the mash down into individual proteins and sugars.

When the enzymes are at their height, the second stage of fermentation starts. At this point the oxygen in the mash has been depleted. A salt brine is added and the molds die, but their enzymes continue to work. Over the six months to a year that the soy sauce is aged, lactic acid bacteria and yeasts that thrive in an anaerobic environment flourish, feeding on the sugar and protein in the mixture and creating their own flavorful by-products. When the fermentation is done, the sauce is pressed and pasteurized.

China and Japan produce almost all of the world's soy sauce. Chinese soy sauces are made with more soy than wheat, Japanese with more wheat than soy. The higher the proportion of wheat in the fermentation, the sweeter the finished product will be. Tamari Japanese soy sauce is made entirely from soy, which is why it is touted for people with wheat allergies.

Both Japanese and Chinese soy sauces come in dark and light varieties. Light soy sauces are lighter in color, saltier, and thinner, and are used in smaller amounts as condiments. Dark soy is more pungent but less salty. It is used more often in cooking, where it lends its flavor and mahogany color to whatever food is simmered in it. "Lite" soy sauce is low in sodium; it should not be confused with light soy.

Buy only naturally fermented soy sauces. If the label doesn't say "fermented" or "brewed," it probably isn't. Many brands of cheap soy sauce are made by hydrolyzing softened, crushed soybeans with hydrochloric acid, neutralizing the acid, and filtering the result. This product never develops the depth of flavor of the real thing.

1   cup chipotle salsa

½   cup raspberry vinaigrette

2   tablespoons garlic-flavored oil

1   boneless turkey breast, about
    3 pounds

chipotle raspberry turkey breast

Sugar soothes and spice excites, a contrast that creates the allure of this lightly smoky, slightly sweet roasted turkey breast. The turkey can be marinated for as long as a day, or for as little as a few hours; the results will not be markedly different, so select a timing that suits your schedule. It is best if you use a turkey breast that still has its skin on. The skin will protect the surface of the meat, helping to keep it moist, and as the skin crisps its juices will continually baste the meat as it roasts.

DIRECTIONS

Mix the chipotle, vinaigrette, and garlic oil in a small bowl. Pour half into a large zipper bag and add the turkey. Seal the bag and massage the marinade into the meat. Refrigerate for 2 to 24 hours. Refrigerate the remaining sauce separately.

Heat the oven to 425°F. Remove the turkey from its marinade. Place skin side up in a baking dish and pour half of the reserved sauce over the top. Roast until an instant-read meat thermometer inserted into the thickest part of the meat reads 160°F, about 1 hour and 15 minutes. Remove from the oven, pour the remaining sauce over the top, and let rest for 10 minutes. Slice and serve.

MAKING SUBSTITUTIONS: SALSA AND DRESSING

Sometimes your market will not have all of the flavors of a line of salsa or salad dressing. If that is the case with this recipe, you can mimic the flavor of a chipotle salsa by adding 1 tablespoon chipotle hot sauce, or half of a chopped chipotle pepper en adobo, to 1 cup mild or medium salsa. Make raspberry vinaigrette by mixing 2 teaspoons raspberry preserves with ½ cup of any simple vinaigrette dressing. If you don't have any garlic oil, substitute an equivalent amount of olive oil and ½ teaspoon minced garlic.

red-cooked chicken wings

MAKES 4 SERVINGS

- ⅓ cup teriyaki sauce
- ¼ cup honey
- ¼ cup water
- ½ teaspoon minced garlic, fresh or jarred organic
- Pinch of crushed red pepper flakes, or 1 teaspoon hot pepper sauce
- 1¾ pounds sectioned chicken wings; do not include wing tips

Red cooking is a traditional form of braising in China in which large pieces of meat are simmered in dark soy sauce, which is less salty and more fermented than the light soy that we are used to using as a condiment and cooking ingredient. This recipe attempts to approach the flavor of red cooking by concentrating the natural balance of salt, sweet, and tang in teriyaki sauce.

DIRECTIONS

Combine the teriyaki sauce, honey, water, garlic, and hot pepper in a large skillet; heat to boiling. Add the chicken, cover, and simmer for 5 minutes. Turn the wings, cover, and simmer for 5 more minutes.

Uncover and continue to boil and turn the chicken pieces until the liquid has reduced to a thick syrup and is coating the wings. You will need to turn and stir frequently near the end of cooking to coat the wings evenly and to keep the syrup from burning in spots. Serve.

chicken sausage roasted with corn and rosemary

MAKES 4 SERVINGS

- 12 ounces chicken sausages, any type, cut into 2-inch lengths
- 1 can (about 10 ounces) corn, drained
- 1 can (about 14 ounces) diced tomatoes, drained
- 1 tablespoon (1 sprig) fresh rosemary leaves
- 1 cup chopped onion, fresh or frozen
- 1 tablespoon olive oil
- Kosher salt and coarsely ground black pepper to taste

This fragrant and colorful mélange takes about half an hour to roast but less than a minute of your time. Its flair comes from the juxtaposition of ingredients and the magic of giving them some privacy in the caramelizing warmth of a hot oven.

DIRECTIONS

Heat the oven to 425°F. Combine all ingredients in a 9-by-13-inch baking dish, and roast for 15 minutes. Flip the sausages and roast for another 15 minutes; serve.

2   cans (about 8 ounces each) Red
    Bull or other energy drink

¼   cup Southwest seasoning

2   game hens, 1½ to 2 pounds
    each, cleaned and giblets removed

    No-stick spray oil

bull-butted game hens

This rendition of the invasive barbecue technique known as beer-butt chicken involves roasting poultry on the grill perched upon a can of some beverage, inserted into its internal cavity in such a way that the bird's legs and the can form a tripod that holds the roast upright. It is a grand technique, for it lifts the bulk of the bird away from the coals so that it roasts gently, and while it cooks, the beverage in the can bubbles, steaming and basting the interior to keep the bird moist. Because game hens are small, I've used a can of energy drink in place of the beer.

DIRECTIONS

Heat a grill for indirect grilling over medium heat.

Open the cans of Red Bull; pour out one fourth of each can (about ¼ cup) and drink or discard. Spoon 1 teaspoon of the seasoning into each can of Red Bull. Rub the game hens with the remaining seasoning, inside and out.

Spray the outside of the cans of Red Bull with the oil and place on a sturdy tray or sheet pan. Lower a game hen onto each can, inserting the can into the internal cavity of the hen. Position the hen so that the front legs and the can form a tripod holding the hen upright. Transfer from the tray to the grill, placing the hens on the grill out of direct contact with the fire. Cover the grill and cook until the hens are golden brown and a thermometer inserted into a thick part of the breast or thigh registers 165°F, 40 to 45 minutes.

Transfer the hens, still on the cans, to a tray and, holding the can with tongs and gripping the hen with a towel, twist and lift each hen off of its can. Cut the hens in half to serve, and baste with a little bit of the liquid from the can.

4   turkey thighs, skinned

     Salt and ground black pepper
     to taste

2   tablespoons vegetable oil

1   onion, diced

1½   pounds sweet potatoes, peeled
     and cut into chunks

1   box (about 17 ounces) mole
     cooking sauce, such as Knorr,
     or ¼ cup mole paste dissolved
     in 2 cups water

1   cup salsa, any heat level

1   cup water

2   tablespoons chopped cilantro

sweet potato turkey mole

Mole is the most elaborate of the Mexican sauces. A compilation of cooked chiles, toasted spices, ground nuts, chopped fruit, and broth, even a simple mole can take more than a day to prepare. But jarred mole pastes and sauces do all of that work for you, cutting the cooking time to however long it takes to cook the meat and vegetables in the sauce. Turkey is the most traditional meat to use in mole; this recipes twists tradition by adding sweet potato.

DIRECTIONS

Season the turkey with salt and pepper. Heat the oil in a Dutch oven over medium-high heat and brown the turkey on both sides. Remove to a plate. Add the onion and cook until it loses its raw look. Add the sweet potatoes and continue to cook until the onion and potatoes begin to brown. Add the mole, salsa, and water and heat to boiling. Reduce the heat so that the liquid simmers. Return the turkey to the pan, along with the juices that have collected on the plate. Cover and simmer until the turkey and potatoes are cooked through, about 45 minutes. Stir in the cilantro before serving.

MOLE PASTE

Mole is the communal name for the thick, pureed sauces of Mexico. They are typically composed of four elements: chiles, vegetables, spices, and nuts, which are prepared separately, combined, and simmered for several hours until their flavors meld. To help modern cooks in Mexico, several Hispanic food manufacturers market mole paste. It includes all of the ingredients you would add to a mole, precooked and ready to go; all you do is add water. The only problem with the paste is that it tends to separate, like non-homogenized peanut butter, so you must stir it to bring the oil back into suspension. Depending on how old the mole is, this can be a little laborious. So recently Knorr has come out with a line of fully prepared Mexican sauces that don't need hydration. You can find them in Hispanic markets.

Although there are dozens of mole recipes, the only two types that are available commercially are red (or brown) mole, which has ancho chile, and often a little chocolate, and green mole, made from green chiles and herbs. Pipian sauces are very similar to moles, but they have a higher proportion of nuts and seeds.

1½ cups almond meal

½ teaspoon garlic salt

½ teaspoon dried poultry seasoning

½ cup sour cream

¼ cup honey Dijon mustard

4 turkey cutlets, 5 to 6 ounces each

2 tablespoons olive oil

1 cup chicken broth

almond-crusted turkey cutlets with mustard cream

This simple breaded turkey cutlet is anything but ordinary. The breading is seasoned almond meal, which is nothing more than finely ground almonds. It is sold by several manufacturers but is not a popular item and therefore is not always available. You can make your own easily using a food processor (see page 341). A mixture of sour cream and mustard adheres the almond coating to the cutlets and forms a pungent, creamy pan sauce.

DIRECTIONS

Set a rack on a sheet pan. Mix the almond meal, garlic salt, and poultry seasoning on a large sheet of plastic wrap or wax paper. Mix the sour cream and mustard in a small bowl.

Brush a turkey cutlet with a thin coat of the sour cream mixture. Dredge in the almond mixture until thoroughly coated and place on the rack to rest. Repeat with all of the cutlets.

Heat the oil in a large, nonstick skillet over medium heat. Brown the cutlets on both sides, reduce the heat, and cook on medium-low until the cutlets are firm to the touch, 5 to 8 minutes (depending on the thickness), turning twice during cooking.

Remove the cutlets to a serving platter, and drain off any oil left in the pan. Add the broth to the skillet and heat to simmering. Stir in the remaining sour cream mixture and heat through (don't boil, or the sour cream will split). Pour over the cutlets, and serve.

LEFTOVERS: TURKEY SALAD REINVENTED

Turkey breasts are buxom. If you have leftovers, turn them into an exotic entrée salad by tossing about 8 ounces of leftover chopped turkey breast (about 1½ cups), ½ cup fruit (like mangoes, raspberries, halved orange sections, or diced peaches), ¼ cup nuts (I like pistachios, but sliced almonds or chopped walnuts are good too), and 2 sliced scallions. Mix in a dressing made from 1 tablespoon mayonnaise or ranch dressing and 2 tablespoons fruity vinegar or leftover vinaigrette. Season with salt and pepper to taste.

2 game hens, 1½ to 2 pounds each, cleaned and giblets removed

   Kosher salt and coarsely ground black pepper to taste

2 tablespoons olive oil

¼ cup tapenade, jarred or homemade (page 347)

⅓ cup extra-virgin olive oil

2 tablespoons chopped Italian (flat-leaf) parsley

olive poached game hens

A game hen is a diminutive chicken, which here is transformed, in a balm of olive oil and tapenade, into something ethereal. The technique is a form of roasting, but because the cooking is so gentle the effect is more like poaching the birds in oil. They emerge succulent, anointed with the essence of ripe olives.

DIRECTIONS

Heat the oven to 300°F.

Cut the game hens in half lengthwise; remove and discard the backbones. Season with salt and pepper.

Heat the 2 tablespoons olive oil over medium-high heat in a large skillet that has a tight-fitting lid and a metal handle. Place the game hen halves, skin-side down, in the hot oil, and cook until browned, about 5 minutes.

Mix the tapenade and ⅓ cup extra-virgin olive oil; turn the game hens skin-side up and spoon the tapenade-oil mixture over and around the game hen halves. Cover the skillet and place in the oven; roast until the game hens are cooked through (165°F internal temperature), about 40 minutes. Remove the skillet from the oven, using a thick potholder. Top the hens with the parsley and baste with some of the oil in the skillet just before serving.

MAKES 6 SERVINGS

1   cup stuffing mix, any flavor

½   cup milk

¼   cup ketchup

2   teaspoons spicy brown mustard

2   eggs, large or extra-large

2   tablespoons apple butter

2   tablespoons soy sauce

2   pounds ground turkey

turkey meatloaf with wild mushroom gravy

Once meat has been ground, its texture is destroyed, and any moisture it once contained is on the run. The only way to save it is to add liquid and starch. In this recipe there is the added challenge of supplementing the flavor of ground turkey, which is notoriously bland. It is done with little effort by using a seasoned stuffing mix and highly flavored, moist ingredients like ketchup, apple butter, and soy sauce.

DIRECTIONS

Heat the oven to 375°F. Mix the stuffing and milk in a medium mixing bowl; set aside until the stuffing is soft, about 5 minutes. Add the remaining ingredients and mix thoroughly. Form into a long loaf on a rimmed sheet pan. Bake until the loaf is firm in the center, about 1 hour. Allow to rest for at least 5 minutes before slicing.

MAKES 6 SERVINGS

1   boneless turkey breast, about 4 pounds

     Salt and ground black pepper to taste

1   tablespoon vegetable oil

1   onion, halved and sliced

1   cup bourbon

1   can (about 10 ounces) condensed chicken broth

bourbon-braised turkey breast

Braising is usually reserved for tough cuts. It is the perfect technique for getting meat fibers to relax and infusing a roast with nuanced flavor. It is also helpful for speeding up the cooking of more tender meats. The trick is to use a minimum of liquid, cover the pan tightly, and keep the heat low. There is less shrinkage than in traditional roasting, and the flavor is spectacular.

DIRECTIONS

Season the turkey with salt and pepper. Heat the oil in a large Dutch oven over medium-high heat. Place the turkey breast in the pan, skin-side down; cook until well browned, scattering the onion around the turkey halfway through. Turn the turkey, pour the bourbon over the top, and boil for 1 minute. Add the chicken broth, reduce the heat to a simmer, cover, and cook until a thermometer inserted into the center registers 165°F, 40 to 50 minutes. Rest for about 5 minutes, then slice and serve.

1   jar (about 12 ounces)
    mango chutney

1½ cups mango juice or nectar

1   tablespoon kosher salt

¼   teaspoon cayenne pepper

1   whole turkey breast, about
    5½ pounds, bone-in

mango-marinated turkey breast

Mangoes contain tenderizing enzymes similar to those in papaya, which gives this marinade a powerful effect. It opens up the structure of the protein in the turkey, encouraging the meat to bind to the flavorful components in the marinade.

DIRECTIONS

Combine the chutney, mango juice, salt, and cayenne in a blender or food processor and puree until smooth. Remove the skin from the turkey breast and place the breast and its skin in a large zippered plastic bag. Pour the mango mixture into the bag, seal it, and massage so that all of the turkey is submerged in liquid. Refrigerate for at least 2 hours, but no longer than 6 hours.

Heat the oven to 350°F. Remove the turkey from the marinade and place it bone-side down on a rack set in a roasting pan. Drape the skin over the top of the breast meat and discard the remaining marinade. Roast until a thermometer inserted into the thickest part registers 160°F, about 2 hours. Let rest for 10 minutes; remove the skin before carving.

2 game hens, 1½ to 2 pounds each, cleaned and giblets removed

2 teaspoons dried poultry seasoning

Salt and ground black pepper to taste

1 tablespoon olive oil

1 teaspoon minced garlic, fresh or jarred organic

1 cup white wine

½ cup minced onion, fresh or frozen

2 tablespoons fresh lemon juice

2 ounces liver pâté, such as pâté de foie gras

roasted game hens with foie gras "butter"

Liver pâté is rich, especially when made with the fatted goose liver known as foie gras. In this recipe we use the plushness of pâté to create a creamy sauce that can be assembled in minutes and that transforms perfectly ordinary roast chickens into something extraordinary.

DIRECTIONS

Heat the oven to 450°F. Season the interior cavities of the game hens with the poultry seasoning, salt, and pepper. Mix the olive oil and garlic and rub all over the outside of the hens, or rub under the skin (see box). Set on a rack in a roasting pan and roast until a thermometer inserted in the thickest part of the thigh registers 165°F, about 45 minutes. Let rest for 5 minutes, and split in half lengthwise.

While the hens are roasting, make the foie butter. Combine the wine and onion in a small skillet and boil over medium-high heat until the liquid reduces to ¼ cup, about 10 minutes. Add the lemon juice and puree in a mini food processor with the pâté until smooth. Top each portion of roasted hen with some of the "butter."

KEEP YOUR SKIN ON

It is essential that a roasted bird keep its skin during cooking. If it's stripped bare, there is nothing to protect the meat from dehydrating. Whenever meat cooks, juices flow to the surface. If the skin is missing, these juices will rise up and out, and trying to seal the surface by slapping on a sweet glaze or rubbing it with a salty seasoning mix will only exacerbate the problem. The only logical solution is to keep the skin in place during cooking, and to season the meat under the skin.

This is easier to do than it appears: simply lift (but don't remove) the skin from the breast and leg sections, by sliding your fingers under it. Start at either end of the breast and use a small knife to slit any membranes that might be too thick to break with your fingers. Once the skin is loosened, rub your seasonings directly on the meat underneath. That way, even if someone removes the skin before eating, the meat will still be fully flavored.

2   teaspoons steak seasoning

1   teaspoon ground dried orange peel

¼   cup barbecue sauce

¼   cup orange juice

1   tablespoon orange marmalade

2   boneless Muscovy duck breasts
    (skin on), weighing 12 ounces to
    1 pound each

barbecued duck breast à l'orange

Duck used to be for special occasions, until several producers started selling duck parts, most commonly the breast. Two types of duck are sold for cooking. The most common is called Peking duck or Long Island duck; the other, which we are seeing more and more of, is Muscovy duck. It is the one I recommend for grilling. The breast is larger and has far less fat under the skin, which reduces flare-ups and makes it possible to cook the meat medium-rare without worrying that all of the fat will be cooked out.

DIRECTIONS

Mix the steak seasoning and orange peel in a small bowl. Mix the barbecue sauce, orange juice, and orange marmalade in a separate bowl. Prepare a grill for direct medium heat, or preheat a broiler.

Score the skin of the duck breasts in a crosshatched pattern, cutting through the fat layer under the skin but not into the meat. Rub the duck breasts on both sides with the spice mixture. Grill or broil the duck over medium heat, skin-side first, until the meat is firm but still deep pink, 12 to 15 minutes, turning the breasts twice so that they start and finish on their skin side. Brush the meat side with sauce after it is cooked; brush the skin side with sauce just before serving.

Allow the duck to rest for a few minutes before slicing; pour the remaining sauce over the sliced meat.

6 fish & shellfish

In an age of dietary doomsaying, where everything from three square meals a day to the goodness of milk is being reevaluated, fish has emerged as the new messiah. Even its fat content, which is the bane of many other animal proteins, seems blessed with health benefits.

Fish is naturally low in cholesterol and calories. It cooks quickly and radiates flavor even in the simplest presentations. It lends itself to every known cooking technique and hundreds of seasonings, and it comes in more varieties than flavored potato chips. The only problem is that most of us don't know the first thing about cooking fish. Reared on frozen flounder and tinned tuna, even good cooks in America frequently find themselves at a loss when confronted with a swordfish steak or a red snapper shining crimson beneath its scales. Add to this the phenomenal number of new fish varieties constantly appearing in the market and it is easy to see why fish cookery in most homes amounts to preheating the broiler and juicing a lemon. May the following recipes put an end to all that.

grilled halibut escabèche

Escabèche, marinating seared fish in citrus juice with onions, chiles, and garlic, is a passion in South America, where it is made in large quantities and served cold or at room temperature. Feel free to substitute any fish for the halibut. Chicken breast also works well, except that you must simmer the chicken in the marinade until it cooks through.

MAKES 4 SERVINGS

1½–2 pounds halibut fillet

Salt and ground black pepper to taste

2 tablespoons olive oil

1 large onion, halved and thinly sliced

1 tablespoon chopped garlic, fresh or jarred organic

¼ teaspoon dried thyme

Large pinch of crushed red pepper flakes

1 cup orange juice

⅓ cup lime juice, fresh or bottled organic

DIRECTIONS

Heat a grill to high. Season the fish with salt and pepper and coat with 1 tablespoon of the oil. Grill until marked on both sides and still raw in the center. Set aside.

Heat the remaining tablespoon of oil in a skillet over medium-high heat. Add the onion and sauté until tender. Add the garlic, thyme, and crushed red pepper; stir to heat through. Add the juices and heat to boiling; season with salt and pepper. Place the fish in the boiling liquid, remove from the heat, cover, and let rest for 5 to 10 minutes, depending on the thickness of the fish. When done the fish will flake to gentle pressure. Serve portions of fish with some of the onion and liquid. It can be chilled and served cold or at room temperature.

½ cup jarred chimichurri sauce

¾ cup orange juice

1½ pounds mahi mahi fillet, about ¾ inch thick, bones removed

Oil for coating the grill rack

No-stick spray oil

1 teaspoon hot pepper sauce, preferably Thai, such as sriracha

1 teaspoon garlic-flavored oil

orange chimichurri mahi mahi

Chimichurri, the tangy herbal barbecue marinade from Argentina, is most typically served with meat, but its clean, green flavor is a natural with fish. Here jarred chimichurri is sweetened with orange juice for a marinade, and then more orange juice is spiced with Thai hot pepper sauce and enriched with garlic oil for a tingling finish.

DIRECTIONS

Combine the chimichurri sauce and ½ cup of the orange juice in a plastic zipper bag. Add the fish, seal the bag, massage it to make sure the fish is completely moistened, and refrigerate for 30 minutes.

Set up a grill for direct grilling, and heat to medium-high. Brush the grill rack with oil before the grill is hot.

Meanwhile, mix the remaining orange juice, hot sauce, and garlic oil in a bowl, and set aside.

Remove the fish from the marinade, allowing a good amount of the herbs from the marinade to remain on its surface. Spray the flesh side of the fish with oil. Grill flesh-side down in a covered grill until browned, 3 to 4 minutes. Turn with a spatula and grill, covered, until the fish flakes to gentle pressure, 5 to 6 minutes more.

Transfer the fish to a platter by slipping a spatula between the skin and the flesh of the fish, allowing the skin to stay stuck to the grill rack (you can scrape it off later). Pour the reserved hot pepper sauce mixture over the fish before serving.

1 tablespoon vegetable oil

1½ pounds tuna steaks, cut at least 1½ inches thick

Kosher salt and coarsely ground black pepper to taste

1 onion, halved and thickly sliced

1 rib celery, peeled and sliced

1 teaspoon five-spice powder

2 cups seafood broth (see box)

1 package (about 12 ounces) frozen shelled edamame, thawed

1 teaspoon soy sauce

1 teaspoon balsamic vinegar

2 tablespoons chopped pickled (sushi) ginger

tuna braised with edamame

Japanese cooking is more than sushi and tempura. This recipe is in the style of the simmered dishes of Japan, known as *nimono*. Thick steaks of tuna fillet are seared and then lightly poached with green soybeans in a clear spiced broth.

DIRECTIONS

Heat the oil in a large, deep skillet or Dutch oven over high heat. Season the tuna with salt and pepper and brown quickly on both sides in the hot oil (no more than 2 minutes per side). Remove from the pan and set aside.

Reduce the heat to medium, add the onion and celery to the pan, and sauté until barely tender, about 5 minutes. Add the five-spice powder and broth, and heat until simmering. Stir in the edamame, and return the tuna to the pan. Simmer until the edamame are tender, 3 to 4 minutes.

Transfer the tuna to a cutting board. Add the soy sauce and vinegar to the edamame and transfer to a serving platter with a slotted spoon. Slice the tuna against its grain and arrange the slices over the edamame; spoon the broth over the top and garnish with the chopped pickled ginger.

FISHING FOR BROTH

Although the broth aisle is bursting with new varieties of high-quality organic, vegan, and flavored broth, the few examples of fully prepared ready-to-use seafood broth that have emerged on the market so far have been very disappointing, forcing us to rely on the old standards, of which there are two formats:

• Concentrates—These high-end products come frozen and on the shelf. Mostly they are made from fish stock (fumet) that has been highly reduced. They can be reconstituted with water or used full strength to boost seafood flavors in a sauce or soup. They are very high in quality, and very expensive; most people find them too costly to use on a regular basis.

• Cubes—Although bouillon cubes and powders are my last choice for chicken, beef, and vegetable broths (because they are very salty and there are many better alternatives), when it comes to fish and seafood broths they are my product of choice. Knorr makes a particularly good-quality fish bouillon cube.

ginger-crusted roasted tuna

1   tablespoon minced ginger, fresh or jarred

1   tablespoon minced garlic, fresh or jarred organic

1   teaspoon red curry paste

1   teaspoon toasted sesame oil

½   teaspoon salt

   About 1½ pounds tuna, 2 inches thick, preferably yellow fin

¼   cup pickled (sushi) ginger, finely chopped

2   scallions, trimmed and thinly sliced

   Juice of ½ lemon

1   teaspoon soy sauce

This is a dramatic and flavorful way to cook tuna. However, try it only if you have a large, thick slab of the best-quality tuna. You want the fish to still be swimmingly rare at its center when it is served. Roasting tuna until it is cooked through ruins its texture and subtle flavors—you might as well serve it out of a can.

DIRECTIONS

Heat the oven to 500°F. Place a rack in a small roasting pan.

Mix the ginger, garlic, curry paste, sesame oil, and salt in a small bowl. Pat the tuna dry with paper towels and rub the ginger paste all over the surface. Roast for 15 minutes.

While the tuna is roasting, mix the pickled ginger, scallions, lemon juice, and soy sauce. When the tuna is done, cut it into 4 slices with a razor-sharp knife. Top each slice with a portion of the pickled ginger mixture, and serve at once.

roasted mussels with salsa

2   pounds fresh mussels, cleaned

1   jar (16 ounces) chunky salsa, medium-hot

2   tablespoons extra-virgin olive oil

   Crusty bread, for serving

Cooking mussels was never easier. The only care you have to take is to make sure all of the mussels are tightly closed, alive, and fresh when you throw them into the oven. As they cook, their juices will mingle with the fragrant oil and spicy salsa into a bread-sopping sauce.

DIRECTIONS

Heat the oven to 450°F.

Combine all of the ingredients in a large baking dish and roast until the mussels open, about 15 minutes. Serve with bread.

Oil for coating the grill rack

1 partially ripe mango

3/4 cup salsa verde

1/3 cup chopped parsley or cilantro

1/2 medium red onion, peeled, quartered, and thinly sliced

1 1/2 pounds salmon fillet, skin on, pin bones removed

1 tablespoon olive oil

Salt and ground black pepper to taste

Juice of 1/2 lemon

grilled salmon with green mango salsa

The pastel peach and green of this salsa highlights the color and flavor of salmon beautifully. It is difficult to find perfectly ripe mangoes, which is one of the assets of this sauce: it works well with any mango, from green to ripe, but is best if the fruit is still a bit firm. The salsa can be thrown together several hours ahead, but try to use it on the day it is made.

DIRECTIONS

Heat a grill for hot, direct grilling. Coat the grill rack with oil.

There is a long, flat pit in the center of the mango; to remove it, start by cutting the mango into two "halves" along either side of the pit. Discard the pit and any fruit clinging to it. Peel both halves and slice the fruit into very thin strips. Combine with the salsa, parsley, and onion in a bowl.

Rub the salmon with the olive oil, and season the flesh side with salt and pepper. Grill the fish flesh-side down, covered, until the surface is golden brown, about 4 minutes. Carefully flip over, cover the grill, and continue to grill until the fish flakes to gentle pressure, 8 to 10 minutes. The skin will burn; don't worry. Slide a spatula between the cooked fish and the skin and transfer to a platter. The skin will stick to the grill; scrape it off when the grill is cool.

Squirt the lemon juice over the salmon and serve each portion topped with some of the mango salsa.

LEAN FISH/FAT FISH

The main culinary differences among fish are reflected in their fat content, and for that reason fish are classified for cooking purposes as lean or oily. A lean fish has a fat content of less than 5 percent. This would include all flatfish, cod, snappers, perch, whiting, catfish, and drum. Oily fish can have fat percentages of up to 45 percent. Salmon, shark, bluefish, tuna, and mackerel are examples.

Typically, as a fish's fat content increases, so does the color of the flesh, its aroma, and its flavor. For that reason high-fat fish tend to work best with dry cooking techniques, like grilling and baking, where their natural oils keep the meat moist, and they are typically served with stronger-flavored sauces.

Lean fish are better suited for wet cooking methods. Poaching and steaming delicately softens the flesh of these fish while keeping the meat moist in a bath of warm liquid. After cooking they are usually served with buttery and creamy sauces to lend needed richness.

Of course, there are exceptions, both in cooking techniques and between fish. For example, both lean and oily fish fry and sauté well, provided the fillet is thin enough, and salmon (the most popular of all oily fish) is equally good whether grilled or poached.

½ cup liquid eggs or egg whites
(or 2 beaten eggs)

2 tablespoons dried chives or
sliced fresh chives

1 cup instant mashed potato flakes

1 teaspoon seasoning salt

4 flounder or sole fillets, about
6 ounces each

2 tablespoons olive oil

2 tablespoons unsalted butter

2 tablespoons balsamic vinegar

1 tablespoon drained capers

potato-crusted flounder with balsamic brown "butter"

I don't suggest that you ever make mashed potatoes from potato flakes, but I do think every kitchen should have a box on hand at all times, and this recipe is one of the reasons why. Easier to use and more distinctive than a coating of flour or breadcrumbs, potato crusts have the flavor of fried potatoes, and the same crunchy-on-the-outside, flaky-on-the-inside appeal. Here they coat a sautéed flounder fillet, creating an update on flounder meunière, which is served classically with brown butter and capers.

DIRECTIONS

Combine the eggs and chives in a pie plate or wide, shallow soup bowl. Place the potato flakes on a sheet of foil or wax paper, or a plate, and mix with the seasoning salt. Dip the fillets in the egg and dredge in the potato flakes until thoroughly coated; set on a rack while you heat the oil in a large, nonstick skillet over medium-high heat.

Cook the fillets until browned on both sides and cooked through, about 3 minutes per side. Transfer to a platter. Wipe out the skillet and return to the heat. Add the butter and cook until foamy; add the vinegar and capers and boil for a few seconds. Pour over the fish and serve immediately.

2 cups water

½ cup chopped onion, frozen or fresh

1 teaspoon chopped garlic, fresh or jarred organic

4 ginger tea teabags

Salt to taste

2 tablespoons lime juice, fresh or bottled organic

4 pieces salmon fillet, about 6 ounces each

4 ounces soft or silken tofu

1 tablespoon prepared wasabi in a tube

Ground black pepper to taste

ginger poached salmon with wasabi "hollandaise"

This recipe is an utter scam. The ginger-flavored poaching liquid comes from a teabag, the wasabi from a tube, and the hollandaise . . . well, it's as rich as a hollandaise, but the butter has been replaced by soft tofu and the lime juice is straight from a bottle. I won't tell anyone if you won't.

DIRECTIONS

Combine the water, onion, and garlic in a medium skillet. Heat to boiling, add the teabags and salt, and simmer for 2 minutes. Remove the teabags, and add 1 tablespoon of the lime juice and the salmon. Return to a simmer, cover, and simmer gently until the salmon flakes to gentle pressure, about 8 minutes per inch of thickness of the fillets.

Remove the fish to a serving plate. Boil the poaching liquid until its volume is about ¾ cup. Combine the poaching liquid, tofu, wasabi, remaining tablespoon of lime juice, and additional salt and pepper to taste in a blender or food processor. Process until smooth, and pour over the poached fish. Serve immediately.

Oil for coating the grill rack

¼ cup hoisin sauce

1 tablespoon basil pesto, jarred or homemade (page 339)

½ teaspoon minced garlic, fresh or jarred organic

1 tablespoon soy sauce

1 teaspoon balsamic vinegar

1 pound extra-large (21–25 or larger) shrimp, peeled and cleaned, thawed if frozen

No-stick spray olive oil

2 cups water

1 large seafood bouillon cube (about 9 grams) or 2 tablespoons jarred or frozen fish fumet glace

1 pound seafood (any combination of bay scallops, small shrimp, squid rings, or fish fillets cut into bite-size pieces)

1 box (about 7 ounces) vegetable-flavored couscous, such as roasted pepper, spinach, or mushroom)

1 tablespoon olive oil

1 tablespoon chopped Italian (flat-leaf) parsley

hoisin pesto shrimp

Don't balk. The act of combining Chinese hoisin sauce and Italian basil pesto is brazen in thought only. On the palate the sweet, pungent, fermented flavor of hoisin and the anise hint of basil meet pleasantly, helped along by some soy sauce and a sweet hit of balsamic vinegar.

DIRECTIONS

Set up a grill for direct cooking, oil the grill rack, and heat to high.

Mix the hoisin, pesto, garlic, soy sauce, and vinegar in a bowl. Toss with the shrimp until thoroughly coated. Set aside for 10 minutes, and grill until browned and firm, about 2 minutes per side. Serve immediately.

seafood couscous

Couscous cooks so fast it inspires the instantaneous. Use this recipe as a template for endless quick meals—it will work with any type of fish, any flavor of couscous, a variety of broths, your choice of flavorful oil, and whatever herb you have on hand.

DIRECTIONS

Heat the water in a medium saucepan until boiling. Stir in the bouillon or glace until dissolved. Stir in the seafood and boil for 30 seconds. Stir in the couscous, oil, and parsley. Cover, remove from the heat, and set aside until all of the liquid has been absorbed, about 4 minutes. Fluff with a fork, and serve.

Oil for coating the grill rack

½ cup ranch dressing

1 tablespoon hot pepper sauce

4 catfish fillets, about 6 ounces each

No-stick spray oil

2 tablespoons Cajun seasoning

8 taco-size flour or corn tortillas

2 cups refrigerated coleslaw mix

½ cup finely chopped fresh tomato or salsa

grilled cajun catfish tacos

I'm addicted to fish tacos. The only thing that keeps me from having several a week is that often the fish is fried, and being at the age of the expanding waistline, I try not to eat an excess of fried food. These are quick (streamlined with bottled dressing, bagged coleslaw mix, and a jar of salsa) and relatively slimming because they're grilled (you can reduce the calories further by using reduced-calorie dressing).

DIRECTIONS

Heat a grill for direct grilling; coat the grill rack with oil. While the grill is heating, mix the ranch dressing and hot pepper sauce in a small bowl; set aside.

Season the catfish with the seasoning, and spray with oil. Grill until cooked through, about 3 minutes per side. Transfer to a plate, and cut each fillet in half lengthwise.

Wrap the tortillas in a clean dish towel and microwave at full power for about 1 minute, until heated through.

Spread each tortilla with 1 teaspoon of the sauce. Top each with a piece of fish, ¼ cup coleslaw, 1 tablespoon tomato, and 2 more teaspoons sauce. Fold or roll to eat.

2 cups water

½ cup chopped onion

1 teaspoon chopped garlic, fresh or jarred organic

Ground black pepper to taste

2 teaspoons lemon juice, fresh or bottled organic

4 pieces salmon fillet, about 6 ounces each

8 ounces Brie, rind removed

1 tablespoon basil pesto, jarred or homemade (page 339)

poached salmon with creamed brie

Although no one would consider Brie a miracle ingredient, it works wonders in this recipe. Unlike traditional hard cheeses, Brie is surfaced ripened, which means it ages from the outside in at the same time that it is aging from the inside out, allowing it to develop lots of flavor without becoming firm the way other aged cheeses do. Because Brie is moist and creamy, it will melt into a silken sauce when combined with simmering liquid. Make sure that you reduce the poaching liquid to concentrate its flavor sufficiently so that it is assertive enough to serve as a counterpoint to the aroma of the cheese.

DIRECTIONS

Combine the water, onion, garlic, pepper, and lemon juice in a large skillet; heat to boiling. Add the salmon; reduce the heat to a simmer, cover, and simmer gently until the salmon flakes to gentle pressure, about 8 minutes per inch of thickness of the fillets.

Remove the fish to a serving plate. Boil the poaching liquid until its volume is reduced to about ½ cup. Reduce the heat to low; add the Brie and stir until the cheese melts. Stir in the pesto and spoon over the fish. Serve immediately.

HOW DO YOU KNOW WHEN THE FISH IS DONE?

However you cook fish, beware of flaking. A fish is not perfectly cooked when you can see its flesh flake. It is overcooked. Flaking occurs when the membrane that supports the muscle fiber of a fish breaks down. When this happens, any juices held within these membranes will run out, leaving the fish hopelessly dry. When properly cooked the surface of a fish will still look smooth (meaning that the membranes are still intact), but it will break into flakes at the slightest pressure. A good rule of thumb is to cook fish for 8 minutes per inch of thickness, regardless of the cooking method.

2–2½ pounds salmon fillet, skin
      and pin bones removed

⅓   cup garlic-flavored oil

¼   cup chopped fresh herbs,
     parsley, dill, chives, thyme,
     tarragon, or a combination

     Kosher salt and coarsely
     ground black pepper to taste

     Juice of 1 lemon

slow-poached salmon in garlic oil and herbs

This method of poaching fish in a low oven in fragrant oil is a rendition of a classic French technique called poêle, which involves poaching fish, poultry, or vegetables in broth and butter. The results are incredibly succulent because the fibers of the food never get hot enough to break down, and as the ingredients warm in the herb-infused oil they quietly absorb its flavor.

DIRECTIONS

Heat the oven to 250°F. Place the fish in a baking dish large enough to hold it snugly. Pour the oil over the top and lift the sides of the fish so some oil runs underneath. Sprinkle the herbs over the top and season liberally with salt and pepper. Cover the dish with foil and bake until the salmon barely flakes to gentle pressure, 50 minutes to 1 hour. Do not uncover for at least 45 minutes while baking.

Uncover and drizzle with lemon juice; serve with some of the cooking juices spooned over the top.

1½ pounds salmon fillet, at least
    1 inch thick, bones and
    skin removed

    Salt and ground black pepper
    to taste

4   ounces (about 1 cup) crumbled
    feta cheese

½   teaspoon minced garlic, fresh
    or jarred organic

2   teaspoons chopped fresh dill

2   ounces smoked salmon,
    finely chopped

2   tablespoons extra-virgin olive oil

salmon sandwiched with feta and smoked salmon

This elaborate layered fish dish looks as though it took a lot of work, but the hardest part is cutting the fish. You need to section a thick fillet of salmon into two thinner fillets by slicing it in half horizontally. If you feel uncomfortable doing this, your fish store can do it for you.

DIRECTIONS

Heat the oven to 500°F.

Cut the fish fillet in half horizontally into 2 thin fillets, and season with salt and pepper. Mix the cheese, garlic, dill, smoked salmon, and 1 tablespoon of the olive oil in a bowl; season with salt and pepper. Sandwich the cheese mixture between the 2 fillets.

Grease a baking pan with some of the remaining olive oil. Place the sandwiched fillets in the pan and coat with the remaining oil. Bake until the fish browns on the surface and flakes to gentle pressure, about 10 minutes (8 minutes in a convection oven). Serve immediately.

1   whole sea bass (about 1½ pounds), cleaned and gills and scales removed

½   teaspoon salt

¼   teaspoon coarsely ground black pepper

2   tablespoons orange juice

1   tablespoon extra-virgin olive oil

1   large roasted red bell pepper, jarred, frozen, or homemade (page 337), coarsely chopped

1½ teaspoons minced garlic, fresh or jarred organic

steamed sea bass with oranges and red pepper

The delicate black-and-white mosaic of sea bass is beautifully framed by a sunburst of a sauce inflamed with orange juice and a puree of red pepper. No one will guess that the whole thing took less than 10 minutes to cook in the microwave.

DIRECTIONS

Make 4 slits through the fleshy parts of the fish on each side, cutting through to the bone. Rub the fish inside and out with the salt and pepper. Combine the orange juice and oil in a microwavable baking dish large enough to hold the fish. Place the fish in the dish as if it were swimming, spreading open the sides of the interior cavity to help the fish balance. Cover tightly with plastic wrap and microwave at full power until cooked through, 6 to 7 minutes.

Meanwhile, puree the pepper and garlic in a food processor or mini-chopper. When the fish is done, transfer it to a platter, using 2 spatulas. Stir the pepper mixture into the juices in the baking dish. Lift the flesh of the fish from the bone with a spatula, using the cuts in the sides to help separate it into portions. Serve with some of the sauce.

JUDGING FRESHNESS

Fresh fish have firm flesh. To test for freshness, poke the side of a fish in its thickest portion. The imprint of your finger should spring right back. If it leaves an impression, it is an indication that the flesh has already begun to decompose.

An even better freshness indicator is smell. Perfectly fresh fish has no odor whatsoever, except possibly the faint aroma of sea water. Any fishy odor is an indication of decay, which is why you should always ask to smell the fish you are about to buy. If the fish seller balks, there's probably something fishy going on.

The same fishy odor rule applies to purchasing shellfish. Clams and mussels should be relatively clean and have tightly closed shells. Lobsters and crabs, if they have not already been boiled and shelled, should be alive and kicking. It is not safe to cook a fresh lobster, crab, mussel, or clam that is not alive.

2   tablespoons mayonnaise

1   tablespoon minced garlic, fresh or jarred organic

2   teaspoons lemon juice, fresh or bottled organic

1   teaspoon hot pepper sauce

     Salt and ground black pepper to taste

1/2–2/3   cup almond meal or finely ground almonds (page 341)

1   whole red snapper or other firm white-fleshed fish, about 2 1/2 pounds, cleaned and gills and scales removed

     No-stick spray oil

FISH ON THE BONE

Bones contain a lot of flavor and rich proteins, which is why we use them to make stock and broth, and why savvy cooks know that whatever you're cooking, meat, poultry, or fish, you will get fuller flavor and richer sauces if you keep the meat on the bone while it's cooking. Especially fish. Because fish bones are so tender, they break down quickly during cooking, releasing their flavor and nutrients into the surrounding flesh. In contrast, beef, pork, and poultry bones, which are harder, don't have the chance to transfer nearly as much of their components into the meat in the time it takes to roast.

snapper encrusted with almonds

If you don't like looking dinner in the eye, turn the page. In this recipe a whole fish (head, tail, fins–the works) is roasted upright, as if it were swimming across the plate. It makes a dramatic presentation, but that's not why we're doing it. The fish is crusted with ground almonds. If it were roasted on its side, the almonds would crisp on one side and become soggy on the other. To keep that from happening, the fish is perched stomach-down, propped up and balanced by spreading out the walls of its belly. Sounds odd–looks great–tastes better.

DIRECTIONS

Heat the oven to 500°F.

Mix the mayonnaise, garlic, lemon juice, hot pepper sauce, salt, and pepper in a bowl; set aside. Place the almonds on a length of plastic wrap or wax paper.

Make 4 slits through the fleshy parts of the fish on each side, cutting through to the bone. Brush the mayonnaise mixture over both sides of the fish, leaving the head and tail uncoated. Roll the fish in the almond meal, making sure that all of the mayonnaise-coated parts are covered. Place the fish on a rack set on a rimmed sheet pan, as if it were swimming, spreading open the sides of the interior cavity to help the fish balance; spray with oil. Bake until the nut-covered skin is crisp and the flesh exposed by the slits appears cooked, 15 to 20 minutes.

Transfer the fish to a platter, using 2 spatulas. To serve, lift the flesh of the fish from the bone with a spatula, using the cuts in the sides to help separate it into portions.

1   egg, any size

1   package (9 ounces) frozen
    creamed spinach, thawed

½   teaspoon minced garlic, fresh or
    jarred organic

⅓   cup grated imported
    Parmesan cheese

1   cup seasoned breadcrumbs

1   pound cooked fish (cod, perch,
    snapper, haddock, flounder,
    salmon, etc.)

    Vegetable oil for frying

1   lemon, cut into 4 wedges

fish cakes florentine

Like meatloaf and sausage, fish cakes need ingredients to keep them moist, give them texture, and bulk up the flavor. Usually that takes a litany of ingredients, but in this case all you need are six—a box of creamed spinach for color, nutrition, and moisture; seasoned breadcrumbs for texture and herbs; cheese and garlic to punch up the flavor; and an egg to hold it all together.

DIRECTIONS

Mix the egg, spinach, garlic, cheese, and ¼ cup of the breadcrumbs in a large bowl. Break the fish into small flakes and fold into the spinach mixture.

Place the remaining crumbs on a length of plastic wrap or wax paper. Divide the fish mixture into 8 balls. Place the balls, one at a time, in the breadcrumbs, flattening them to about ½ inch thick and turning several times to thoroughly coat each cake.

Heat ¼ inch of oil in a large skillet over medium-high heat, and brown the cakes on both sides until they are golden brown and heated through, about 4 minutes per side. Serve with the lemon wedges.

Olive oil, as needed

1   jar (about 12 ounces) mango salsa

½   cup white wine

4   tablespoons unsalted butter, cut into small pieces

Salt and ground black pepper to taste

1¼ pounds large unsoaked sea scallops

mango beurre blanc with grilled scallops

Beurre blanc is a classic French sauce made from white wine, shallots, and an excess of sweet butter that is typically teamed with poached or baked seafood. By starting with mango salsa, we are able to make a more assertive rendition that is sweet, spicy, and tart, and made with a fraction of the butter called for in the original. It is perfect with the caramelized flavor of charcoal-seared scallops.

DIRECTIONS

Heat a grill set up for direct grilling until hot; brush the grill rack with oil.

Puree the salsa until smooth in a blender or food processor. Boil the wine in a medium skillet over high heat until reduced by half. Add the salsa and heat to boiling. Reduce the heat to a simmer; stir in the butter until melted and incorporated into the sauce. Season with salt and pepper and keep warm.

Remove any short, hard strips from the short edge of the scallops. Pat the scallops dry with paper towels, and season with salt and pepper. Coat with oil and grill until the scallops are resilient and browned on both sides, about 2 minutes per side. Serve the scallops topped with sauce.

DRY-PACK, DAY-BOAT, UNSOAKED SCALLOPS

Unlike clams, oysters, and mussels, scallops cannot survive for long outside of the sea, so they are usually shucked on board and kept chilled until they can be sold. Many scallop fishing grounds are so far offshore that fishing trips commonly take several days, which is why wholesale scallop buyers will pay a premium price for the "last of the catch" or the "top of the catch." The same applies to scallops caught on shorter trips, where the entire catch is guaranteed to have been harvested within the last 24 hours; these scallops are often sold as "day-boat scallops."

For years, inexpensive scallops have been treated with sodium tripolyphosphate (STP) to reduce the amount of water that seeps from the scallops as they sit. STP, along with other phosphates, is part of a group of acceptable food additives categorized as GRAS (generally recognized as safe).

It wasn't long before fish sellers figured out that if a little STP could keep scallops from weeping, a lot could cause them to soak up extra water. And since water is cheaper than scallops, it started to make economic sense to "soak" scallops, which meant loading them up with STP and setting them in water until they absorbed as much water as they could hold. The FDA has put a limit on the level of soaking, but for culinary purposes, any amount is a bad idea.

When soaked scallops are cooked, the bonds that hold the water in suspension are broken and the added soaking liquid comes pouring out, causing the scallops to steam and making it impossible to sear them. In addition, phosphates have a briny flavor that muffles any sweetness that the scallop possesses naturally.

So buy only scallops with a descriptor on the label. It could say "dry-pack," "diver," "chemical-free," "day-boat," "unsoaked," "100% natural," or anything else that indicates the scallops have not been treated. If there is no descriptor, you can assume that the scallops have been soaked, and if they are labeled "water added," which means they have been soaked until their weight is more than 80 percent water, run in the opposite direction.

½ package (about 3 ounces) pâté de foie gras or other liver pâté

2 tablespoons aged balsamic vinegar

2 tablespoons orange juice

2 tablespoons (plus a little more) extra-virgin olive oil

½ teaspoon minced garlic, fresh or jarred organic

½ teaspoon minced ginger, fresh or jarred

Salt and ground black pepper to taste

16 large wild-caught sea scallops, about 1¼ pounds

roasted scallops with foie vinaigrette

This dish is pure decadence. The sauce is plusher than butter, with a subtle flavor of barely poached liver and a sweet twang of balsamic vinegar. The scallops are cooked so hot and fast they have no time to sweat, but you will. It's that good.

DIRECTIONS

Heat the oven to 500°F. Place a large iron skillet or other heavy pan in the oven to heat for at least 10 minutes.

Puree the pâté, vinegar, orange juice, 2 tablespoons oil, garlic, ginger, salt, and pepper in a food processor or blender; set aside.

Remove any firm strips from the short edge of the scallops, and pat dry with paper towels. Season with salt and pepper. Remove the hot pan from the oven (use a thick pot holder), and coat the bottom with a little olive oil. Place the scallops, flat-sides down, in the pan, leaving as much space as possible between them. Roast for 2 to 3 minutes; turn and roast for 2 minutes more.

Serve 4 scallops per person; top each with a spoonful of the pâté mixture.

DON'T OVERCOOK

The big trick to cooking seafood is knowing when to stop. Shrimp, crab, scallops, squid, and lobster are done as soon as their flesh firms; most of the time this takes no more than a few minutes. Small shrimp and scallops can even cook through off of the heat from the residual warmth of a boiling sauce. Mussels and clams are done cooking as soon as their shells open.

2 skeins (two thirds of a 6-ounce package) rice stick noodles

12 wild-caught large sea scallops (about 1 pound), trimmed

2 tablespoons teriyaki sauce

1/3 cup water

1 large fish-flavored bouillon cube (9 grams)

1 can (about 13 ounces) coconut milk, light or regular

1 teaspoon Chinese chili paste with garlic

1/4 teaspoon dried ground lemongrass, such as Thai Kitchen

1/2 teaspoon toasted sesame oil

1 tablespoon chopped cilantro

No-stick spray oil

1 lime, cut into 4 wedges

mahogany sea scallops in coconut broth

Get ready to cook like a chef! This multidimensional recipe has several parts, but none of them are difficult or time-consuming. Here's what you will end up with: a tiny nest of pristine white noodles bathed in a fragrant, spicy broth enriched with coconut milk and topped with lacquered roasted scallops and a thin wedge of lime. It looks regal. Its flavors are exquisite, and it cooks in 20 minutes (including preheating the oven).

DIRECTIONS

Place a large iron skillet on the lowest rack in an oven; heat the oven to 500°F.

Meanwhile, place the noodles in a large bowl and cover with very hot tap water; stir to moisten and soak until softened, about 15 minutes. Toss the scallops in the teriyaki sauce in a separate bowl.

At the same time, heat the water to boiling in a saucepan; add the bouillon cube and stir until dissolved. Add the coconut milk, chili paste, and lemongrass and heat until boiling. Reduce the heat to a simmer and stir in the sesame oil and cilantro; keep warm.

Remove the hot skillet from the oven, using a thick pot holder. Spray the bottom of the skillet with oil, and arrange the scallops, flat-sides down, in the skillet, leaving as much space between them as possible. Return the skillet to the oven and roast the scallops for 5 minutes. Turn the scallops over and roast for 1 minute more.

To serve, drain the noodles and place a small pile on each of 4 dinner plates (or use wide, shallow bowls). Top each with a portion of the coconut broth and 3 scallops. Garnish each with a lime wedge.

7 meatless meals

In the decades when good nutrition meant meat, potatoes, and a green vegetable on every plate, little attention was paid to cuisines that produced perfectly healthy populations with hardly a speck of animal protein in their diets. Billions of Asians over the centuries have fed their bodies on bowls of rice, sesame seeds, soybeans, and vegetables. South Americans have been doing the same thing with cornmeal tortillas and beans for just as long. West Africans have learned to stave off starvation with a combination of peanuts and grains, and Caribbean cultures get high-quality proteins by eating beans and rice together.

The argument that beans and grains are high-calorie starches has recently been used against them by carb-fearing dieters. But look at the facts. A pound of beef steak has more than three times the calories found in a pound of cooked kidney beans, and considering that an average serving of meat is between 6 and 10 ounces and an average portion of beans or rice is closer to 5 ounces, the "starch is fattening" argument loses much of its weight.

In this chapter you will find dozens of recipes that deliver high-quality protein and powerful flavors without a speck of meat.

MAKES 4 SERVINGS

- 1 large poblano chile pepper
- 1 large red bell pepper
- 1 can (about 14 ounces) vegetable broth
- 1 can (about 16 ounces) cannellini beans, drained and rinsed
- 1/2 cup chunky salsa, medium or hotter
- 1 zucchini, stem removed, cut into 1/2-inch-thick slices
- 1 yellow squash, stem removed, cut into 1/2-inch-thick slices
- 3 tablespoons green mole paste or pipian paste
- 2 tablespoons chopped cilantro

vegan mole poblano

Normally I would use jarred or frozen roasted red peppers in a mole, but since a poblano pepper is essential for this mole, and poblanos don't come preroasted, you might as well roast the bell pepper at the same time. Once that job is done the mole is almost made; just simmer everything together. The complex spicing of the mole paste will permeate the stew in minutes.

DIRECTIONS

Char the skin of the poblano and bell peppers by placing them directly onto the grate of a gas burner set on high, at the highest setting of a broiler, or over a hot grill. As the skin on one side of the peppers burns, turn them over until the skin is uniformly burnt. Be careful to keep them moving so that the flesh under the skin doesn't char. Place the peppers in a bowl, cover, and set aside until cool. Peel off the burnt skin. Remove the stems and seeds, and cut the flesh into strips.

Combine the peppers, broth, beans, salsa, and squashes in a large saucepan and simmer for 5 minutes. Stir in the mole paste and cilantro and simmer until the vegetables are tender, about 5 minutes more; serve.

thai tofu tabbouleh (tabouli)

1   pound extra-firm or firm tofu, cut into 1/4-inch-thick slices

3/4 cup bottled Thai peanut sauce or salad dressing

1   tablespoon minced ginger, jarred, from a tube, or fresh

1   teaspoon ground dried lemongrass, such as Thai Kitchen

1/2 teaspoon minced garlic, fresh or jarred organic

2   teaspoons toasted sesame oil

1   box (about 6 ounces) tabbouleh or tabouli (bulgur wheat)

1 1/4 cups boiling water

Tofu is whatever you want it to be. Season it with soy and ginger and its home is China, but slather on the pit sauce and it's ready for the barbecue. One of the best ways to give it character is by charring its surface on a hot grill. In this recipe grilled tofu is paired with a quick grain salad to create a high-grade protein.

DIRECTIONS

Heat a grill set up for hot, direct grilling, or preheat the oven to 450°F. Coat the tofu slices with 1/2 cup of the peanut sauce; set aside for 10 minutes.

Mix the ginger, lemongrass, garlic, sesame oil, and tabbouleh in a medium bowl. Add the water and set aside for 15 minutes, until the grain is tender and the liquid has been absorbed.

Grill or bake the tofu until browned, 2 minutes per side if grilling, 10 minutes if baking. Serve the grilled tofu on a bed of tabbouleh. Top the tofu slices with the remaining peanut sauce.

TOFU

Just as cheese is made by separating milk into curds (solids) and whey (liquid), so tofu is made by separating soy milk into its solid (bean curd) and liquid (bean whey) components. The more whey that is extracted, the firmer the curd will be. In cheese-making this yields a variety of textures: soft, semisoft, firm, hard, and grating cheese. In tofu the range runs from silken to extra-firm.

Firm and extra-firm tofu are best for stir-frying, baking, or grilling. Soft or silken tofu is best for garnishing a soup or for making sauces. When silken tofu is pureed it is smooth and creamy, and it can be flavored in any number of ways. If you can find only firm tofu, you can still use it in a sauce recipe by reducing the amount by half and adding a few tablespoons of water. The adjustment is important because firm tofu has a greater amount of curd and less liquid in it than silken tofu, so it will cause the sauce to thicken more. Even with the adjustments, the results will not be quite as smooth as when the sauce is made with soft tofu.

¾ cup ricotta cheese, whole milk or part-skim

3 tablespoons grated imported Parmesan cheese

⅛ teaspoon minced garlic, fresh or jarred organic

½ teaspoon hot pepper sauce

2 tablespoons basil pesto, jarred or homemade (page 339)

Salt and ground black pepper to taste

1 loaf (about 8 ounces) French bread, cut into 24 thin slices

1 egg, large or extra-large

½ cup milk, any fat content

No-stick spray oil, butter, or oil for the pan

herbed ricotta sandwiches

These herb-infused dairy-fresh cheese confections exist somewhere between blintzes, French toast, and grilled cheese. They could be the centerpiece of a creative brunch, an aside to a soup for a simple supper, or a brilliant après-party snack.

DIRECTIONS

Combine the ricotta, Parmesan, garlic, hot pepper sauce, and all but 1 teaspoon of the pesto in a bowl. Season with salt and pepper. Make 12 small sandwiches, using 1 tablespoon of the ricotta mixture and 2 slices of bread for each.

Mix the egg, milk, remaining pesto, and salt and pepper in a wide, shallow bowl or pie plate.

Heat a large, nonstick skillet over medium heat. Coat with no-stick spray oil or a small amount of butter or oil. Dip the sandwiches in the custard, a few at a time, and cook until browned and cooked through, 2 to 3 minutes on each side; serve.

1   bag (12 ounces) micro-ready
    broccoli rabe

2   tablespoons vegetable oil

1   roll (about 18 ounces) cooked
    polenta, cut into 8 1/2-inch-
    thick slices

4   ounces spicy vegan sausage,
    such as Soyrizo, crumbled

1   cup tomato pasta sauce

2   tablespoons sun-dried
    tomato pesto

2   tablespoons garlic-flavored oil

1   teaspoon salt

3   tablespoons grated imported
    Parmesan cheese (optional)

grilled polenta with rabe and spicy sun-dried tomato sauce

This vegan version of the classic Italian triumvirate—broccoli rabe, hot sausage, and polenta—can be prepared in less than 10 minutes. Although its antecedents are ancient, its method is purely modern, because the polenta comes precooked in a log for slicing, the broccoli is already washed and chopped and ready to cook, and the "sausage" needs only to be heated.

DIRECTIONS

Cook the bag of broccoli rabe in a microwave at full power for 4 minutes.

Meanwhile, heat the oil in a large, nonstick skillet over medium-high heat. Brown the polenta slices on both sides in the hot oil. Transfer to a plate, cover, and keep warm. Add the sausage to the pan and cook until browned, about 2 minutes. Add the tomato sauce and sun-dried tomato pesto, and simmer for a few minutes.

Toss the cooked broccoli rabe, garlic oil, and salt in a bowl.

Serve by placing 2 polenta slices on a pool of sauce on each plate. Top each slice with a spoonful of sauce and a mound of broccoli rabe. Serve with the cheese, if desired.

1   bag (about 12 ounces) frozen Quorn Grounds

1   can (about 16 ounces) white, red, or pink kidney beans, drained and rinsed

1   jar (about 16 ounces) chunky salsa, any heat level

1   tablespoon ground cumin

1/4   teaspoon dried oregano

1   tablespoon chili powder

1/4   cup instant refried bean powder

1/4   cup chopped cilantro

quorn chili

Don't let the seeming simplicity of chili cause you to dismiss it; the stuff is more complex than you might expect. Fragrant with spices, vegetables, and beans, a good chili is not unlike a good curry—looks like slop, tastes like nirvana. This recipe is vegan. The meat substitute in it, Quorn, is a remarkable product developed in England that is made from isolated mushroom protein (see box), and unlike everything else that purports to taste like chicken, this product actually does.

DIRECTIONS

Combine everything in a large saucepan and simmer for 10 minutes over medium heat. Serve hot.

QUORN

Quorn is the brand name of a meat substitute that originated in England. It is made from a protein extracted from mushrooms. The fermented mycoprotein has a cell structure that is very similar to animal muscle cells. In muscle tissue, cells are bound together by connective tissue. So the manufacturers of Quorn have created a method to bind the cells of mycoprotein into fibers that, after cooking, have a natural meatlike texture similar to that of chicken. The raw Quorn is formed into a variety of meat shapes (nuggets, cutlets, ground, etc.) and is sold frozen. The amino acid structure of chicken eggs is the gold standard against which all other proteins are measured. Of all the nonanimal proteins (soy, peanuts, grains), Quorn comes closest to the balance of amino acids in eggs.

2   boxes (about 10 ounces) frozen creamed spinach, thawed

2   cups (8 ounces) ricotta cheese, whole milk or part-skim

½   cup (about 4 ounces) basil pesto, jarred or homemade (page 339)

1   jar (about 24 ounces) tomato pasta sauce

9   sheets (about two thirds of a box) no-boil lasagna noodles

1   box (about 1 pound) frozen breaded eggplant cutlets (slices)

1   package (about 6 ounces) shredded mozzarella

spinach and eggplant lasagna

One of the untold secrets of lasagna is that you can make it without precooking the noodles. Any noodle works, but the ones designated as "no-boil" are best. They look a bit odd; some are rippled and translucent like corrugated fiberglass, while others look like hardened sheets of fresh pasta. But they cook up thin and tender—more like fresh pasta than dried.

DIRECTIONS

Heat the oven to 375°F. Mix the spinach, ricotta, and pesto in a bowl.

Pour ½ cup of the tomato sauce in the bottom of a 9-by-13-inch baking pan. Place 3 noodles across the bottom of the pan. Top with half of the spinach mixture, half of the eggplant slices, ½ cup of the pasta sauce, and one third of the mozzarella. Repeat the layers one more time. Finish with the remaining 3 noodles. Add ½ cup water to the remaining tomato sauce, seal the jar, and shake to combine; pour over the top of the lasagna. Cover with foil and bake for 40 minutes. Uncover and top with the remaining mozzarella; bake for 10 minutes more. Let the lasagna rest for at least 10 minutes before cutting. It will slice more cleanly if refrigerated overnight and reheated.

- 1 cup diced onion, frozen or fresh
- 2 teaspoons chopped garlic, fresh or jarred organic
- ¼ teaspoon dried oregano
- 1 package (about 6 ounces) refrigerated or frozen soy "chicken" strips
- 1 jar (about 12 ounces) salsa verde
- 1 can (about 14 ounces) vegetable broth
- 1 can (about 4 ounces) diced green chiles
- 1 can (about 15 ounces) white posole (whole hominy), drained
- 1 tablespoon ancho chile powder or other chili powder
- 1 tablespoon lime juice, fresh or bottled organic

  Cooked white rice, for serving (optional)

vegan menudo

Every cuisine has its restorative dishes. In Mexico it is menudo, a humble stew of tripe, posole (whole hominy), and chiles. It simmers for hours until it is fragrant and spicy, slicked with fat. This version is vegan, its fat content is nil, and it takes less than 10 minutes to cook, but its ability to clear a stuffy head and excite the senses is undiminished.

DIRECTIONS

Heat the onion, garlic, and oregano in a large, covered saucepan over medium heat until soft, about 4 minutes, stirring once or twice. Add the remaining ingredients and simmer for 5 minutes. Serve with rice, if desired.

- 2 bundles (about 5 ounces) rice stick pasta
- 1 tablespoon toasted sesame oil
- 1 tablespoon minced garlic, preferably fresh
- 2 tablespoons minced ginger, jarred or fresh
- 1 package (about 18 ounces) chicken-style seitan, in bite-size pieces
- 1 container (32 ounces) vegetable broth
- 1 cup (about 3 ounces) sliced mushrooms
- 1 cup (about 3 ounces) snow peas, each cut into 3 sections
- 1 cup refrigerated coleslaw mix
- 1 teaspoon hot pepper sauce
- 1 teaspoon soy sauce

seitan big bowl

The curative power of this gigantic soup lacks credentials, but the aroma alone inspires health. Fragrant with garlic, ginger, and sesame, it is made from seitan that has been processed to resemble chicken. Although seitan (wheat protein) has the best meatlike texture, if you are sensitive to wheat products you can substitute a soy-based or Quorn-based "chicken" product without ill effect.

DIRECTIONS

Cover the rice sticks with hot tap water in a large bowl and set aside until tender, about 15 minutes; drain.

Combine the sesame oil, garlic, and ginger in a large saucepan and warm over medium heat until the aroma of the ginger and garlic is strong. Toss the seitan with this mixture, and add the broth. Raise the heat to medium-high and bring the liquid to a boil. Add the mushrooms, snow peas, and coleslaw and simmer until the vegetables are tender, about 5 minutes. Stir in the hot pepper sauce and soy sauce.

Place a portion of the soaked noodles in each of 4 large soup bowls. Ladle the soup over the noodles, and serve.

ASIAN QUICK-SOAK NOODLES

Unlike European pasta, which is made exclusively from wheat, Asian noodles are manufactured from many sources, including wheat, buckwheat, rice, bean starch, and seaweeds. The wheat and buckwheat noodles are cooked like Western pasta in boiling water, but the other noodles are not sturdy enough to stand up to boiling. All they need is to be soaked in hot water until they are tender.

When you visit the noodle section of an Asian grocery, the variety can be overwhelming, but most of the noodles you see will be made from either rice flour or bean starch. Rice noodles, also called rice sticks, banh pho, or chantaboon, are white. Bean starch noodles, also called bean thread, glass, transparent, or bai fun noodles, are thin and translucent. Both rice noodles and bean starch noodles come in a variety of shapes, but they are all prepared in the same way. Place the amount you need in a bowl and cover with very hot tap water. Allow them to soak until tender, about 15 minutes.

6   eggs, large or extra-large

Salt and ground black pepper to taste

No-stick spray oil

4   ounces crumbled vegetarian chorizo, such as Soyrizo

1   can (about 10 ounces) corn kernels, drained

1   can (about 10 ounces) diced tomatoes with chiles, drained

1/2 cup (about 2 ounces) shredded Monterey Jack cheese

2   tablespoons finely chopped cilantro

corn, tomato, and "chorizo" frittata

Southwest flavors dominate this hearty frittata. If you can't find vegetarian chorizo, any Mexican-seasoned meat substitute will do, such as tempeh or Quorn.

DIRECTIONS

Heat the broiler to high; set the rack at medium height. Beat the eggs, salt, and pepper in a bowl until well blended.

Spray a large, oven-safe, nonstick skillet with oil and heat over medium-high heat. Brown the chorizo. Add the corn and tomatoes and simmer for several minutes, until fairly dry. Reduce the heat to medium and add the beaten egg, tilting the pan and lifting the vegetables so that it flows evenly across the bottom of the pan. Make sure the vegetables are distributed evenly. As the egg sets, lift the edges and tilt the pan so that the liquid egg flows under the set sections; cook until just the top 1/2 inch of egg is liquid.

Place the pan under the broiler and broil until the surface is puffed and browned, 2 to 4 minutes. Remove from the broiler, using a thick pot holder. Sprinkle with the cheese, cover, and let rest for 5 minutes to melt the cheese. Scatter the cilantro over the top, cut into wedges, and serve.

No-stick spray olive oil

1 medium onion, halved and cut into 1/2-inch-thick slices

1 large sweet potato, peeled, halved, and cut into wedges

3 cups (about 10 ounces) precut fresh broccoli and cauliflower mix

1 medium red bell pepper, cored, stemmed, and cut into 1-inch-wide strips

Salt and ground black pepper to taste

3/4 cup (about 3 ounces) shredded Monterey Jack or cheddar cheese

1/2 cup (about 4 ounces) hummus, purchased or homemade (page 348)

2 tablespoons chopped cilantro (optional)

roasted vegetables with hummus queso

Several years ago in a bar in Phoenix, I was served a pot of queso with a few mashed white beans in it. It was a revelation (the earthiness of the beans were a perfect counterpoint to the rich, creamy cheese) and the inspiration for the sauce that cloaks this simple dish of roasted vegetables.

DIRECTIONS

Heat the oven to 425ºF. Spray a rimmed sheet pan with olive oil, and toss the onion, sweet potato, broccoli and cauliflower, and bell pepper together on the pan. Spray with more oil, and roast until the edges are browned and the vegetables are tender but not mushy, about 20 minutes.

While the vegetables are roasting, combine the cheese and hummus in a microwave-safe bowl; cover.

When the vegetables are roasted, transfer to a platter; microwave the cheese sauce at full power until the cheese melts, 1 to 2 minutes. Stir with a fork until well combined, and spoon over the vegetables. Top with chopped cilantro, if desired, before serving.

Variations: There are dozens of types of hummus in the deli case of your local supermarket, and almost any of them will work well in this recipe. Try garlic hummus, red pepper hummus, lemon hummus, or olive hummus. You can also modify the cheese to suit the flavor of your hummus; try pepper Jack with red pepper hummus, goat cheese with olive hummus, and Brie with lemon hummus.

2 tablespoons vegetable oil

1 cup diced onion, fresh or frozen

1 teaspoon minced garlic, fresh or jarred organic

1 can (about 14 ounces) pinto beans, drained and rinsed

1 can (about 14 ounces) green enchilada sauce

1/2 roasted red bell pepper, frozen, jarred, or homemade (page 337), diced

Salt and ground black pepper to taste

3 cups boiling water

3/4 cup instant polenta, such as Bellino or Favero

2 tablespoons chopped cilantro

1/2 cup shredded Cheddar Jack cheese

chili bean polenta

Preparing polenta used to be a big deal involving half an hour of stirring, sputtering, and scorching. Then there arrived precooked polenta in loaves and logs, which was a great alternative if you wanted to slice and fry it, but not for creamy, silken, soft polenta. Recently I found instant polenta. Innately suspicious of anything instant, I didn't expect much, but I was floored. This stuff is good. It cooks up in less than 5 minutes and has a creamy, appropriately grainy consistency and bold corn flavor, similar to what one would expect from long-simmered polenta.

DIRECTIONS

Heat the oil in a large saucepan over medium-high heat. Add the onion and cook until tender, about 2 minutes. Add the garlic, beans, enchilada sauce, and red pepper. Heat until simmering, season with salt and pepper, and simmer for 5 minutes.

Bring the water to a vigorous boil in a separate saucepan. Stir in the polenta and simmer until thick, about 3 minutes. Season assertively with salt.

Stir the cilantro into the beans and serve over a bed of polenta; top with the cheese.

- 3 tablespoons vegetable oil
- 8 ounces seitan, cut into bite-size chunks
- 1 cup diced onion, fresh or frozen
- 1 red bell pepper, stemmed, seeded, and diced
- 1 medium sweet potato, peeled and cut into bite-size chunks
- 2 tablespoons minced ginger, jarred or fresh
- 1 tablespoon minced garlic, preferably fresh
- 3 cups vegetable broth
- Salt and ground black pepper to taste
- 1/2 cup peanut butter, chunky or creamy
- 2 teaspoons hot pepper sauce
- 2 tablespoons chopped cilantro (optional)

seared seitan stew

Seitan is the meatiest of meat substitutes, and it should be treated that way. Sear it, grill it, brown it, roast it—it will reward you with a satisfying chewy texture and protein-rich flavor. I can't tell you it tastes like chicken or pork or beef; it doesn't. Like most meat substitutes, it tastes like whatever you cook it with. This recipe gives it the flavor of an Indonesian satay with the addition of hot peppers, cilantro, and peanut butter.

DIRECTIONS

Heat the oil in a deep skillet over medium-high heat. Add the seitan and brown on both sides, about 3 minutes; remove. Add the onion and red pepper to the oil remaining in the skillet, and sauté until tender. Add the sweet potato, ginger, and garlic; toss to coat with oil. Add the broth, and salt and pepper, and simmer until the sweet potato is tender, about 15 minutes.

Remove a ladleful of broth to a small bowl. Add the peanut butter and hot sauce and stir until the peanut butter is thinned to the consistency of cream. Stir into the stew and finish with cilantro, if desired.

SEITAN

Vegetarian cooks have long used grains, beans, and nuts to make foods that imitate the chewy texture of meat and provide high-grade protein. When the protein is extracted from wheat, it is known as seitan or gluten (it is also sold as "wheat protein" or "wheat meat"). Grain proteins, like seitan, yield a meatier texture than bean proteins like tofu or tempeh. Because seitan is naturally bland, it often has flavorful ingredients added to it, most commonly soy sauce. Seitan stays firm during cooking and is a good choice for soups or for grilling.

1   cup (about 4 ounces) shredded
    Cheddar Jack cheese

½   cup plus 2 tablespoons
    sour cream

½   cup chunky salsa, any heat level

1   roasted red bell pepper, jarred,
    frozen, or homemade (page 337),
    diced

1   tablespoon chopped cilantro

9   corn tortillas (from a package of 10)

1   can (about 16 ounces) vegetarian
    refried beans, black or red

bean burrito torta

This elaborate-looking tortilla "cake" makes a fun appetizer or
vegetarian entrée. It requires no particular skills other than the
ability to stack evenly, turn on the oven, and tell time.

DIRECTIONS

Heat the oven to 375°F.

Mix the cheese and ½ cup sour cream in a small bowl. Mix the
salsa, pepper, and cilantro in a separate bowl.

Stack the ingredients on a pie plate or an oven-safe plate in this order:

1. 1 tortilla
2. ¼ cup refried beans spread over the tortilla
3. 3 tablespoons salsa mixture spread over the beans
4. 1 tortilla
5. ¼ cup cheese mixture spread over the tortilla

Repeat the sequence 3 more times. Top with the last tortilla, and
cover with foil. Bake until heated through, about 25 minutes. Ice
the top with the remaining 2 tablespoons sour cream and a dollop
of the remaining salsa mixture in the center. Let cool for 5 to
10 minutes before cutting into quarters to serve.

MEATLESS PROTEIN

There are lots of ways to get high-quality protein without eating animal products. Proteins are built from
amino acids (eight of which are essential), and in order for our bodies to build protein from the foods we
eat, we need all of the essential amino acids present in our bloodstream at the same time. Only animal
products contain all eight essential amino acids, but if you eat certain vegetable products together, the
amino acids in one can make up for the deficiencies in another, giving your body all of the amino acids
it needs to build protein. Many classic vegan dishes are built on this system of complementary proteins:
tofu and rice, chickpeas and sesame seeds, peanut butter and bread, and, in the case of this recipe, beans
and corn.

greens and beans

MAKES 4 SERVINGS

2½ cups water

1 bag (about 1 pound) frozen or refrigerated chopped collard

1 package (about 10 ounces) frozen or refrigerated cooked black-eyed peas

⅓ cup hickory-flavored barbecue sauce

4 ounces extra-firm tofu, cut into ¼-inch cubes

Salt and ground black pepper to taste

A vegan takeoff on a soulful boil of collard greens and black-eyed peas, this one-pot meal will not win a beauty pageant, but it is loaded with protein. It's also quite tasty, easy to cook, and easier to love—a likely candidate for Miss Congeniality.

DIRECTIONS

Heat the water to boiling over medium-high heat in a large skillet. Add the collard and black-eyed peas and simmer until both are tender, about 15 minutes. Stir in the barbecue sauce and tofu and cook for another 2 to 3 minutes. Season with salt and pepper before serving.

eggplant steaks with bruschetta steak sauce

MAKES 4 SERVINGS

1 box (about 1 pound) frozen breaded eggplant cutlets (slices)

1 jar (about 12 ounces) tomato bruschetta

3 tablespoons steak sauce

1 tablespoon extra-virgin olive oil

Bruschetta, which once meant toast with an Italian salsa on top, has come to mean the salsa itself. Now sold in jars and refrigerated cases, tomato bruschetta is hawked as a pasta sauce, a garnish, and a pizza topping. In this recipe, its blend of garlic, herbs, and extra-virgin olive is are transformed by a jolt of steak sauce into something bold and hearty, the perfect foil to send a slice of breaded eggplant onto the center of the plate.

DIRECTIONS

Heat the oven to 425°F. Arrange the eggplant in a single layer on a large sheet pan and bake until browned and crisp, about 15 minutes. Meanwhile, heat the bruschetta to a simmer over medium heat. Stir in the steak sauce and olive oil and keep warm. Serve the eggplant slices topped with some of the sauce.

No-stick spray oil

1 cup (about 4 ounces) finely grated imported Parmesan cheese

2 pounds ricotta cheese, preferably whole milk

1 teaspoon minced garlic, fresh or jarred organic

3 tablespoons basil pesto, jarred or homemade (page 339)

½ teaspoon salt

½ teaspoon ground black pepper

Pinch of cayenne pepper

1 tablespoon white wine vinegar

4 eggs, large or extra-large

slow-baked savory ricotta pudding

This herb-infused ricotta pudding is whatever you want it to be: cheese soufflé, savory custard, or herbed cheesecake. Cut into slender wedges and served with toasted black bread, it is an elegant hors d'oeuvre. Make the slices thicker and accompany them with shaved prosciutto and fruit, and it becomes a light appetizer. Serve it with fresh tomato sauce and a green salad for a sophisticated luncheon, or team it with a side of ratatouille and pasta for a vegetarian entrée.

DIRECTIONS

Heat the oven to 325°F. Spray a 2-quart soufflé dish or an 8- or 9-inch cheesecake pan with oil, and dust with 3 tablespoons of the Parmesan cheese.

Combine the remaining ingredients, including the remaining Parmesan, in a bowl, and mix until well blended. Pour into the prepared pan and bake until a tester inserted in the center comes out with a bit of set batter clinging to it, about 1 hour and 15 minutes. Cool to warm room temperature, 30 minutes to 1 hour. Cover with a serving plate, invert and shake slightly to release the pudding, and remove the baking pan. Slice to serve.

1 package (about 9 ounces) buckwheat soba noodles

1/2 cup chipotle salsa

1/3 cup teriyaki sauce

1 package (about 8 ounces) spicy
tofu (Mexican or Southwest), cut
into 1/2-inch cubes

2 tablespoons extra-virgin olive oil

4 scallions, trimmed and sliced

soba noodles with spicy tofu

Soba noodles, made from buckwheat flour, are darker and heartier than your typical pasta—the perfect choice to go with a spicy, tangy sauce radiating with smoked chiles, spiced tofu, and teriyaki.

DIRECTIONS

Bring a large pot of salted water to a boil. Add the soba, stirring a few times to ensure that the pasta does not stick to itself. Boil vigorously for the time recommended on the pasta package or until the pasta is tender, about 4 minutes. Drain.

Meanwhile, combine the chipotle salsa, teriyaki sauce, tofu, and olive oil in a microwave-safe serving bowl. Cover and heat in a microwave at full power until simmering, about 2 to 3 minutes (or heat to simmering in a saucepan). Toss the cooked noodles, scallions, and sauce until the noodles are coated with sauce.

FLAVORED SALSA

Salsa contains just three ingredients: tomatoes, onions, and peppers. Everything else is flavoring. Cilantro, garlic, lime, corn, chipotle, black beans, white beans, and artichoke all can give salsa a distinctive taste profile or a stylistic panache, but they limit its versatility as a cooking ingredient. Use flavored salsas where appropriate to streamline the number of ingredients in a recipe, but always feel free to substitute an all-purpose salsa amended with a flavorful addition.

To make a flavored salsa, add the following to 1 cup salsa:

• For chipotle salsa, add 1 teaspoon chipotle hot sauce, or 1/2 teaspoon ground chipotle, or 1/4 chipotle pepper en adobo, finely chopped.

• For cilantro salsa, add 1 teaspoon cilantro pesto or 2 tablespoons chopped cilantro.

• For lime salsa, add 2 teaspoons fresh lime juice.

• For corn and black bean (Southwest) salsa, add 1/2 teaspoon ground cumin and 2 tablespoons each rinsed canned black beans and drained canned or frozen corn kernels.

1   tablespoon olive oil

4   frozen veggie burgers, thawed

1   cup tomato pasta sauce

1   teaspoon ground cinnamon

2   ounces (about 1/2 cup) shredded Italian cheese (mozzarella, provolone, Asiago, or a blend)

veggie burgers parmesan

Vegetarian cooking tends to be labor intensive. There's usually a lengthy list of ingredients, considerable chopping, and exotic seasoning; eventually everyone gets burnt out. And that's when you want a recipe like this. No chopping, no thinking, no effort, no time. Put it together, stick it in the oven, turn on the TV, and eat.

DIRECTIONS

Heat the oven to 375°F. Coat the bottom of an 8- or 9-inch square baking pan with the olive oil. Place the burgers in the oil and turn over to coat on both sides. Bake until browned, about 10 minutes.

Mix the sauce and cinnamon and heat in a saucepan or in a microwave. Pour the sauce over the browned burgers. Top with the cheese and bake until the sauce is bubbling and the cheese is melted, about 10 minutes; serve.

THE TWO FACES OF VEGGIE BURGERS

There are two types of non-meat burgers. Those made from TVP (textured vegetable protein) have been processed from beans to resemble meat, either ground beef or chicken, depending on the burger's design. The other type doesn't attempt to imitate meat in texture, flavor, or appearance. It is made from grain and vegetables and is more fragile than the ersatz meat patties. Either one will work well in the Veggie Burger Parmesan recipe.

2 tablespoons olive oil

1 cup diced onion, fresh or frozen

½ cup (about 2 ounces) shredded carrot

½ teaspoon pumpkin pie spice

1 teaspoon ground coriander

1 teaspoon ground cumin

1 can (about 14 ounces) vegetable broth

1 cup canned chickpeas, drained and rinsed

¾ cup instant couscous

Salt and ground black pepper to taste

2 red bell peppers, split lengthwise and seeds removed

6 ounces fresh goat cheese (chèvre)

couscous stuffed peppers

These cups of carmine-red peppers overflowing with Moroccan-scented couscous are a far cry from the drab, flabby stuffed peppers that Mom used to make. There is a nubbin of goat cheese hidden in the stuffing; if you want to make the recipe vegan, you can omit the cheese.

DIRECTIONS

Heat the oil in a saucepan over medium heat. Add the onion and carrot and sauté until tender, about 4 minutes. Add the spices and cook briefly, just until the aroma of the spices is pronounced. Add 1 cup of the broth and heat to boiling. Stir in the chickpeas and couscous to moisten; remove from the heat, cover, and let rest until the couscous is tender, about 5 minutes.

Place the peppers, cut-sides up, in a shallow baking dish just large enough to hold them snugly. Spoon ¼ cup couscous into each pepper shell; nestle an ounce of chèvre in the center of each pepper. Fill with the remaining couscous and top with a small nugget of the remaining chèvre. Pour the remaining broth around the peppers, cover tightly with foil, and bake until steaming and tender, about 45 minutes; serve.

4   large eggs, lightly beaten

1   unbaked 9-inch pie crust in a
    pie pan

1   cup (about 4 ounces) shredded
    Swiss cheese

2½ cups roasted vegetables,
    purchased or homemade
    (pages 342 and 343)

2   tablespoons spicy
    brown mustard

½   cup milk

roasted vegetable cheese tart

Roasted vegetables are sold in the prepared foods section of many supermarkets, or you can make your own; there are recipes on pages 342 and 343. Whenever you are roasting vegetables, change the mixture according to what is freshest and cheapest, but try to keep the selection similar in texture. Hard vegetables (like beets) take longer to roast than soft ones (like tomatoes). So you must either precook the hard ones or add the soft ones near the end of roasting. Roasted vegetables can be stored in the refrigerator for about 10 days and tossed with pasta, served as a side dish, or baked into a savory pie.

DIRECTIONS

Heat the oven to 375°F. Brush a thin film of beaten egg over the interior of the unbaked crust. Scatter half of the cheese over the bottom of the crust; top with the roasted vegetables, followed by the remaining cheese. Mix the remaining egg, mustard, and milk in a bowl, and pour into the pie; it should just cover the solid ingredients. Bake until the custard is set and the crust has browned, 35 to 40 minutes. Rest for about 5 minutes, then cut into 6 or 8 wedges and serve.

feta and potato pizza

MAKES 2 ENTRÉE SERVINGS

1   prepared pizza crust, such as Boboli

½   cup roasted pepper spread or pesto

1   package (about 9 ounces) frozen roasted potatoes with garlic and herbs, thawed

4   ounces (about 1 cup) crumbled feta, with or without herbs

Anyone who professes to starch addiction and has never tried potatoes on pizza has no business in my twelve-step program. This recipe is embarrassingly easy and, shame of all shames, everything in it is packaged. Mea culpa; it's sinfully good.

DIRECTIONS

Heat the oven to 450°F. Place the pizza crust on a sheet pan. Spread the pepper spread over the crust, up to the rim. Top with the potatoes and feta and bake until bubbling, 10 to 12 minutes. Rest for about 5 minutes, then cut into wedges and serve.

polenta pan pizza

MAKES 2 ENTRÉE SERVINGS

1¼   cups water

½   teaspoon salt

¼   teaspoon ground black pepper

½   cup instant polenta, such as Bellino or Favero

1   cup diced fresh tomato (about 2 tomatoes)

½   cup (about 2 ounces) shredded mozzarella cheese

¼   cup (about ½ ounce) shredded imported Parmesan cheese

    Pinch of dried oregano

This dish is pizza in name only. Instant polenta, which should be in the pantry of anyone with a passing fondness for Italian home cooking, is spread into a disk and baked, then topped with fresh tomatoes and cheese. Serve it as a simple entrée or an upscale snack. It is good right out of the oven or at room temperature.

DIRECTIONS

Heat the oven to 375°F. Heat the water, salt, and pepper in a saucepan over medium-high heat until boiling. Stir in the polenta and cook until thick, about 4 minutes. Spread across the bottom of a 9-inch pie pan. Top with the tomato, cheeses, and oregano. Bake until the polenta is crisp on the edges and the cheese is melted, about 15 minutes. Cut into wedges to serve.

6   eggs, large or extra-large

     Salt and ground black pepper
     to taste

     No-stick spray olive oil

4   slices (about 5 ounces) frozen
     breaded eggplant cutlets, cut
     into quarters

½   cup muffaletta or olive salad,
     purchased or homemade
     (page 339)

⅓   cup (about 2 ounces) crumbled
     feta cheese

2   tablespoons finely chopped
     Italian (flat-leaf) parsley

eggplant, olive, and feta frittata

Frittata is the contemporary deviled egg. Easy to make, nostalgic, and casual, a homey dinner or an elegant appetizer, and ultimately versatile, it is equally comfortable with a filling of potatoes and cheese as it is speckled with smoked salmon and caviar. Like most frittatas, this one is good served hot or at room temperature.

DIRECTIONS

Heat the broiler to high; set the rack at medium height. Beat the eggs, salt, and pepper in a bowl until well blended.

Spray a large, oven-safe, nonstick skillet with oil and heat over medium-high heat. Brown the eggplant pieces on both sides. Reduce the heat to medium and add the beaten egg, tilting the pan and lifting the eggplant so that it flows evenly across the bottom of the pan. Make sure the eggplant pieces are distributed evenly. As the egg sets, lift the edges and tilt the pan so that the liquid egg flows under the set sections; cook until just the top ½ inch of egg is liquid.

Place spoonfuls of olive mixture evenly over the top of the egg. Scatter the feta evenly over all. Place the pan under the broiler and broil until the surface is puffed and browned, 2 to 4 minutes. Remove from the broiler, using a thick pot holder. Sprinkle with parsley, cut into wedges, and serve.

- 1   bag (about 16 ounces) broccoli and cauliflower florets
- 1   bag (about 8 ounces) bell pepper strips, preferably multicolored
- 8   ounces small white mushrooms, trimmed and cleaned
- 1   bag (about 8 ounces) baby-cut carrots
- 1   can (about 14 ounces) chickpeas, drained and rinsed
- 1   jar (about 15 ounces) curry cooking (simmer) sauce, or 2 cups homemade (page 349)
- 1   cup vegetable broth
- 1   tablespoon chopped cilantro
- 4   rounds pita bread
-     No-stick spray olive oil

ten-minute vegetable curry with grilled flatbread

Curry takes time: time to toast the spices, grind them, and simmer them with aromatic vegetables into a fragrant paste. But use a jar of curry sauce and all of the work is done for you, and the results are far more authentic than what usually takes place with a spoonful of curry powder in most American kitchens.

DIRECTIONS

Heat a grill set up for direct grilling to medium; or heat a broiler with the rack placed at the closest setting.

Combine the broccoli and cauliflower, bell pepper strips, mushrooms, carrots, chickpeas, curry sauce, and vegetable broth in a large saucepan, and heat to boiling over medium-high heat. Simmer until the vegetables are tender, about 15 minutes; stir in the cilantro.

Shortly before the vegetables are done cooking, spray the pitas with olive oil spray and grill or broil until toasted but not crisp, about 1 minute per side. Wrap in a clean towel or cloth napkin. Serve the stew with the pitas for scooping.

8 vegetable accompaniments

There is nothing so ingratiating as a vegetable. Happy to sit on the sidelines, letting a fillet of sole get all the attention, vegetables are equally able to take center stage. All they need is your imagination and a little pizzazz to attract attention.

Don't go crazy. Remember, the recipes in this chapter are side dishes; they are accompaniments to the main attraction, so they should complement, not compete. When choosing vegetables to escort an entrée, think about the flavorful, colorful, and textural combinations you are creating on the plate.

chèvre mashed sweet potatoes

MAKES 4 SERVINGS

- 2 pounds sweet potatoes or yams, peeled and cut into chunks
- 1/3 cup half-and-half or whole milk
- 1 1/2 tablespoons honey

  Salt and ground black pepper to taste
- 2 ounces goat cheese (chèvre), crumbled

Preparations for sweet potatoes are too often redundantly sweet. Here I've added a little honey to underscore the natural sugars in the potato and, in contrast, a swirl of goat cheese for a little tang. The effect is rich and subtle; most people won't quite know what's going on, except that the results are delicious.

DIRECTIONS

Place the sweet potatoes in a saucepan and cover with water. Cover and boil gently until tender, about 15 minutes. Drain. Add the half-and-half, honey, salt, and pepper, and mash until smooth. Stir in the cheese, leaving the mixture streaky.

roasted teriyaki fries

MAKES 4 SERVINGS

- 1 bag (about 16 ounces) frozen French fries, any shape
- 3 tablespoons teriyaki sauce

Teriyaki sauce is salty, sweet, and tangy. When exposed to high heat, its sugars caramelize and the salinity and acidity intensify. An intriguing coating for French fries, don't you think?

DIRECTIONS

Heat the oven to 450°F. Crumple a sheet of heavy-duty foil, uncrumple it, and place on a sheet pan. Toss the potatoes and teriyaki sauce and scatter on the foil, trying to avoid having one French fry touching another. Bake until browned and heated through, 15 to 20 minutes; the longer they cook, the crisper they will be.

1   package (about 16 ounces) frozen French fries, any shape

1   tablespoon dried oregano

2   tablespoons fresh lemon juice

4   ounces (about 1 cup) crumbled feta cheese

feta fries

I first had "Greek Fries" in a sandwich shop in Seattle, and the combination of fried potatoes, oregano, lemon, and feta was a mind-altering experience. Here is my attempt to duplicate the sensation.

DIRECTIONS

Heat the oven to 450°F. Crumple a sheet of heavy-duty foil, uncrumple it, place on a sheet pan, and scatter the fries on the foil. Bake until browned and crisp, 16 to 18 minutes. Toss with the oregano, lemon juice, and cheese.

FROZEN POTATOES

Mealy potatoes, like russets, which are best for roasting and frying, benefit from a rest period between an initial phase of cooking to soften their fibers and a second flash of heat to make them fluffy and crisp just before they are served. It is this two-phase cooking cycle that has created an opportunity for the mass production of frozen French fries and roasted potatoes. Manufacturers cook the potatoes through the first phase and freeze them, and consumers complete the second step at home.

During the initial cooking (done at a relatively cool 250°F to 325°) the starch in the outer cells dissolves and gathers on the surface, where it reinforces the cell walls into a thicker, stronger layer. At the same time, the cell walls in the interior of the potato break down, softening the texture of the vegetable.

At that point the cooked potatoes are seasoned and frozen in giant flash freezers. After they are purchased and reheated, the interiors steam and fluff, while the starch on the surface dries, browns, and crisps. Some French fry products are coated with extra starch to make them crisper.

3   pounds russet potatoes, peeled and cut into small chunks

1/4 ounce (about 8 grams) dried portobello mushrooms, finely chopped

3   cups water

1   can (about 10 ounces) condensed cream of mushroom soup

Salt and ground black pepper to taste

portobello mashed potatoes

The concentrated flavor of dried portobello mushrooms inhabits this exotic version of mashed potatoes. If you have a mini-chopper, use it to mince the mushrooms; if not, you will have to use a knife, as most full-size food processors are too large to chop small quantities evenly. The mushrooms don't require presoaking, because they will hydrate as they cook with the potatoes.

DIRECTIONS

Combine the potatoes and mushrooms with the water in a large, covered saucepan, and bring to a boil over medium-high heat. Boil until the potatoes are tender, about 15 minutes; drain. Mash the potatoes right in the pot, using a potato masher or fork, adding the soup and mixing until the mixture is fluffy and creamy. Season with salt and pepper.

3–4 large russet potatoes (about 1 1/2 pounds), unpeeled, washed- and cut into chunks

6   tablespoons extra-virgin olive oil

1   teaspoon salt

1/2 teaspoon chopped garlic, fresh or jarred organic

1/4 teaspoon ground black pepper

mashed roasted potatoes with garlic "butter"

If you have dined only on potatoes mashed with cream and butter, get ready for something radically different. Roasting potatoes develops browned meaty flavors that are the antithesis of your typical mash, so to intensify that difference I've traded in the richness of sweet dairy for an aromatic jolt of garlic and extra-virgin olive oil.

DIRECTIONS

Heat the oven to 450°F. Toss the potatoes with 2 tablespoons of the oil and the salt on a rimmed sheet pan or large roasting pan. Roast until tender and lightly browned, about 25 minutes. Mash with the remaining 4 tablespoons oil, the garlic, and the pepper.

1   pound russet potatoes, unpeeled, washed, and cut into chunks

1   can (about 15 ounces) sliced pickled beets, drained and quartered

1   tablespoon prepared horseradish

¼   cup sour cream

    Salt and ground black pepper to taste

beet 'n' smashed potatoes

The outrageous magenta glow of these mashed potatoes makes it clear that they're probably not for everyone, but if you grew up, as I did, on pickles and herring, and sour cream and horseradish, this fanciful combination will bring you home.

DIRECTIONS

Boil the potatoes in a generous amount of water until tender. Add the beets to the undrained potatoes and warm through. Drain and add the horseradish, sour cream, salt, and pepper. Smash until well combined but not smooth. Adjust the seasoning.

TECHNIQUES FOR COOKING VEGETABLES

Choosing the best method for cooking a vegetable is contingent on its texture. Hard, tough vegetables, like carrots, potatoes, or beets, must be boiled or steamed. Softer, moister vegetables, like tomatoes, mushrooms, and spinach, can be sautéed, baked, or grilled. If you want to sauté or grill a tough vegetable, you must either chop it finely to break it down, or boil it briefly to soften its fibers.

4   large russet potatoes, about
    8 ounces each, washed and dried

1   tablespoon vegetable oil

**SMOKED SALMON, CHIVE, AND CREAM
CHEESE TOPPING**

4   ounces smoked salmon, chopped

3/4 cup (about 3 ounces) cream
    cheese chive spread

**PICKLED BEET, SOUR CREAM, AND
HORSERADISH TOPPING**

1/2 15-ounce can pickled beets,
    drained and diced

1/4 cup sour cream

1   tablespoon prepared horseradish

**SHRIMP AND RUSSIAN DRESSING
TOPPING**

1   package (about 4 ounces) tiny
    shrimp, drained

1/4 cup bottled Russian dressing

baked potatoes with toppings

A baked potato is a blank canvas. If baked correctly, it provides a fluffy, flaky, fairly bland background for your creativity. The possibilities are profuse; I'm starting you off with three.

DIRECTIONS

Heat the oven to 400°F. Place the potatoes on a rack in a roasting pan and bake until tender, about 45 minutes. Meanwhile, prepare one of the toppings by mixing the ingredients together in a bowl.

To serve, split open the potatoes and top with some of the topping.

SPEED-BAKING POTATOES

One of the greatest travesties in the history of quick cooking is the erroneous notion that a baked potato and a microwave-baked potato have any similarity, other than the fact that they are both hot. The flesh of a properly baked potato is fluffy and dry, while the interior of the same potato cooked in a microwave will be flabby and damp. What's happening?

There are two types of potatoes when it comes to cooking. Mealy potatoes, which include russets (such as Idaho), purple potatoes, and fingerling potatoes, are preferred for baking because they have a high concentration of dry starch in their cells. As they cook, the moisture in the potato starts to steam, and at about 150°F the starch starts to absorb that moisture, causing the starch cells to swell and separate from one another. Because there is so much starch in mealy potatoes, any moisture that doesn't evaporate through the skin gets absorbed, resulting in a fluffy, tender, and relatively dry texture.

Unfortunately, this doesn't happen in a microwave, but there is a compromise that yields moderately fluffy results. Turn on the oven to 450°F. While it is heating, set the potatoes in a microwave oven and cook at full power for about 8 minutes, which is approximately the time it will take for your oven to preheat. Transfer the partially cooked potatoes to the oven until they are cooked through, about 20 minutes for large russet potatoes.

MAKES 6 SERVINGS

3 pounds sweet potatoes or yams, peeled and cut into chunks

1 jar mango chutney or sweet tamarind chutney, chunks finely chopped

2 tablespoons butter, salted or unsalted, melted

Salt and ground black pepper to taste

roasted yams with chutney glaze

This simple three-ingredient recipe (excluding salt and pepper) is bursting with sweetness and spice. The trick is a jar of chutney, which seasons the yams and caramelizes as they roast.

DIRECTIONS

Heat the oven to 400°F. Toss all of the ingredients together in a large roasting pan and roast until the sweet potatoes are tender and crisp on the edges, 45 to 50 minutes; serve.

MAKES 12 SERVINGS

2 large yellow onions, peeled and cut into bite-size chunks

2 pounds turnips or rutabagas, peeled and cut into bite-size chunks

1/4 cup garlic-flavored olive oil

Salt and ground black pepper to taste

2 boxes (12 ounces each) frozen scalloped apples or Harvest apples, thawed

Leaves from 2 large sprigs rosemary

roasted turnips and apples

Turnips are coarse, requiring a little finesse to smooth their rough edges. Straight sugar is too strong, but a few mild root vegetables or orchard fruits can work wonders. The combination of caramelized onions, apples, and turnips is hard to beat. These take their time (about an hour) roasting, but all you have to do is pop them in an oven and wait until they're done.

DIRECTIONS

Heat the oven to 425°F. Toss the onions, turnips, and half of the oil in a large roasting pan or rimmed sheet pan; season with salt and pepper. Roast until the turnips just begin to soften and the edges start to brown, about 30 minutes.

Add the apples and rosemary, and toss with the vegetables. Roast until the vegetables are lightly caramelized and tender, 20 to 25 minutes more. Toss with the remaining 2 tablespoons oil before serving.

¼ cup extra-virgin olive oil

¼ cup tabbouleh (bulgur wheat), with a separate seasoning packet

2 boxes (12 ounces each) grape or cherry tomatoes

1 teaspoon chopped garlic, preferably fresh

Salt and ground black pepper to taste

stir-fried tomatoes with toasted tabbouleh

Cooked tomatoes tend toward mush, which has always been my problem with stewed tomatoes. I liked the flavor, but the texture left me bored. Stir-frying these tomatoes retains a little more of their firmness, but the real revelation is the crunch of toasted tabbouleh. Wonderfully crisp, it even absorbs some of the tomatoes' juices without becoming soggy.

DIRECTIONS

Heat a wok over high heat. Add 2 tablespoons of the oil and the tabbouleh and toast until golden brown, about 1 minute. Remove and set aside. Reserve the seasoning packet from the tabbouleh.

Add the remaining 2 tablespoons oil to the wok and heat until smoking. Add the tomatoes, garlic, salt, pepper, and 1 tablespoon of the reserved seasoning packet, and stir-fry until the tomatoes are heated through and a few of them burst. Add the toasted tabbouleh and serve.

Note: If you want to make the remaining tabbouleh according to the package directions, add ¾ cup boiling water to the tabbouleh and the remainder of its seasoning packet.

vanilla cauliflower poached in almond milk

MAKES 4 SERVINGS

1 cup almond milk

½ teaspoon salt

¼ teaspoon ground black pepper

1 teaspoon vanilla extract

1 head cauliflower, greens removed and stem cut flush

This delicately perfumed and meltingly creamy vegetable takes time but no attention. The almond milk sweetens the more pungent elements of the cauliflower, and the hint of vanilla lends it a floral perfume that is otherworldly.

DIRECTIONS

Heat the oven to 400°F.

Combine the almond milk, salt, pepper, and vanilla in a small casserole just big enough to hold the cauliflower. Place the whole head of cauliflower in the almond milk, upside down, and bake until browned, about 30 minutes. Turn the cauliflower over and baste the top with some of the almond milk in the casserole. Bake, basting 2 or 3 more times, until the cauliflower is browned and very soft, about 30 minutes more. Remove from the casserole and cut into wedges to serve.

roasted balsamic tomatoes

MAKES 4 SERVINGS

1½ pounds ripe tomatoes (4 or 5 medium), cut into large wedges

¼ cup extra-virgin olive oil

1 teaspoon kosher salt

½ teaspoon ground black pepper

4 teaspoons aged balsamic vinegar, preferably at least 15 years

This fragrant, pungent tomato compote is the perfect accompaniment to a roasted chicken or a char-grilled steak.

DIRECTIONS

Heat the oven to 450°F. Toss the tomatoes, half the oil, the salt, and pepper on a rimmed sheet pan or in a large roasting pan and roast until the tomatoes are just beginning to break down, 6 to 8 minutes. Toss with the remaining oil and the vinegar before serving.

- - - - - - - - - - - - - - - - - - - -

1   bag (about 16 ounces) frozen
    shelled edamame

¼   cup soy sauce

2   teaspoons grated ginger, fresh
    or jarred

2   teaspoons chopped pickled
    (sushi) ginger

gingered edamame

As you might have guessed by the proliferation of recipes in this cookbook for edamame, I am a big fan of fresh soybeans. Fortunately, as my penchant has grown, so has their availability. Once sold only at Asian groceries, they are now available frozen, in and out of their pods, at every supermarket. This highly flavored, easy side dish shows them off beautifully.

DIRECTIONS

Warm the edamame in a large, covered nonstick skillet over medium-low heat until tender, 5 to 7 minutes. Turn the heat to medium-high until the pan is very hot. Add the soy sauce and ginger and toss until the edamame are coated. Serve garnished with the pickled ginger.

EDAMAME

- -

Edamame (pronounced ed-dah-MAH-may) are immature soybeans that are harvested while the beans are still green and have grown to between 80 and 90 percent of the full size. At harvest, edamame have less indigestible ogliosaccharides and more vitamins than mature soybeans. They are slightly higher in oils and sugars, and slightly lower in protein, which accounts for their sweet flavor, creamy texture, and fresh green vegetable aroma.

Although edamame are available fresh, they are very perishable and are more commonly sold frozen, in their pods or already shelled. Unshelled edamame are mostly eaten for snacks; boil them for 5 minutes, toss with salt, and pop the beans from the pod directly into your mouth. Shelled beans are more convenient for all other edamame recipes. The shells are indigestible.

1½ cups (about 8 ounces) frozen shelled edamame

1 can (about 15 ounces) corn kernels, drained and rinsed

¼ cup chicken or vegetable broth

¼ cup salsa, any heat level

1 tablespoon chopped cilantro, or 1 teaspoon cilantro pesto or chutney

soy succotash

Succotash is the early American colonists' rendition of a native Narragansett dish made by stewing corn and beans together. Although there were many variations on the theme, the one that stuck was fresh lima beans and corn, often drenched in melted butter. This recipe ups the nutrition and (if you ask me) the flavor and texture by introducing fresh green soybeans (edamame) in place of the limas. Edamame are available frozen in their pods or shelled. The shelled ones are much more convenient for dishes like this.

DIRECTIONS

Combine the edamame, corn, broth, and salsa in a medium saucepan. Heat through, stirring often. Stir in the cilantro, and serve.

2 tablespoons olive oil

¼ cup (1 ounce) diced prosciutto

1 can (about 15 ounces) corn kernels, drained

1 can (about 15 ounces) cannellini beans, drained and rinsed

Salt and ground black pepper to taste

4 scallions, trimmed and thinly sliced

cannellini succotash

Think succotash Italian-style. It's not so far-fetched. Italians are big on beans and grains. Switch from limas to cannellini, throw in a little prosciutto, and you're there.

DIRECTIONS

Heat 1 tablespoon of the oil in a large saucepan over medium heat. Add the prosciutto and brown lightly. Add the corn, beans, salt, and pepper. Heat through and stir in the scallions and the remaining tablespoon of oil before serving.

almond miso green beans

1   tablespoon miso, any type

2   tablespoons almond butter

1   tablespoon soy sauce

1   tablespoon vegetable oil

1/4   cup water

2   teaspoons finely chopped pickled (sushi) ginger

1   bag (about 16 ounces) frozen green beans

1   tablespoon water

1   tablespoon sesame seeds

This Asian twist on green beans amandine is simplified by using almond butter, enhanced with fermented soy miso and some sweetness from chopped pickled ginger.

DIRECTIONS

Mix the miso, almond butter, soy sauce, vegetable oil, water, and ginger in a bowl. Place the beans and the water in a covered microwave-safe container and cook in a microwave at full power until tender, 3 to 4 minutes. Toss with the miso mixture, and scatter the sesame seeds over the top.

bananas broiled with chutney

2   large bananas, peeled and halved lengthwise

1   tablespoon unsalted butter, melted

1/4   cup Major Grey's chutney

We tend to shy away from fruit as a side dish, but these creamy, spicy bananas might be just the thing to embolden a staid dinner. Serve them with a simple grilled fish or a garlic-infused roast chicken for a startling tropical tease.

DIRECTIONS

Heat a broiler to high and set the rack at its top setting. Place the bananas cut-sides up on a broiler pan. Mix the butter and chutney and spoon evenly over the bananas. Broil until browned and bubbly and the bananas are tender, about 8 minutes; serve.

1   teaspoon spicy brown mustard

2   teaspoons red wine vinegar

⅓   cup olive oil

¼   teaspoon sugar

½   teaspoon hot water

    Salt and ground black pepper
    to taste

8   ounces frozen or fresh haricots
    verts or other tender green beans

1   tablespoon water

haricots verts with mustard vinaigrette

Haricots verts are French green beans that are longer and slimmer than American string beans. For many years, fancy recipes called for "French-cut" green beans, which were string beans sliced lengthwise to resemble haricots verts. Now you can buy the real thing, fresh or frozen, in most supermarkets. If you have not tried them, seek them out; there's a huge difference.

DIRECTIONS

Combine the mustard, vinegar, olive oil, sugar, hot water, salt, and pepper in a bowl with a whisk.

Place the green beans in a microwave-safe bowl, add the water, cover, and cook at full power for about 3 minutes. Drain and toss with the mustard mixture before serving.

COOK YOUR VEGETABLES BY COLOR

Enhancing the color of a vegetable requires a different technique for each hue. Chlorophyll, the pigment in green vegetables, is destroyed by excessive heat or by exposure to acid. This means that greens cannot be marinated, cooked for long periods, or cooked with wine or lemon. Less obviously, green vegetables should not be boiled for long in a covered pot. During boiling the natural acids of the vegetable are released into the water. If the pot is covered, these acids become trapped, causing the water to grow increasingly acidic. After about 7 minutes, the water will become acidic enough to cause the vegetable to discolor.

The phenomenon is reversed when cooking red and purple vegetables. Their pigment, called anthocyanin, is enhanced by exposure to acid and turns blue when heated with an alkaline substance or when not enough acid is present. That is why recipes for red cabbage or red peppers often add a bit of vinegar or lemon to the mixture, or instruct you to keep the lid on the pot.

White vegetables discolor with long storage or overcooking. Both of these situations allow oxygen to mix with the pigment, causing it to turn gray or brown. That is why mushrooms and cauliflower are best cooked quickly, and why potatoes must be cooked as soon as they are peeled. It is also why leftover potatoes turn gray if they are not coated with butter or oil.

Orange-colored vegetables, like carrots and squash, are almost impervious to hue abuse. Nothing short of culinary conflagration could cause their color to change.

6 ounces soft tofu

2 tablespoons rice wine vinegar

1 tablespoon toasted sesame oil

1/4 teaspoon salt

1/2 teaspoon hot pepper sauce

1/2 teaspoon minced garlic, fresh or jarred organic

1 1/2 pounds asparagus, hard ends trimmed

2 tablespoons chopped pickled (sushi) ginger

asparagus with tofu vinaigrette

This low-fat creamy vegan sauce is similar to mayonnaise or hollandaise, and is a guilt-free sauce for dressing up any steamed vegetable. Here it is napped over asparagus that has been steamed in a microwave.

DIRECTIONS

Puree the tofu, vinegar, sesame oil, salt, hot pepper sauce, and garlic in a blender or mini food processor. Place the asparagus in a single layer in a microwave-safe baking dish. Add a few tablespoons of water and cover; cook in a microwave at full power until tender, 4 to 5 minutes. Drain the water; arrange the asparagus on a serving platter and pour the tofu sauce over the top. Garnish with the pickled ginger.

1 pound medium-thick asparagus, trimmed

1/4 cup extra-virgin olive oil

Salt and ground black pepper to taste

2 tablespoons freshly grated pecorino Romano cheese

grilled asparagus with pecorino

Asparagus gains flavor on the grill. Perhaps it is the slight dehydration that concentrates its natural juices, or the interplay of smoke and fresh greenery. The results are addictive. The intensity of the grilled vegetable is offset with a garnish of freshly grated Romano cheese.

DIRECTIONS

Set up a grill for direct grilling and heat to medium-high. Coat the asparagus with half the oil and grill until bright green and lightly seared, about 2 minutes per side. Place on a platter and season with salt and pepper. Drizzle with the remaining olive oil and scatter the cheese over the top before serving.

6   medium beets (about 2 pounds)

Oil for coating the grill rack

No-stick spray oil

¼ cup fig preserves, such as
Adriatic Fig Spread, strained

1   tablespoon balsamic vinegar

grilled beets with fig molasses

In this recipe, microwave-cooked beets are seared over hot coals for a few minutes to get a delicate charred flavor that is an exciting contrast to the sweet and pungent fig glaze. Serve with grilled fish, poultry, or meat.

DIRECTIONS

Wash the beets and trim them of greens, stems, and any long taproots. Place the beets in a shallow, microwave-safe casserole or pie plate. Add ¼ inch of water and cover tightly. Microwave at full power until the largest of the beets are tender, 8 to 10 minutes. Uncover, drain, and allow to cool. Peel the cooled beets by cutting off the stem end and rubbing the skin; it will slip off. If any pieces of skin stick, trim with a small knife. The recipe can be completed up to this point a day ahead, if desired.

Heat a charcoal or gas grill to high and coat the grill rack with oil before placing 4 inches from the fire. Cut the beets into thick (about ½ inch) slices, and coat with spray oil. Grill the beets until browned, about 3 minutes per side.

Mix the fig preserves and vinegar until smooth in a serving bowl. Toss the hot beets with this mixture. Serve immediately.

1 pound Brussels sprouts, wilted leaves discarded

3 tablespoons (about 1 ounce) diced prosciutto

1 tablespoon extra-virgin olive oil

1/4 teaspoon dried thyme

Salt and ground black pepper to taste

stir-fried brussels leaves with prosciutto

Brussels sprouts have a tendency to get sulfury and acrid when they are overcooked. In this recipe the sprouts are shredded, which allows you to sauté them super-fast. Because you don't have to wait for the whole sprout to cook through, the surface doesn't overcook, and off-flavors don't get a chance to develop.

DIRECTIONS

Starting at the rounded ends, cut the Brussels sprouts into thin slices, discarding the hard stem ends. Heat a wok over high heat until hot. Add the prosciutto and oil and stir-fry for 10 seconds. Add the Brussels sprouts and thyme and stir-fry until bright green and tender, about 3 minutes. Season with salt and pepper before serving.

BUYING LEAFY VEGETABLES

Leaves are the most common and the most perishable of vegetables. They include lettuces, spinach, endives, cabbages, cresses, herbs, rabe, and sprouts. Although leaf vegetables vary in color, toughness, and flavor, all of them are prone to wilting because of their unique structure.

Leaves are energy factories, producing sugar via photosynthesis. Photosynthesis uses water, carbon dioxide, and sunlight from the atmosphere and turns them into oxygen, which is released back into the air, and sugar, which is stored as starch. To do their job, leaves need to be broad and flat, exposing maximum surface area to sunlight and water. Inside the leaf, a network of air pockets increases the number of cells that come into contact with the air. This allows optimal transfer of carbon dioxide and oxygen through the cell walls where photosynthesis takes place.

This unique framework makes leaves much more susceptible to dehydration and bruising than other vegetables. It also causes them to shrink dramatically during cooking. Most of a leaf is air and water. As it is heated its cell structure collapses. The leaf wilts and all its water and air are released, which is why a gallon of fresh spinach collapses into less than a cup of cooked vegetable and a sea of water.

Because leaves are prone to dehydration, it is best to store them in loosely closed plastic bags and use them as soon as possible. Do not seal them too tightly, or the leaves may absorb excess water and become soggy. Wash leafy vegetables as close to serving time as possible.

MAKES 4 SERVINGS

- 1 bag (about 1 pound) refrigerated diced potatoes
- 1 bag (about 16 ounces) cleaned and cut broccoli rabe
- 2 teaspoons minced garlic, fresh or jarred organic
- 2 tablespoons extra-virgin olive oil
- 6 ounces (1 1/2 cups) crumbled feta cheese
- 1/2 teaspoon cracked black pepper

rabe with potatoes and feta

The appearance of bags of cleaned and cut broccoli rabe displayed alongside precut carrots, prepared lettuces, and washed baby spinach has signaled the mainstream acceptance of this nutritious and flavorful vegetable. This recipe is pure convenience–everything is precut. All you do is simmer the ingredients together. The slight bitterness of the rabe, the bland, starchy potatoes, and the pungent bits of feta cheese play off of one another beautifully.

DIRECTIONS

Bring a large pot of salted water to a boil over high heat. Add the potatoes and boil until barely tender, about 10 minutes. While the potatoes are cooking, wash the rabe and drain. Add to the boiling water and continue cooking until the rabe is tender, about 5 minutes. Drain well and toss with the garlic, oil, cheese, and pepper before serving.

MAKES 4 SERVINGS

- 2 tablespoons vegetable oil
- 2 teaspoons minced ginger, fresh or jarred
- 12 ounces broccoli florets
- 2 tablespoons water
- 2 tablespoons soy sauce
- 1/2 cup toasted walnuts

stir-fried broccoli with ginger and walnuts

This extremely simple and delicious preparation is made even faster by purchasing precut broccoli florets, jarred minced ginger, and toasted walnuts.

DIRECTIONS

Heat the oil in a large wok over medium-high heat. Add the ginger and stir-fry for 20 seconds. Add the broccoli and toss to coat with oil. Add the water and cover the wok; steam until the broccoli is barely tender, about 3 minutes. Add the soy sauce and walnuts, and toss to combine before serving.

roasted corn and tomatoes

1 bag (about 16 ounces) frozen corn kernels

4 medium tomatoes, about 12 ounces total, cut into chunks

Salt and ground black pepper to taste

1/2 teaspoon minced garlic, fresh or jarred organic

2 tablespoons butter, salted or unsalted

2 tablespoons chopped Italian (flat-leaf) parsley

Roasting concentrates flavor. In addition to browning the edges and giving each corn kernel a little bit more texture, roasting corn makes it incredibly sweet. The tomatoes provide a flavorful counterpoint and help to keep the corn moist.

DIRECTIONS

Heat the oven to 450°F. Toss the corn and tomatoes in a baking dish large enough to hold them in a single layer; season with salt and pepper. Roast until the tomatoes are almost dry but not brown, about 20 minutes. Toss with the garlic, butter, and parsley before serving.

corn pilaf

1 tablespoon vegetable oil

2 tablespoons pine nuts (pignoli)

1/2 cup diced onion

1/2 red bell pepper, diced

1 rib celery, diced

1 teaspoon chopped garlic, fresh or jarred organic

1/4 teaspoon dried thyme

About 1 pound frozen or canned corn kernels, drained

Salt and ground black pepper to taste

This confetti of corn, pignoli, and fragrant vegetables gets an added flavor boost by browning all of the ingredients with a cooking method that is reminiscent of making a rice pilaf.

DIRECTIONS

Heat the oil in a large, nonstick skillet over medium heat. Add the pine nuts and stir until lightly toasted. Remove with a slotted spoon. Add the onion to the oil remaining in the pan and sauté until light brown. Add the pepper and celery and sauté until tender. Add the garlic, thyme, and corn and sauté until the corn browns in spots. Return the pine nuts to the pan and season with salt and pepper before serving.

1   pint mini red and yellow bell
    peppers, stemmed, seeded,
    and cut in half, or 1 large red
    or yellow bell pepper, stemmed,
    seeded, and cut into strips

8   ounces (about 2 cups) baby carrots

1   tablespoon extra-virgin olive oil

½   teaspoon chopped garlic, fresh
    or jarred organic

    Salt and coarsely ground black
    pepper to taste

roasted peppers and carrots

The raucous confluence of red peppers and carrots is a love affair for the eye and the palate. And the match-making couldn't be easier. All you do is introduce them in a baking dish, set them in a hot oven, and let nature take its course.

DIRECTIONS

Heat the oven to 425°F. Combine the bell peppers, carrots, olive oil, and garlic in a baking dish. Season with salt and pepper and bake until some of the edges are browned and the vegetables are tender, about 25 minutes; serve.

VEGETABLES THAT ARE FRUIT

There are countless vegetables that are botanically fruits. Fruit is the pulpy part of a plant that houses the seed. Tomatoes, cucumbers, squashes, eggplant, bell peppers, and avocados are all fruits.

The botanical purpose of a fruit is to protect and nurture a seed until it is ready to grow into a new plant. When the seed is mature, the fruit ripens, making it attractive to animals. Hopefully they will eat the fruit, thus scattering its seed and helping the plant species to flourish. As a fruit ripens, its skin blushes with color; it gets softer and juicier; its starch is converted to sugar, making the fruit sweeter; and enzymes break down its cell walls, releasing a characteristic perfume. For fruits like tomatoes, corn, and avocados, full ripeness is the essence of quality, but for most fruit-vegetables ripening is a process of diminishing returns.

Think about the qualities of full ripeness, such as soft flesh, sweetness, and pronounced aroma. They are the very attributes that make a cucumber or zucchini undesirable. Ripe cucumbers are yellow and soft. Ripe zucchini are flaccid and full of seeds. Completely ripened eggplants are flabby and bitter. These fruits are judged by the opposite criteria—firmness, smallness, greenness, and a clean, fresh aroma.

Bell peppers are the trickiest of all fruit-vegetables in which to judge quality. Part of the problem is that the desirable degree of ripeness changes with the pepper. Green bell peppers are underripe. They should be very firm, be heavy for their size, and give off a characteristic acrid aroma. Red, yellow, and orange bell peppers are green peppers that have been left to ripen. They should have vivid color and a heady, sweet fragrance, but unlike other ripe fruits, peppers should never be soft. The line between a ripe bell pepper and a rotten one is very thin. Choose carefully, avoiding ones with bruises, soft spots, or a musty odor.

1 tablespoon vegetable oil

1 can (about 15 ounces) corn kernels, drained

1 teaspoon ground ginger

3 scallions, trimmed and sliced

Salt and ground black pepper to taste

1 tablespoon minced pickled (sushi) ginger

2 bunches broccoli rabe

½ cup raisins, golden or mixed golden and dark

2 tablespoons extra-virgin olive oil

2 ounces prosciutto, finely diced (about ⅓ cup)

2 teaspoons minced garlic, fresh or jarred organic

Kosher salt and coarsely ground black pepper to taste

wok-seared corn and ginger

Another method to enhance the sweetness of corn is to brown it quickly in a wok. The kernels emerge peppered with hundreds of caramelized freckles and, if you're using a well-seasoned wok, a subtle smoky essence.

DIRECTIONS

Heat a wok over high heat until very hot. Add the oil and heat until smoking, about 5 seconds. Add the corn and ginger and stir-fry until the corn is browned. Add the scallions and salt and pepper, and heat through. Remove from the heat and stir in the pickled ginger before serving.

broccoli rabe with prosciutto and raisins

Broccoli rabe can be bitter, so in this recipe I've taken several precautions. First, the rabe is blanched before sautéing, which helps to quiet its more acrid elements. Then it is paired with prosciutto and raisins to counteract any residual bitterness with their own assertive salty and sweet flavors.

DIRECTIONS

Bring a large pot of salted water to a boil. Meanwhile, cut the hard ends from the broccoli rabe and cut the rest into 2-inch-long pieces. Wash thoroughly in a large bowl or a sink filled with cold water; drain. Boil the rabe until barely tender, about 5 minutes. During the last minute, add the raisins; drain. Set aside for up to several hours.

Just before serving, heat the oil in a large, deep skillet over high heat. Add the prosciutto and garlic and sauté until lightly browned, about a minute. Add the cooked rabe and season liberally with salt and pepper. Sauté until heated through.

1   pound Brussels sprouts, stem
    ends and wilted leaves removed

2   teaspoons garlic-flavored oil

    Salt and ground black pepper
    to taste

¼   cup onion marmalade, such
    as Vidalia, Stonewall Kitchen, or
    Trader Joe's, or finely chopped
    Roasted Caramelized Onions
    (page 336)

brussels sprouts roasted with onion jam

A wonderful way to cook Brussels sprouts is to roast them in an extremely hot oven. The outsides get browned and sweet, and the interiors barely soften to al dente. Here their sweetness is enhanced by coating them in a glaze of caramelized onions. If you can't find onion marmalade or jam (it's an esoteric item, I admit), you can use a little bit of homemade caramelized onion.

DIRECTIONS

Heat the oven to 450°F. Cut any large Brussels sprouts in half lengthwise. Toss on a rimmed baking sheet with the oil, salt, pepper, and marmalade. Roast until the marmalade caramelizes and the Brussels sprouts are just tender, about 20 minutes; serve.

6 medium beets (about 2 pounds)

1 teaspoon lemon juice, fresh or bottled organic

2 tablespoons real maple syrup

2 teaspoons garlic-flavored oil

"roasted" maple-glazed beets

Roasting beets takes several hours and frequent visits to the oven to ensure that they do not burn. The results are sweeter than boiling, and, though time-consuming, you will never return to simmering beets again. But there is an easier way. Cooking beets in a microwave doesn't yield quite the intensity of flavor of roasting, but it is a huge improvement over boiling.

DIRECTIONS

Wash the beets and trim them of greens, stems, and any long taproots. Place the beets in a shallow microwave-safe casserole or pie plate. Add ¼ inch of water and cover tightly. Microwave at full power until the largest of the beets are tender, 8 to 10 minutes. Uncover, drain, and allow to cool. Peel the cooled beets by cutting off the stem end and rubbing the skin; it will slip off. If any pieces of skin stick, trim with a small knife. The recipe can be completed up to this point a day ahead, if desired.

Meanwhile, mix the lemon juice, syrup, and garlic oil in a microwave-safe bowl. Cut the beets into wedges and toss with the syrup mixture; reheat in a microwave at full power or in a 400°F oven until hot, about 10 minutes; serve.

SHOPPING FOR ROOT VEGETABLES

Roots are the way plants absorb nutrients from the soil. They anchor the plant into the ground and act as a storehouse of starch and free sugar, which the plant or a passing animal can use for food. Like all storage units, roots need strong walls and lots of space. Hard fibers are interspersed with large, starch-storing chambers (vacuoles). As the plant matures, the vacuoles get bigger (making the root sweeter), and the fibers get harder. Quality walks a tightrope between sweetness and toughness. Harvest it too soon and it will lack size and flavor. Let it get too old and its fiber will turn to wood.

Judge root vegetables by their size. Smaller specimens will be milder and more tender; larger and thicker roots will be tougher and more robust. In any bunch or package of root vegetables, it is likely that you will get roots of different sizes. Use the larger ones for soup and stew, and save the smaller ones for shredding into a salad or for quick cooking methods, like stir-frying and sautéing.

Avoid root vegetables that blush green near their tops. This indicates that part of the root grew above the soil line, where it was exposed to sunlight, giving the green part a bitter aftertaste. However, green leaves or a green stub emerging from a root can give you helpful information about the vegetable's freshness. Look for tops that are bright green and moist, but not damp.

Hairlike sprouts growing from a root indicate that the vegetable has been kept too moist for too long. Although this is not a disastrous sign, it means that the vegetable has given some of its nutrition up to the sprouts. Softness is an indication of dehydration. Depending on its severity, it can be relieved by soaking the vegetable in cold water.

zucchini and wild mushrooms

MAKES 4 SERVINGS

- 2 tablespoons olive oil
- 1 tablespoon butter, salted or unsalted
- 1 bag (about 16 ounces) refrigerated sliced squash
- 1 package (about 6 ounces) sliced wild mushrooms
- 1 teaspoon dried Italian seasoning
- 1 teaspoon chopped garlic, fresh or jarred organic
- 2 teaspoons tomato paste

   Salt and ground black pepper to taste

Zucchini needs help. Like most squash, it is watery and bland, but it is also ubiquitous and we need as many ways to give it flavor as we can get. This is a simple one and takes advantage of the ready availability of both sliced fresh squash and sliced wild mushrooms in the produce section of your local supermarket.

DIRECTIONS

Heat the olive oil and butter in a large skillet over medium heat. Add the squash and mushrooms and sauté until they lose their raw look. Add the seasoning, garlic, tomato paste, salt, and pepper. Cover and cook until the vegetables are tender, about 7 minutes; serve.

baked acorn squash with spiced applesauce

MAKES 4 SERVINGS

- 1 large acorn squash, weighing about 1 1/2 pounds
- 2 tablespoons butter, salted or unsalted, melted
- 1 teaspoon pumpkin pie spice
- 1/4 cup water
- 1 cup applesauce
- 1/2 teaspoon vanilla extract

Put away that tired-out recipe for baked winter squash with cinnamon butter and try this lower-fat version, in which roasted sections of squash are filled with warm vanilla-scented applesauce.

DIRECTIONS

Heat the oven to 400°F. Cut the squash into quarters and scrape out the seeds and the stringy pulp surrounding them. Place the squash flesh-side up in a baking dish sized to fit them snugly. Drizzle with 1 tablespoon of the butter and half the pumpkin pie spice. Pour the water into the baking dish around the squash, cover with foil, and bake until tender, about 40 minutes.

Just before the squash is done baking, mix the applesauce, remaining butter, and remaining pumpkin pie spice in a saucepan and heat to simmering; stir in the vanilla. Fill the cavity in each portion of squash with some of the applesauce, and serve.

roman-fried artichoke hearts

MAKES 4 SERVINGS

Oil for frying

1   lemon, cut in half

1   can (about 14 ounces) artichoke
    hearts, drained

2   tablespoons flour

    Salt and ground black pepper
    to taste

1   extra-large egg, beaten

Cooking the glorified blossoms known as *carciofi alla giudia*, which are the poster child of Roman Jewish cooking, takes time and a heedless disregard for personal safety. You see traditional recipes call for deep-frying the artichokes as you sprinkle them with water, which helps them steam as they brown but unfortunately also causes hot oil to fly about the room. I have discovered something much saner: start with precooked canned artichoke hearts and leave the daredevil tactics to the culinary cavalier.

DIRECTIONS

Heat ½ inch of oil in a large, deep skillet to 375°F, or until the end of a wooden spoon dipped into the oil bubbles within 10 seconds.

While the oil is heating, squirt half the lemon over the artichoke hearts and toss with the flour until the artichokes are uniformly coated. Sprinkle with salt and pepper.

When the oil is hot, toss half the artichoke hearts in the egg and fry in the hot oil until golden brown, turning as needed to brown evenly, about 1 minute. Drain on paper towels and repeat with the remaining artichoke hearts. Serve with the remaining lemon half, cut into wedges.

2   large fennel bulbs, stems and
    core trimmed

2   tablespoons extra-virgin olive oil

½   onion, sliced

    Salt and ground black pepper
    to taste

    Leaves from 1 branch fresh
    rosemary

¾   cup apple juice

1   cup chicken broth

½   cup chunky applesauce

1   teaspoon apple cider vinegar

fennel braised with apples and rosemary

Braising, browning an ingredient in oil and then simmering it to tenderness, is usually reserved for tough cuts of meat, but it is also a succulent technique for hearty vegetables. Here, the subtle anise flavor of fresh fennel bulbs is sweetened with apples and scented with a piney whiff of rosemary.

DIRECTIONS

Slice the fennel bulbs lengthwise into ½-inch-thick slices.

Heat the olive oil in a large skillet over medium-high heat. Brown the fennel and the onion, trying to keep the fennel slices intact. Season with salt and pepper and scatter the rosemary around the vegetables. Add the apple juice and broth, cover, and simmer until the fennel is tender, about 10 minutes. Stir in the applesauce and vinegar, and heat through before serving.

FENNEL, CELERY, AND OTHER STEM VEGETABLES

Stems fulfill two functions for a plant. They hold the upper parts of the plant aloft, exposing leaves to sunlight, flowers to pollinating insects, and fruits to passing animals. And they contain the circulatory system through which nutrients move up from the root and sugars manufactured in the leaves descend back down into the roots to be stored as starch.

To complete their dual job, stems are structured much like roots. Strong support fibers are interspersed with hollow veins, but unlike roots the support fibers are not tough enough to do the job alone. They must be helped by a turgid flow of fluid in the veins. It is this combination of firm fiber and lots of water that gives stem vegetables their snap—a brief resistance followed by a burst of juice. If the vascular tissue dehydrates, the stem will lose this crispness, causing the vegetable to become limp.

Stem vegetables don't usually stand alone. Most often they're connected to other plant parts. For instance, broccoli is part stem, part flower. Asparagus is both stem and bud. Chard and celery are stem and leaf. Because different plant parts differ in structure, it is important to judge each part respectively. For instance, the stem of broccoli should be judged on its firmness and juiciness, but the flower should be looked at for color and shape. Swollen or open buds indicate the broccoli is about to flower, and yellowness means it has begun to bloom (a sign that the broccoli is past its prime).

lime-a-beans

MAKES 4 SERVINGS

1 tablespoon olive oil

½ teaspoon chopped garlic, fresh or jarred organic

1 can (about 16 ounces) cannellini beans, drained and rinsed

Salt and ground black pepper to taste

2 teaspoons lime juice, fresh or bottled organic

2 tablespoons chopped Italian (flat-leaf) parsley

These citrus-bright lime-scented white beans are a great complement to grilled fish or chicken. And they take less than 3 minutes to prepare.

DIRECTIONS

Heat the oil in a saucepan over medium heat. Add the garlic and cook until aromatic, about 30 seconds. Add the beans, salt, pepper, and lime juice and heat through, about 2 minutes. Stir in the parsley before serving.

roasted romanesco with capers

MAKES 4 SERVINGS

1 large head Romanesco cauliflower or Broccoflower

2 tablespoons garlic-flavored oil

Salt and ground black pepper to taste

1 tablespoon mayonnaise

2 tablespoons drained small capers, smashed

Cauliflower is kept white by tying its leaves over the head so that sunlight can't reach the curd, which would cause chlorophyll to develop and turn the cauliflower green. Romanesco is an Italian form of cauliflower in which the leaf covering is removed near the end of the growing season. The tips of the curd start to grow, covering the bulbous head with dozens of pale green cones. If you can't find Romanesco, Broccoflower or green cauliflower is a perfectly good alternative.

DIRECTIONS

Heat the oven to 400°F. Cut the cauliflower into bite-size pieces. Toss with half of the garlic oil, salt, and pepper in a roasting pan. Roast until brown and tender, about 20 minutes. Meanwhile, mix the mayonnaise, remaining oil, and capers in a large bowl. Toss with the cooked cauliflower before serving.

⑨ rice & other grains

Grain is basic to every cuisine on earth. It is rice in Asia, millet in Africa, bulgur in the Middle East, semolina in Italy, masa in Mexico, barley in Scotland, and a humble slice of wheat bread practically anywhere. Grain is basic to nutrition, yielding necessary fiber, protein, B vitamins, and healthful unsaturated fat; and it is basic to world agriculture, forming the great bulk of all edible crops. Yet in America, whole grains are blatantly missing from our diets, and grain cookery remains a mystery. Though doctors and nutritionists continue to chide us to eat more whole grains, few have much advice on how to do it.

All that is about to change. Quick-cooking whole grains have arrived. There is instant brown rice, quick-cooking wild rice, and quick-cooking barley. Couscous is now whole wheat, and whole-grain polenta is available premade, and instantized.

2   cups chicken broth

1   tablespoon olive oil

$\frac{1}{2}$ cup chopped onion

1   teaspoon minced garlic, fresh
    or jarred organic

$\frac{1}{2}$ cup whole wheat couscous

1   cup instant brown rice

    Salt and ground black pepper
    to taste

2   tablespoons chopped Italian
    (flat-leaf) parsley

whole-grain rice-a-bruni

This whole-grain impersonation of prepackaged sautéed rice and pasta has the same toasty allure of the original, but with a lot more nutrition. Both the rice and pasta are whole grain, and using pre-cooked ingredients cuts the time on the stove to less than 10 minutes.

DIRECTIONS

Heat the chicken broth in a small saucepan until simmering; cover and keep warm.

Heat the oil in a large saucepan. Add the onion and sauté over medium-high heat until browned. Add the garlic and couscous and sauté until toasted, about 2 minutes. Add the rice, chicken broth, salt, and pepper; stir to combine. Reduce the heat, cover, and simmer until the liquid is absorbed and the grain is tender but chewy, about 5 minutes. Stir in the parsley before serving.

2 teaspoons butter, salted or unsalted

1 small onion, finely chopped

Leaves from 1 sprig rosemary

2 cups chicken broth

1/2 cup dried cranberries

2 cups instant brown rice

cranberry brown rice pilaf

Pilaf is a method of cooking dried grain (like rice) by browning it and then simmering it until it is tender. The browning helps to create a nutty flavor and to lock the starch inside the kernels so that the finished grains of rice remain separate. The process takes time and considerable attention, but by switching to instant brown rice (in which separate grains are guaranteed), you can simply sauté some onion, add the remaining ingredients, and simmer for 5 minutes.

DIRECTIONS

Melt the butter in a saucepan over medium heat; add the onion and sauté until tender. Add the rosemary, chicken broth, cranberries, and rice. Simmer, covered, for 5 minutes; remove from the heat and let rest for 3 minutes before serving.

2 tablespoons butter, salted or unsalted

1/2 cup chopped onion, fresh or frozen

2 teaspoons minced garlic, fresh or jarred organic

1 cup long-grain rice

2 1/2 cups chicken broth

1/2 teaspoon salt

1/4 teaspoon ground black pepper

Pinch of grated nutmeg

1 cup Libby's 100% pure pumpkin

1/4 cup grated imported Parmesan cheese

1/2 cup cream or half-and-half

creamy pumpkin risotto

You may be inspired to save this luscious risotto for Thanksgiving (and you wouldn't be disappointed if you did so), but I urge you to throw caution to the wind and dive in. Because it is made with canned pumpkin, there is no need to wait until the frost is on the vine, and because the pumpkin naturally thickens the sauce, the risotto can be made with long-grain rice, rather than a more expensive risotto variety, like Arborio.

DIRECTIONS

Melt the butter in a large saucepan over medium heat. Add the onion and cook until tender; add the garlic and rice and sauté for about 1 minute. Add 2 cups of the chicken broth, the salt, pepper, and nutmeg; cover and simmer for 10 minutes. Add the remaining 1/2 cup broth and the pumpkin, and cook for another 5 minutes. The rice will be tender and slightly moist; remove from the heat and stir in the cheese and cream. Adjust the seasoning before serving.

1   cup Chinese black rice
    (Forbidden Rice)

1³/₄ cups water

1   teaspoon extra-virgin olive oil

    Salt and ground black pepper
    to taste

1   can (about 15 ounces) cannellini
    beans, drained and rinsed

1   cup canned petite diced
    tomatoes, drained

2   scallions, trimmed and
    thinly sliced

black rice and white beans

The jet black of Chinese black rice blooms into a deep violet after cooking. It has a nutty flavor that is reminiscent of wild rice, but the medium-long grains cook much quicker, in about 30 minutes. The brand that I see most often is packaged by Lotus Foods and is sold under the name Forbidden Rice, alluding to a legend that says the rice was once reserved exclusively for the emperor. Do not confuse Chinese black rice with Thai black sticky rice, which needs to be soaked overnight and takes much longer to cook.

DIRECTIONS

Combine the rice, water, oil, salt, and pepper in a medium saucepan; cover and bring to a boil over medium-high heat. Reduce the heat to a simmer and cook until the rice is tender and the liquid is absorbed, about 30 minutes. Stir in the beans, tomatoes, and scallions, cover, and heat through, about 2 minutes. Fluff with a fork and adjust the seasoning before serving.

2   tablespoons vegetable oil

¹/₂ cup chopped onion, fresh
    or frozen

1   rib celery, trimmed and
    finely diced

8   ounces chicken livers, finely
    chopped

2   cups instant brown rice

2   cups chicken broth

2   cups chunky salsa,
    any heat level

    Salt and ground black
    pepper to taste

dirty brown rice

Dirty rice is soul food pilaf, in which a pot of rice is inundated with vegetables and chicken giblets (it's the crumbled liver that gives it its dirty appearance and moniker). Traditionally made with white rice, it takes about 20 minutes to cook, by which time the chopped chicken liver has turned to gustatory gravel. Switching to instant brown rice cuts the cooking time by 75 percent and keeps the liver moist and tender.

DIRECTIONS

Heat the oven to 350°F. Heat the oil in a large skillet over medium heat. Add the onion and celery and cook until tender. Add the chicken livers and sauté until the liver loses its raw look. Add the rice and stir to coat. Add the broth, salsa, salt, and pepper and heat to boiling. Reduce the heat, cover, and simmer until the liquid is absorbed and the rice is tender, about 5 minutes. Toss with a fork to combine everything evenly before serving.

2 cups instant brown rice

1 can (about 14 ounces)
   vegetable broth

4 ounces broccoli florets

½ cup shredded carrot

½ red bell pepper, diced

6 ounces (about 2 cups)
   sliced mushrooms

1 teaspoon toasted sesame oil

½ teaspoon salt

¼ teaspoon ground black pepper

instant brown rice steamed with vegetables

Instant brown rice is parboiled and dried, which means that all you have to do is heat it and hydrate it. In this recipe the process does double duty by steaming a slew of vegetables in the same pot at the same time.

DIRECTIONS

Combine everything in a large microwave-safe bowl, cover, and microwave at full power for 9 minutes. Let rest for 3 minutes before serving.

QUICK-COOKING WHOLE-GRAIN RICE

Dietary guidelines tout the advantage of whole grains, but no one tells you where you are going to find the time to cook them. Enter quick-cooking whole-grain rices. Like their milled and polished white rice instant brethren, quick-cooking brown rice is parboiled until tender and then fissured before it is dried, to allow boiling water to infiltrate it faster when it is cooked by the consumer. The fissuring can be done with dry heat to crack the surface, by rolling to crush it, or by freeze-drying, which causes the grain to become porous.

The process changes the texture of the finished rice and diminishes its flavor and nutrition slightly. But it also creates an opportunity for consumers who otherwise would never cook a whole grain to start bringing brown rice into their diets on a regular basis.

Nutritional Comparison Between Long-Cooking and Quick-Cooking Rices (for 1 cup cooked rice)

TYPE OF RICE	Calories (kcal)	Fat (grams)	Cholesterol (milligrams)	Sodium (milligrams)	Carbohydrates (grams)	Fiber (grams)	Protein (grams)
Brown rice	216	1.5	0	10	45	3.5	5
Instant brown rice	150	1	0	5	44	2	4
White rice	205	0.4	0	2	44	0.6	4
Instant white rice	170	0	0	10	45	1	4
Wild rice	200	0.7	0	0	44	3	6
Quick wild rice	200	0.7	0	0	44	3	6

hoppin' john risotto

Hoppin' John, a Southern dish of black-eyed peas and rice, is traditionally served on New Year's Day for good luck. This recipe translates the traditional flavors of hoppin' John into a creamy risotto. The addition of Cheddar cheese complements the spiciness of the sausage and gives the risotto a plush consistency.

1   teaspoon vegetable oil

1   hot Italian sausage (about 3 ounces), finely chopped

1   cup chopped onion, fresh or frozen

1   cup Arborio rice or packaged risotto

1   teaspoon minced garlic, fresh or jarred organic

3   cups chicken broth

    Salt and ground black pepper to taste

1   can (about 15 ounces) black-eyed peas, drained and rinsed

½   cup shredded sharp Cheddar cheese

DIRECTIONS

Heat the oil in a large saucepan. Add the sausage and onion and cook over medium-high heat until lightly browned. Add the rice and garlic and sauté for a little less than a minute. Add half the broth, reduce the heat so that the broth simmers, cover, and cook until the broth is absorbed, about 10 minutes. Add the remaining broth, the salt, pepper, and black-eyed peas, cover, and cook until the rice is tender but some liquid is still visible, another 5 minutes. Remove from the heat, adjust the seasoning, and stir in the cheese. Serve immediately.

RISOTTO

Risotto is made from rice, such as Arborio or Carnaroli, that has a sturdy core surrounded by a fragile layer of starch. As the rice is simmered and stirred, the starch rubs off, thickening the liquid surrounding it into a sauce. Usually that liquid is broth, and since risotto is made in an open pot, the broth evaporates as the rice cooks. More broth is added, and by the end an intensely flavored concentrated sauce surrounds each grain of rice.

When you buy a box of premixed risotto, the broth flavors are mixed into the rice so that evaporation is not necessary to achieve full flavor. And since the rice is formulated to make a sauce without constant stirring, the time you have to spend at the stove is greatly reduced.

1 egg, any size

1 cup kasha

2 cups chicken broth

Salt and ground black pepper to taste

½ cup Vidalia onion relish or homemade roasted caramelized onions (page 336)

¼ cup chopped Italian (flat-leaf) parsley

kasha with onion relish

The Vidalia onion folks of Vidalia, Georgia, spend lots of time and money making sure that you buy their onions. One of the best ways they have come up with is manufacturing a sweet and tangy saffron-hued relish sold under the Vidalia label. It is a great way to flavor a hearty grain like buckwheat.

DIRECTIONS

Beat the egg in a small bowl; add the kasha and mix until coated. Heat a large, nonstick skillet over medium heat; add the kasha mixture and stir until it separates into individual grains. Add the broth, salt, and pepper, cover, and reduce the heat to a simmer; simmer until the kasha is fluffy, about 10 minutes. Stir in the relish and parsley and heat through, about 1 minute, before serving.

1 tablespoon olive oil

1 cup chopped onion, fresh or frozen

2 teaspoons minced garlic, fresh or jarred organic

1 cup quick-cooking barley

½ cup white wine

2½ cups chicken broth

½ teaspoon salt

¼ teaspoon ground black pepper

2 tablespoons grated imported Parmesan cheese

2 tablespoons finely chopped Italian (flat-leaf) parsley

1 tablespoon butter, salted or unsalted

barley risotto

The most common form of barley is pearled, so called because a deep cleft in whole-grain barley causes millers to grind the grain down until it is almost round in order to remove its bran. Pearled barley is used in soups and stews, where it takes about 45 minutes to soften. This side dish uses quick-cooking rolled barley, which is just flattened pearled barley that cooks in a fraction of the time.

DIRECTIONS

Heat the oil in a heavy, medium saucepan over medium heat. Add the onion and sauté until tender. Add the garlic and barley and stir to coat with oil. Add the wine and boil until the alcohol has boiled away, 1 to 2 minutes. Add half the chicken broth, and the salt and pepper. Cover and simmer until most of the liquid has been absorbed, about 5 minutes. Add the remaining broth, cover, and simmer until the barley is tender but still wet, about another 6 minutes. Remove from the heat and stir in the cheese, parsley, and butter before serving.

spiced brown rice with figs

MAKES 4 SERVINGS

2 chai tea bags, such as Celestial Seasonings Bengal Spice

2 cups boiling water

2 tablespoons unsalted butter

1/2 cup chopped onion, fresh or frozen

1 cup brown rice

1 cup chicken broth

1/2 teaspoon salt

1 teaspoon dried dill

4 dried Calimyrna or other light-colored figs, stems removed, finely chopped

This very special rice takes some time, but no attention. Cooking whole-grain brown rice in a mixture of chai tea and broth allows the rice to absorb an array of exotic spices as it simmers. The figs soften into delicate, creamy bits, and the fig seeds disperse through the mixture, creating a slight crunch with every bite.

DIRECTIONS

Steep the tea in the water for 3 minutes. Remove the tea bags.

Melt the butter in a large saucepan over medium heat. Add the onion and cook until tender. Add the rice and stir to coat with butter. Add the tea, broth, salt, dill, and figs and stir to moisten the rice. Heat to boiling; reduce the heat to a simmer, cover, and simmer until the rice is tender and the liquid has been absorbed, about 45 minutes. Fluff with a fork before serving.

orange whole-wheat couscous

MAKES 4 SERVINGS

3/4 cup water

3/4 cup orange juice

1 cup (8 ounces) whole-wheat couscous

1/2 teaspoon ground dried orange peel

Leaves of 1 small sprig rosemary

Salt and ground black pepper to taste

I know that couscous is a pasta, and therefore this recipe should be in the next chapter, but since this couscous is made with whole grain, and it is sold in the grain section of your food store, and it looks like a grain, and it cooks like a grain, and everyone but the culinary elite believe it to be a grain, here it stays. It's ready in 5 minutes, and the combination of whole wheat, orange, and rosemary is spectacular.

DIRECTIONS

Bring the water and orange juice to a boil in a medium saucepan. Stir in the couscous, orange peel, rosemary, and pepper, cover, and remove from the heat. Let rest for 5 minutes, and fluff with a fork before serving.

1 package (about ½ ounce) dried wild mushrooms, such as porcini

2½ cups boiling water

1 tablespoon extra-virgin olive oil

1 medium onion, peeled, halved from top to bottom, and thinly sliced

½ teaspoon dried thyme

1 package (about 8 ounces) organic quick wild rice, such as Lundberg

   Salt and ground black pepper to taste

1 can (about 14 ounces) petite diced tomatoes with garlic and olive oil, drained

2 tablespoons chopped Italian (flat-leaf) parsley

quick wild mushroom wild rice

Wild rice has problems. It takes over an hour to cook, and even then some grains don't ever seem to get tender. Lundberg Family Farms has solved the wild rice dilemma with an amazing organic product. It cooks in about 25 minutes, and every grain puffs perfectly. In this recipe the woodsy flavor of dried wild mushrooms complements its natural nutty flavor propitiously.

DIRECTIONS

Soak the dried mushrooms in the boiling water until softened, about 10 minutes; drain, reserving the soaking liquid and the mushrooms separately. Chop the mushrooms coarsely.

Heat the oil in a heavy saucepan over medium heat. Add the onion and sauté until tender; do not brown. Add the thyme and cook for a few more seconds. Stir in the rice, mushroom soaking liquid, and soaked mushrooms, and season with salt and pepper. Heat to simmering, stirring once. Cover and simmer for 20 minutes. Add the tomatoes and parsley, and simmer until the wild rice is cooked and the liquid has all been absorbed, 5 to 10 minutes; serve.

chèvre polenta

MAKES 6 SERVINGS

- 2 tablespoons extra-virgin olive oil
- 1 tablespoon chopped garlic, fresh or jarred organic
- ¾ cup white wine
- ¾ cup chicken broth
- ½ cup instant polenta, such as Bellino or Favero
- 1 package (about 5 ounces) fresh goat cheese (chèvre), cut into pieces
- Salt and ground black pepper to taste

Beware: This side dish may cause swooning. Porridge-soft polenta is fattened for the table with a plumping of goat cheese. The results are a fusion of whole-grain goodness and unctuous decadence. Serve it right away; it will lose its fluffiness as it sits. I like it accompanying roast chicken, grilled sausages, baked fish, or, better yet, eaten right out of the pot as I stand by the stove.

DIRECTIONS

Heat the oil in a nonstick skillet over medium heat. Add the garlic and cook until aromatic, about 20 seconds. Add the wine and boil for 1 minute. Add the broth and heat to boiling. Stir in the polenta until the mixture is smooth, and cook for 1 minute. Reduce the heat to low; stir in the cheese until fully incorporated and the mixture is fluffy; do not overcook. Remove from the heat, season with salt and pepper, and serve immediately.

INSTANT AND PRECOOKED POLENTA

Polenta has a reputation for being difficult to prepare. Fortunately, there are many prepared alternatives. It comes precooked in tubes and pouches, or instantized and dried, ready to be reconstituted. The type you use depends on the consistency you want in the finished polenta. Polenta can be made firm or soft. Firm polenta is usually sliced and sautéed; soft polenta is served like grits. Precooked polentas are on the firm side. Those in tubes are ready for slicing into rounds; polenta that is packed in a pouch is better for cutting into wedges. When you want soft polenta, it is easier to start with an instant product, but if you can find only the precooked variety, that too can be made soft by chopping it finely and heating it with some water until it dissolves. If you don't want to dirty a pot, the process works great in the microwave.

1½ cups light cream or half-and-half

3 cloves garlic, fresh or jarred organic, halved

¼ teaspoon salt

Pinch of ground cayenne pepper

¼ cup instant polenta, such as Bellino or Favero

Pinch of cayenne pepper

1 large or extra-large egg

1 large or extra-large egg yolk

1 teaspoon butter, salted or unsalted

polenta pots de crème

Pots de crème, those decadent cups of edible ecstasy, are the inspiration for this delicate cornmeal custard. Wonderfully creamy, and rich enough to warrant a diminutive portion, these pots de polenta can be served as an appetizer garnished with a bit of onion relish or salsa, or as a side dish to poached seafood or roasted meats. If you don't have ramekins, bake them in small coffee cups.

DIRECTIONS

Heat the oven to 325°F.

Heat the cream, garlic, salt, and cayenne until simmering. Remove from the heat. Remove the garlic cloves with a slotted spoon, and stir in the polenta until smooth but not thick. Beat in the egg and yolk.

Grease four 4- to 6-ounce ramekins or custard cups with the butter, and divide the polenta mixture among them. Place the ramekins in a baking pan and fill the pan with water halfway up the sides of the ramekins. Cover the pan with foil and bake until set at the edges but still jiggly in the center, about 35 minutes. Cool for 5 minutes before serving.

corn and black bean grits

MAKES 4 SERVINGS

1 container (about 32 ounces) creamy sweet corn soup

1 can (about 15 ounces) corn kernels, drained

1 can (about 15 ounces) black beans, drained and rinsed

1 can (about 4 ounces) diced green chiles

1 cup 5-minute corn grits, white or yellow

1 teaspoon hot pepper sauce

1/2 cup sour cream

If you've never imagined that grits could be sexy, warm up the back burner and get cooking. These velvety grits are punctuated with bits of vegetables and a slow burn of chiles—pucker up.

DIRECTIONS

Heat the soup over medium heat in a large saucepan, stirring often. Stir in the corn, beans, and chiles and heat through. Stir in the grits and continue stirring until smooth and thick, about 5 minutes. Stir in the hot sauce and sour cream before serving.

sticky vanilla rice

MAKES 4 SERVINGS

1 cup basmati rice

2 cups water

3/4 cup coconut milk

1/2 teaspoon salt

2 teaspoons sugar

Dash of cayenne pepper

1 teaspoon vanilla extract

Stickiness is a rice aesthetic that is underrated in the United States. We tend to do everything we can to ensure that every grain we eat is separate and self-contained. However, in the rest of the world, particularly Southeast Asia, stickiness is not only tolerated, it is cultivated. One way it is achieved is by breaking the rice before it is cooked to release some of its internal starch. Broken rice is sold in Asian food stores, and if you can find it you will not need to go through the processing step that starts this recipe.

DIRECTIONS

Process the rice in a food processor until about half of the grains are chopped, about 1 minute. Heat the water to a boil; add the coconut milk, salt, sugar, and cayenne. Stir in the rice and simmer over medium-low heat until the rice is tender and the liquid has been absorbed, about 15 minutes. Stir in the vanilla before serving.

1½ cups whole-groat kasha

1 egg, large or extra-large

1 tablespoon olive oil

½ onion, finely chopped

1 cup Israeli or toasted couscous

4 cups chicken broth

Salt and ground black pepper to taste

kasha and couscous

Kasha and bowtie noodles is a classic combination, but the traditional recipe requires you to cook the noodles in a separate pot, and the size and shape of the bowties make them difficult to eat with the grain. Switching to couscous changes all of that; now everything cooks in the same pot, and because the pasta and kasha are similar in size, every bite is balanced.

DIRECTIONS

Mix the kasha and egg; cook in a large, dry skillet over medium heat until the egg is cooked and the kasha is in separate grains. Transfer to a bowl and set aside.

Add the oil to the skillet and heat over medium-high heat until hot. Add the onion and sauté until lightly browned. Add the couscous and continue to sauté until the onion and couscous are browned. Stir in the kasha, broth, salt, and pepper. Reduce the heat to medium, cover, and simmer until the broth has been absorbed and the couscous and kasha are tender; serve.

BUCKWHEAT

Buckwheat grows fast and tolerates poor growing conditions, which has made it a valued crop in cold parts of the world with rocky soil and a short growing season. The kernels are pyramid shaped and, once hulled, have a starchy surface layer that breaks down easily in cooking. For that reason it is best to coat buckwheat groats (called kasha) with a thin film of protein, such as beaten egg, to keep the starch from leaching out too easily, which would cause the exterior of the grain to become mushy before it is cooked through.

spinach tabbouleh

1 1/4 cups water

1 teaspoon minced garlic, fresh
   or jarred organic

1/2 teaspoon salt

   Pinch of ground black pepper

1 tablespoon olive oil

1 box (about 6 ounces) traditional
   tabbouleh or bulgur wheat
   (3/4 cup)

1 bag (about 9 ounces)
   baby spinach

1/4 cup (about 1 ounce)
   crumbled feta

Tabbouleh is a parsley salad that is traditionally garnished with cracked cooked wheat, called bulgur. In this country, Middle Eastern restaurants (mostly to save money) started to increase the bulgur in the tabbouleh they served and decrease the parsley, until the dish became a grain salad garnished with parsley. That is why people started calling bulgur (the grain) "tabbouleh" and why most of the bulgur sold in the States is labeled as such. Now, to muddy the waters further, I offer you this recipe for Spinach Tabbouleh, which does away with the parsley altogether.

DIRECTIONS

Heat the water to boiling in a large saucepan. Add the garlic, salt, pepper, olive oil, tabbouleh, and spinach; stir until everything is moistened. Cover and set aside for 5 minutes. In that time the spinach will wilt and the water will be absorbed. Stir in the feta, and serve.

YOU SAY TABBOULEH, I SAY TABOULI

It's confusing, but whether you call it tabbouleh, tabouli, bulgur, bulgar, bulghur, or burghul, it's all the same stuff. Bulgur is not a variety of wheat but a way of processing wheat. Bulgur is wheat that has been cleaned, parboiled, dried, and ground into particles. Often confused with cracked wheat, bulgur differs in that it has been precooked, and therefore needs only to be soaked or cooked briefly. Bulgur is prepared similarly to couscous, but because it is a whole grain, it is more nutritious. It can be used in many of the same dishes in which you would use couscous or rice.

1   tablespoon vegetable oil

¼   cup chopped onion, fresh
    or frozen

½   cup steel-cut oats

2   cups broth, vegetable or chicken

½   teaspoon salt

¼   teaspoon ground black pepper

¾   cup (about 3 ounces) shredded
    sharp Cheddar cheese

½   cup walnut pieces, toasted
    (page 340)

1   tablespoon chopped parsley

cheddar cheese oats with toasted walnuts

Oats have been imprisoned at breakfast for so many decades that most people would never think of adding them to a soup or serving them as a side dish. Well, it's time to change your mind! Steel-cut oats (sold as Irish or Scottish oatmeal) are cooked like brown rice (except faster). Here they are prepared pilaf style with onions, enriched with a hefty handful of Cheddar and a garnish of toasted walnuts. It is a wonderful accompaniment to any roast, especially lamb.

DIRECTIONS

Heat the oil in a large saucepan over medium-high heat. Add the onion and cook until tender. Add the oats and cook until the onion is lightly browned and the oats smell toasty.

Add the broth, salt, and pepper and heat to boiling. Cover and simmer until the oats are tender, about 30 minutes. The mixture will still be wet. Remove from the heat, adjust the seasoning, and stir in the cheese until melted. Stir in the walnuts and parsley, and serve immediately.

1   teaspoon olive oil

¼   cup chopped onion, fresh or frozen

½   teaspoon minced garlic, fresh
    or jarred organic

½   teaspoon minced ginger, fresh
    or jarred

1   cup (8 ounces) quinoa, rinsed
    according to the package directions

2   cups vegetable broth

½   teaspoon salt

¼   teaspoon ground black pepper

2   teaspoons lemon juice, fresh
    or bottled organic

1   cup (8 ounces) mung bean sprouts

sprouted quinoa

It is remarkable that after five thousand years of cultivation, more than twenty years of intensive marketing and product development by the Quinoa Corporation, and countless articles in newspaper food sections and culinary magazines, quinoa remains relatively unknown. It's a shame, for the grain is easy to cook (it's faster than rice), it's highly nutritious (with more protein than any other grain), it has a wonderful chewy consistency, and its flavor pairs well with almost anything. I encourage you to give it a try and, if you like it, spread the word.

DIRECTIONS

Heat the oil over medium heat in a medium saucepan. Add the onion and sauté until transparent. Add the garlic and ginger and cook for 30 seconds. Add the quinoa and broth and stir until the quinoa is distributed. Heat to boiling and reduce the heat so that the liquid just simmers. Cover and simmer until the liquid is absorbed, 10 to 12 minutes. Season with salt, pepper, and lemon juice and mix well; toss in the bean sprouts, and serve.

QUINOA

Quinoa (pronounced KEEN wah) was the sacred grain of the Incas. Cultivated for five thousand years in the Andes and for nearly twenty-five years in the United States, it is currently marketed by the Quinoa Corporation, which is billing it as the "super grain of the future."

Judging from its nutritional analysis, their claims don't seem far-fetched. Technically a fruit of the *Chenopodium* genus, quinoa is neither a true grain nor a seed crop, although it has the nutritional and culinary qualities of both. A portion of quinoa packs more protein than any other grain, yielding more than twice the protein of rice and five times more than corn. Quinoa is high in lysine, an amino acid widely deficient among vegetable proteins, and is a good complement to the amino acid structure of most legumes, being naturally high in both methionine and cystine. It has less carbohydrate than any other grain besides corn, and a 6 percent fat content, which gives it a pleasant nutty flavor.

The small round seeds of quinoa, which resemble a cross between sesame and millet, are covered with saponin, a bitter resin that must be removed during processing. By the time you purchase quinoa the saponin is largely gone, but it is a good idea to wash quinoa well before cooking to ensure that no bitterness remains.

Before processing, quinoa seeds are a brilliantly colored raspberry red, dark violet, blue black, or burnt orange, but once the saponin is removed all quinoa is a uniform pale yellow. Each flat, disk-shaped seed is framed with a white band around its periphery. During cooking this band unravels, giving the grain a short, crescent-shaped tail.

⑩ pasta & sauce

Most pastas cook in about 10 minutes, and it is my aim in this chapter to give you a selection of recipes in which all of the sauces cook in less time than it takes to cook the pasta. This isn't as miraculous as it sounds, for there are scores of classic sauces that do just that. The trick is working with highly flavored ingredients—extra-virgin olive oil, jarred pesto, cured olives, sun-dried tomatoes, anchovies, canned tuna in oil, dried mushrooms, fresh arugula, and cheese. With ingredients like these, all you need to do is cook the pasta.

1   pound refrigerated or frozen
    meat tortellini

1/3 cup mayonnaise

1/4 cup extra-virgin olive oil

2   tablespoons lemon juice, fresh or
    bottled organic

2   teaspoons minced garlic,
    preferably fresh

1   teaspoon ground sage

    Salt and ground black pepper
    to taste

2   tablespoons chopped Italian
    (flat-leaf) parsley

meat tortellini with rosemary sage aioli

Freshly made aioli is a wonder, but with the health risks of raw egg yolk and the fact that hardly anyone knows how to make it, homemade aioli is facing extinction. Before it passes into eternity I offer this good-quality ersatz version that is easily whipped up from a spoonful of mayo, some extra-virgin oil, minced garlic, and a healthy squirt of lemon juice.

DIRECTIONS

Bring a large pot of salted water to a boil. Add the tortellini, stirring a few times to ensure that it does not stick to itself. Boil vigorously for the time recommended on the package or until tender. Drain.

Meanwhile, mix the mayonnaise, olive oil, lemon juice, garlic, sage, salt, and pepper in a serving bowl. Toss the cooked pasta with the sauce and the parsley before serving.

1   pound dried fettuccine

1   cup sour cream

½   cup extra-virgin olive oil

⅓   cup basil pesto, jarred or homemade (page 339)

2   teaspoons chopped garlic, preferably fresh

3   tablespoons drained capers, coarsely chopped

    Salt and ground black pepper to taste

1   pound spaghetti

¼   cup mayonnaise

⅓   cup extra-virgin olive oil

    Juice of 1 lemon

2   teaspoons chopped garlic, preferably fresh

2   cans (about 6 ounces each) tuna in olive oil, undrained

2   tablespoons drained capers

    Salt and ground black pepper to taste

1   cup chopped Italian (flat-leaf) parsley

creamy fettuccine with capers and herbs

Dinner doesn't get any quicker than this. Rich, creamy, and completely uncooked, the sauce is mixed in a bowl while the pasta cooks. Make sure you use a good-quality olive oil; its flavor is paramount to the success of the sauce.

DIRECTIONS

Bring a large pot of salted water to a boil. Add the fettuccine, stirring a few times to ensure that it does not stick to itself. Boil vigorously for the time recommended on the package or until tender. Drain.

Meanwhile, mix the sour cream, olive oil, pesto, garlic, capers, salt, and pepper in a serving bowl. Toss the cooked pasta with the sauce before serving.

spaghetti tonnato

Tonnato, or tuna sauce, is served classically with veal in Italy. But since I was raised on tuna noodle casserole, its role as a potential pasta sauce always seemed obvious.

DIRECTIONS

Bring a large pot of salted water to a boil. Add the spaghetti, stirring a few times to ensure that it does not stick to itself. Boil vigorously for the time recommended on the package or until tender. Drain.

Meanwhile, mix the mayonnaise, olive oil, lemon juice, garlic, tuna, capers, salt, and pepper in a serving bowl. Toss the cooked pasta with the sauce and the parsley before serving.

9   ounces vegetable ravioli,
    preferably pumpkin or squash

1   cup roasted caramelized onions
    (page 336)

2   tablespoons basil pesto, jarred
    or homemade (page 339)

2   tablespoons extra-virgin olive oil

1   tablespoon aged balsamic
    vinegar, preferably at least
    15 years

¼   cup chopped Italian
    (flat-leaf) parsley

    Salt and ground black pepper
    to taste

sweet onion ravioli

No one could guess that the amber glaze gilding these ravioli took less time to prepare than it took to cook the pasta. The secret is roasted onions, richly sweet and savory, with a natural ability to lacquer whatever they touch. One day a savvy manufacturer will come up with a jarred or frozen product, but until that day we have to make them ourselves. A recipe is on page 336; they will stay fresh in the refrigerator for several weeks and can be frozen for several months.

DIRECTIONS

Bring a large pot of lightly salted water to a boil. Add the ravioli, stirring a few times to ensure that it does not stick to itself. Boil for the time recommended on the package or until the ravioli is tender, about 8 minutes.

Meanwhile, combine the remaining ingredients in a serving bowl. If they are not room temperature or warmer, warm in a microwave. Drain the ravioli and toss with the onion mixture before serving.

24 frozen cheese ravioli

2 tablespoons extra-virgin olive oil

2 tablespoons basil pesto, jarred or
    homemade (page 339)

   Finely grated zest and juice of
   1/2 lemon (see box)

   Salt and ground black pepper
   to taste

ravioli with lemon basil pesto

Lemon and basil are wondrous together, but the pairing doesn't work in pesto. The acid in the lemon ruins the color of the basil, so the only alternative is to keep the ingredients apart until right before they are served. Note that both the zest (the colorful part of the peel) and the juice of the lemon are used. The zest contains lemon oil, which lends richness to the sauce, and the juice gives it a bright, tart jolt.

DIRECTIONS

Bring a large pot of salted water to a boil. Add the ravioli, stirring a few times to ensure that it does not stick to itself. Boil vigorously for the time recommended on the package or until the ravioli is tender, about 8 minutes.

While the ravioli are cooking, mix the oil, pesto, lemon zest, lemon juice, salt, and pepper in a serving bowl. When the ravioli are tender, drain and toss gently with the pesto mixture before serving.

LEMON ZEST

It is easiest to remove the zest from the lemon while it is still whole. You can rub it against the finest teeth of a grater (a Microplane works great) or remove the zest in strips with a vegetable peeler and then chop it finely. You can also substitute dried lemon peel for fresh zest. The dried product is already grated and is stronger than fresh so use about a third of the amount; approximately 1 teaspoon dried lemon zest equals the grated zest of 1 lemon. Dried zest can be found in the seasonings section of the supermarket.

1   pound spaghetti

2   tablespoons olive oil

1   cup chopped onion, fresh
    or frozen

1   teaspoon chopped garlic, fresh
    or jarred organic

    Pinch of crushed red pepper
    flakes

1   can (about 28 ounces) chopped or
    crushed tomatoes

1   tablespoon tomato paste

    Salt and ground black pepper
    to taste

1   tablespoon basil pesto, jarred or
    homemade (page 339)

    Grated imported Parmesan
    cheese, for serving (optional)

spaghetti with stir-fried tomato sauce

Canned tomatoes are already cooked. Simmering them for any length of time is a process of diminishing returns. So unless you are making a meat-laden ragù that needs to warm for hours in order to break down the meat, there is no reason to cook a tomato sauce for any longer than it takes to boil pasta.

DIRECTIONS

Bring a large pot of salted water to a boil. Add the spaghetti, stirring a few times to ensure that the pasta does not stick to itself. Boil vigorously for the time recommended on the package or until the spaghetti is tender. Drain.

In a wok over medium-high heat, heat the oil. Add the onion and cook until soft, about 1 minute. Add the garlic, pepper flakes, and tomatoes. Cook until the tomatoes bubble vigorously, about 4 minutes. Stir in the tomato paste, salt, and pepper, and simmer for 4 minutes more. Stir in the pesto.

Drain the spaghetti and toss with the sauce. Serve with freshly grated cheese, if desired.

CANNED TOMATOES

Tomatoes for canning are picked ripe and are usually in the can within a day or two of picking. Compared to the hothouse-grown specimens available in many markets, canned tomatoes are not only a better buy, but they are often of better quality. All canned tomatoes are cooked in the can, minimally to sterilize the contents, and at most to concentrate the tomatoes into a paste. So whenever a recipe calls for cooking tomatoes, canned products give you a head start.

The available canned tomato products, from least to most cooked, are as follows:

- **Whole tomatoes** and **diced tomatoes** are cooked in their own juice just long enough to kill any bacteria.
- **Crushed tomatoes in puree** and **tomato puree** are cooked until the fiber of the tomato is broken down.
- **Tomato paste** is concentrated purée.

1 pound orecchiette pasta

1 cup (about 4 ounces) diced
   prosciutto

2 cups (about 5 ounces) frozen
   peas, thawed

3 tablespoons rosemary-flavored oil

1 tablespoon garlic-flavored oil

¼ cup grated imported
   Parmesan cheese

   Salt and ground black pepper
   to taste

rosemary orecchiette with prosciutto and peas

This "sauce" is nothing more than diced prosciutto, garden peas, a ladleful of fragrant oil, and a handful of grated cheese. It requires no cooking, yields less than a cup of sauce, and once on the pasta it practically disappears. That is, until you taste it. Whatever is missing in fluid is made up for in a rush of flavor, for it is the very lack of moisture that makes it so intense and satisfying.

DIRECTIONS

Bring a large pot of salted water to a boil. Add the pasta, stirring a few times to ensure that it does not stick to itself. Boil vigorously for the time recommended on the pasta package or until the pasta is tender. Drain.

Combine the prosciutto, peas, and oils in a serving bowl. Toss with the hot pasta. Add the cheese, salt, and pepper, and toss to coat before serving.

1   pound curly pasta, such as rotini, shells, elbows, or fusilli

1   package (about 6 ounces) tuna in olive oil

1   can (about 14 ounces) diced tomatoes with chiles

1/2 teaspoon crushed red pepper flakes

3   tablespoons pesto, jarred or homemade (page 339)

1/2 teaspoon minced garlic, fresh or jarred organic

3   tablespoons olive spread (tapenade), jarred or homemade (page 347)

1   tablespoon drained capers

1/3 cup coarsely chopped Italian (flat-leaf) parsley

pasta puttanesca

Puttanesca, or "whore's sauce," is made with whatever you have in your pantry. If you practiced your craft in Naples, you obviously would have everything on this ingredient list close at hand. So if you are out of capers or tapenade, don't substitute dill pickles just because they are in the cupboard.

DIRECTIONS

Bring a large pot of salted water to a boil. Add the pasta, stirring a few times to ensure that it does not stick to itself. Boil vigorously for the time recommended on the package or until tender. Drain.

While the pasta is cooking, combine the remaining ingredients in a serving bowl. Add a ladleful of the pasta water to the tuna mixture. Drain the pasta and toss with the tuna mixture while it is still hot; serve.

1 pound farfalle pasta

1 bag (12 ounces) micro-ready chopped and cleaned broccoli rabe

1/4 cup heavy cream

3 tablespoons extra-virgin olive oil

1 teaspoon chopped garlic, fresh or jarred organic

Salt and ground black pepper to taste

1 cup grated pecorino Romano cheese

farfalle with rabe and pecorino pesto

I was delighted and skeptical the first time I saw cleaned, precut broccoli rabe being sold next to the bagged spinach and lettuces in the supermarket. Delighted because it meant that the popularity of this wonderful vegetable had grown to the point that someone was willing to mass-market it, and skeptical because I knew that rabe has a tendency to get bitter if it is not cooked carefully. My skepticism vanished and my delight increased the first time I tried it. The product works brilliantly. My only criticism is that the package has too much stem for the amount of leaf, a flaw that will have no bearing on the success of this pesto.

DIRECTIONS

Bring a large pot of salted water to a boil. Add the pasta, stirring a few times to ensure that it does not stick to itself. Boil vigorously for the time recommended on the package or until tender. Drain.

Meanwhile, cook the broccoli rabe in a microwave in its bag for 4 minutes at full power. Puree the cooked rabe, heavy cream, olive oil, garlic, salt, and pepper in a blender or food processor. Stir in the cheese. Toss with the hot cooked pasta before serving.

MAKES 4 SERVINGS

1   pound penne, fettuccine, or fusilli

1   tablespoon olive oil

1   teaspoon minced garlic, fresh or organic jarred

1   can (about 15 ounces) tomatillos, drained and chopped

2   cups heavy cream

    Salt and ground black pepper to taste

¼   cup tequila

2   teaspoons green hot sauce

½   cup coarsely chopped cilantro

pasta with tomatillos, tequila, and cream

Although most sources describe a tomatillo as a green tomato, the comparison is misleading. It is true that once they are peeled of their papery skins they look like large, pale green cherry tomatoes, but after that all similarity stops. Tomatillos have a delicate lemony-herbal flavor and a natural thickening ability. Since their flavor doesn't emerge until they are cooked, there is no compromise in using canned rather than fresh. However, always buy canned tomatillos whole; crushed tomatillos tend to develop a slimy consistency during canning.

DIRECTIONS

Bring a large pot of salted water to a boil. Add the pasta, stirring a few times to ensure that it does not stick to itself. Boil vigorously for the time recommended on the package or until the pasta is tender. Drain.

Meanwhile, heat the oil in a large skillet over medium heat. Add the garlic and the tomatillos and cook until almost dry. Add the cream, salt, and pepper and simmer until the cream thickens slightly, about 1 minute. Stir in the tequila, hot sauce, and cilantro. Toss with the hot pasta before serving.

TOMATOES AND CREAM

Cooking cream and acidic vegetables together can cause problems if you're not careful. Cream is an emulsion of protein, water, and milk fat. The fat will melt into the sauce, making it smoother and richer, and at the same time the protein will congeal, causing the sauce to thicken. If the protein gets too firm it will break into curds, and the sauce will split. This potential problem is exacerbated by two things that a simmering tomato sauce has in spades—heat and acid. Therefore, you must watch carefully as you mix in the cream. As soon as the sauce starts to thicken, remove it from the heat. It could take 10 seconds or a minute, depending on the freshness of the cream. So be on guard. Older cream sets up faster and has a greater chance of splitting than very fresh cream.

1 pound penne

8 ounces (about 2 cups) crumbled feta cheese

1 jar (about 8 ounces) roasted red bell peppers, drained and cut into strips

½ cup extra-virgin olive oil

1 large bunch (about 12 ounces) arugula leaves, cleaned and dried

   Kosher salt and coarsely ground black pepper to taste

penne with arugula, roasted peppers, and feta

This beautiful bowl of pasta and greens couldn't be easier. All of the sauce ingredients are combined in a serving bowl, waiting for the heat of the pasta to melt the cheese, wilt the greens, and make the perfume of the roasted peppers explode.

DIRECTIONS

Bring a large pot of salted water to a boil. Add the penne, stirring a few times to ensure that it does not stick to itself. Boil vigorously for the time recommended on the package or until the penne is tender.

Meanwhile, combine the remaining ingredients in a large bowl. Drain the penne and immediately toss with the arugula mixture, allowing the heat of the pasta to melt the cheese and wilt the greens before serving.

- ½ ounce dried porcini mushrooms, or 2 tablespoons porcini flour/powder
- ⅓ cup extra-virgin olive oil
- 1 package (about 8 ounces) buckwheat soba noodles
- 1 tablespoon tomato paste
- 1 tablespoon aged balsamic vinegar
- ½ teaspoon kosher salt
- ¼ teaspoon coarsely ground black pepper
- 2 tablespoons chopped Italian (flat-leaf) parsley

buckwheat noodles with porcini oil

Flavorful ingredients need help. Without something to make their flavor flow over the surface of a noodle, they are powerless. You can add wine, or broth or pasta water, but the richest and most effective medium for revealing flavor is oil. In this recipe we go right to the source, infusing extra-virgin oil with finely ground dried porcini mushrooms, which will inundate the pasta on contact.

DIRECTIONS

Bring a large pot of salted water to a boil. Grind the porcini mushrooms in a mini food processor (or use the porcini flour) and combine with the oil in a small saucepan. Warm over low heat for several minutes, until you can smell the porcini.

Meanwhile cook the soba in the boiling water according to the package directions. While the noodles are cooking, add the tomato paste, vinegar, salt, and pepper to the porcini oil. When the pasta is tender, drain and toss with the oil and parsley before serving.

DRIED WILD MUSHROOMS

It takes about 10 pounds of fresh mushrooms to make 1 pound of dried mushrooms, which means that if you are substituting dried for fresh, 1 ounce of dried mushrooms equals about 9 ounces of fresh. Rehydration is easy: just soak as many mushrooms as you would like to cook in warm water that has a pinch of salt and a pinch of sugar in it. As soon as the mushrooms are tender (in about 20 minutes), they are ready to cook. Dried mushrooms never absorb quite as much moisture as they lost, so they tend to have a more concentrated flavor and a slightly tougher texture than fresh.

Some of the more commonly found dried wild mushrooms are:

- **Black trumpet**—This delicate black "chanterelle" is often infused into cream sauces, especially for pasta dishes. It is a delicious accompaniment to game meats.

- **Chanterelle**—The most familiar chanterelle is a golden apricot color and, like its relative the black trumpet, is shaped like a horn. Chanterelles have a natural affinity for light meats—poultry, pork, veal, or quail—and for eggs. They are also delicious in cream sauces and paired with starchy items like pasta or risotto.

- **Morel**—One of the most delicious and meatiest of wild mushroom, the morel also has a distinctive appearance. Its long, narrow cap is covered with deep folds, like a brain. It is a savory accompaniment to red meats and game.

- **Oyster**—Often described as having an oysterlike flavor, these mushrooms are very similar in flavor and texture to white button mushrooms. Like portobello and shiitake, they are so commonly available fresh that using them dried seems unnecessary.

- **Porcini**—Also known as cèpe or *Buletus*, porcini have an extremely rich flavor that complements almost any dish. In Europe, where they are highly prized, fresh porcini are eaten alone with a simple sauce, but the dried specimens are best used in a sauce for pasta or with other bland starches. They can range in color from pale tan to brown and should be flexible even when dried.

- **Portobello**—Known as cremini when young, this hearty mushroom adds flavor, texture, and color to almost any dish. Because portobellos are commonly available fresh, their function as a dried mushroom is negligible.

- **Shiitake**—Unlike other large mushrooms, which are often dried in slices, shiitakes are commonly dried whole. Because their stems are woody, they should be removed after soaking. Shiitakes have a meaty texture but a very delicate flavor; they can be paired with almost anything.

1   tablespoon olive oil

1   pound ground beef

³/₄ cup red wine

    Salt and ground black pepper
    to taste

1   jar (about 16 ounces)
    Alfredo sauce

1   container (about 15 ounces)
    ricotta cheese

8   ounces (about 2 cups) shredded
    mozzarella cheese

1   jar (about 26 ounces)
    marinara sauce

12 sheets (about 12 ounces)
    no-boil lasagna noodles

lasagna bolognese

This classic lasagna has been updated by using jarred Alfredo sauce instead of white sauce, jarred marinara, and no-boil noodles. Judging by the results, no one will guess it took only minutes to throw together.

DIRECTIONS

Heat the oven to 375°F. Heat the olive oil in a medium skillet over medium-high heat. Add the beef and brown, chopping and turning with a spatula to help it brown evenly. Add the wine and simmer until it is mostly evaporated, about 5 minutes. Season with salt and pepper.

In a large bowl, mix the Alfredo sauce, ricotta cheese, 1½ cups of the mozzarella, salt, and pepper.

Spread ½ cup of the marinara sauce over the bottom of a 9-by-13-inch baking dish. Top with a layer of 3 noodles; spread 1 cup sauce over the noodles, and top with one third of the ricotta mixture and one third of the beef. Top with another layer of noodles, another 1 cup sauce, half of the remaining ricotta mixture, and half of the remaining beef. Make another layer of noodles, another cup of sauce, and the remaining ricotta mixture and beef. Cover with the remaining noodles. Add ½ cup water to the remaining pasta sauce in the jar, seal with the lid, and shake to combine. Pour over the top of the lasagna and cover tightly with foil. Bake for 45 minutes.

Uncover, top with the remaining mozzarella, and bake for another 15 minutes. Let rest for at least 15 minutes before serving. Cut into 6 portions. Lasagna slices better after it has been refrigerated or frozen and reheated.

1 pound fettuccine (tagliatelle), dried or fresh

1 cup heavy cream

Large pinch of crushed red pepper flakes

1 teaspoon chopped garlic, fresh or jarred organic

1 cup (4¾ ounces) crumbled Gorgonzola

1 cup coarsely chopped Italian (flat-leaf) parsley

½ cup crushed herb croutons

blue cheese tagliatelle

Ribbon-shaped noodles are called *tagliatelle* in every region of Italy except around Rome, where the most famous dish using this noodle, fettuccine Alfredo, gave it the name that stuck, which is why we call *tagliatelle* fettuccine in this country. Whatever you call it, this simple, pungent sauce coats the pasta beautifully, and the crushed crouton garnish delivers a disarming crunch.

DIRECTIONS

Bring a large pot of salted water to a boil. Add the fettuccine, stirring a few times to ensure that it does not stick to itself. Boil vigorously for the time recommended on the package or until tender. Drain.

Meanwhile, bring the cream to a simmer in a skillet over medium heat. Add the pepper flakes and garlic and simmer until the cream thickens slightly. Remove from the heat and stir in the Gorgonzola until it melts. Toss the cooked pasta with the sauce and parsley. Garnish each portion with some of the crushed croutons before serving.

MAKES 4 SERVINGS

1   container (16 ounces) large-curd
    cottage cheese

    Salt and ground black pepper
    to taste

¼   cup extra-virgin olive oil

¼   teaspoon crushed red
    pepper flakes

1   teaspoon dried Italian seasoning

1   teaspoon minced garlic,
    preferably fresh

1   can (about 14 ounces) small
    diced tomatoes, drained

1   package (about 16 ounces)
    cup-shaped pasta, such as shells,
    tortellini, or orecchiette

pasta with tomatoes and baked cheese curds

When you bake cottage cheese, the curds plump and firm until they separate into hundreds of tiny individual cheese balls. In this simple pasta dish, the warm curds are tossed with tiny diced tomatoes and a small cup-shaped pasta that can cradle the bits of cheese and vegetable in every bite.

DIRECTIONS

Heat the oven to 400°F. Set a large pot of salted water on to boil.

Place the cottage cheese in a strainer and run cold water through the cheese to wash away everything but the curds. Spread the washed curds on a sheet pan, season with salt and pepper, and toss with 1 tablespoon of the oil. Bake for 15 minutes. While still hot, toss the curds, red pepper flakes, Italian seasoning, garlic, and tomatoes together in a serving bowl.

Meanwhile, cook the pasta according to the package directions. Drain and toss with the remaining 3 tablespoons oil and the cheese mixture before serving.

QUICK TOMATO SAUCES

Tomatoes are fruit, and like all fruit, their flavor is robust but their fiber is delicate. A few minutes of cooking are enough to release all a tomato has to offer. More than that starts a process of diminishing returns. What you gain in thickness and consistency you rapidly lose in fragrance, sweetness, and subtlety.

The only flavor component a tomato can retain over hours of cooking is acidity—the bane of all red sauces. To counteract it, cooks through the ages have loaded the pot with caramelized onions, carrots, garlic, herbs, and sugar—anything sweet to kill the unavoidable growth of acid. But what these cooks never realized is that the acid is not growing. Rather, the natural sweetness and perfume of the tomato, which had balanced its tang so perfectly when the fruit was raw, have been simmered away, tipping the flavor scales irreversibly to tartness.

You can avoid all the doctoring that long-simmered sauces go through simply by tasting and turning off the heat as soon as the flavor is right. What you get will taste as fresh and sweet as vine-ripened fruit.

1   pound dried fettuccine

1   can (about 15 ounces) cannellini beans, drained and rinsed

1½   teaspoons minced garlic, fresh or jarred organic

½   cup chopped Italian (flat-leaf) parsley

¼   cup extra-virgin olive oil

    Salt and ground black pepper to taste

½   cup boiling pasta water

pasta fagioli blanco

Pasta and beans are a classic combination that generations of Italians have savored for their subtle flavors and creamy textures, without knowing that the two made a powerful nutritional duo. Even though neither is complete protein alone, together a 1-cup serving delivers more than 14 grams of high-quality protein.

DIRECTIONS

Bring a large pot of salted water to a boil. Add the fettuccine, stirring a few times to ensure that it does not stick to itself. Boil vigorously for the time recommended on the package or until tender. Drain, reserving ½ cup of the pasta water if you haven't yet mixed the sauce.

Meanwhile, mash half the beans, garlic, parsley, oil, pasta water, salt, and pepper. Fold in the remaining beans, and toss with the cooked fettuccine before serving.

1 pound small shell-shaped pasta

2 tablespoons olive oil

1 mild Italian sausage, about
   3 ounces, cut in small slices

1/2 teaspoon chopped garlic, fresh
   or jarred organic

1 cup white wine

1 can (about 15 ounces) clam sauce

4 ounces small cleaned,
   shelled shrimp

4 ounces chopped fresh clams

   Pinch of crushed red
   pepper flakes

   Salt and ground black pepper
   to taste

conchiglie with sausage and seafood

The pairing of sausage and seafood is a tradition in Portugal and Spain. Fresh seafood is best, but you don't need to mess with shells. Chopped fresh clams are available at the seafood department of your supermarket, as are shelled and cleaned shrimp. If you can't find either, pouched baby clams and mini-shrimp can be substituted.

DIRECTIONS

Bring a large pot of salted water to a boil. Add the pasta, stirring a few times to ensure that it does not stick to itself. Boil vigorously for the time recommended on the package or until tender. Drain.

Meanwhile, heat the oil in a large skillet. Sauté the sausage until it loses its raw look, add the garlic, and stir; add the wine and boil for 2 minutes. Stir in the clam sauce, shrimp, clams, and red pepper flakes, and heat through. Drain the pasta, season with salt and pepper, and toss it with the sauce before serving.

1 container (about 32 ounces) ricotta cheese

2 cups muffaletta olive mix, olive salad, or chopped mixed olives, jarred or homemade (page 339)

12 ounces (about 3 cups) shredded mozzarella cheese

¼ cup grated imported Parmesan cheese

   Salt and ground black pepper to taste

1 tablespoon extra-virgin olive oil

1 jar (about 26 ounces) marinara sauce

12 sheets (about 12 ounces) no-boil lasagna noodles

muffaletta lasagna

A muffaletta is an Italian sandwich from New Orleans named for the bread on which it is made. One of the principal flavorings in a muffaletta is olive salad, a mixture of chopped olives, onions, herbs, and oil. Eventually the salad itself became known as muffaletta, which lends its name to this indulgent lasagna, streamlined with a jar of muffaletta, a jar of marinara, and a box of no-boil lasagna noodles.

DIRECTIONS

Heat the oven to 375°F. In a large bowl, mix the ricotta cheese, muffaletta, 2 cups of the mozzarella, the Parmesan, salt, pepper, and olive oil.

Spread ½ cup of the marinara sauce over the bottom of a 9-by-13-inch baking dish. Top with a layer of 3 noodles; spread 1 cup sauce over the noodles, and top with one third of the ricotta mixture. Top with another layer of noodles, another 1 cup sauce, and half of the remaining ricotta mixture. Make another layer of noodles, another cup of sauce, and the remaining ricotta mixture. Cover with the remaining noodles. Add ½ cup water to the remaining pasta sauce in the jar; seal with the lid, and shake to combine. Pour over the top of the lasagna and cover tightly with foil. Bake for 45 minutes.

Uncover, top with the remaining mozzarella, and bake for another 15 minutes. Let rest for at least 15 minutes before serving. Cut into 6 portions. Lasagna slices better after it has been refrigerated or frozen and reheated.

8 ounces short-cut pasta, such as penne, medium shells, or rotini

3 tablespoons extra-virgin olive oil

¼ cup (about 1 ounce) chopped prosciutto

⅓ cup (about ½ ounce) chopped mint

⅔ cup ricotta cheese, preferably whole milk

Salt and ground black pepper to taste

pasta with ricotta, prosciutto, and mint

The salty sweetness of prosciutto is the inspiration that marries fresh ricotta and a cool clipping of mint into a refreshing pasta sauce.

DIRECTIONS

Bring a large pot of salted water to a boil. Add the pasta, stirring a few times to ensure that it does not stick to itself. Boil vigorously for the time recommended on the package or until tender.

Meanwhile, heat 1 tablespoon of the oil in a skillet over high heat. Add the prosciutto and sauté until the edges are crisp, about 1 minute. Combine the cooked prosciutto, mint, ricotta, and remaining olive oil in a serving bowl; season to taste with salt and pepper.

Just before the pasta is done, mix a ladleful of pasta water with the ricotta mixture. Drain the pasta and toss with the sauce. Adjust the seasoning before serving.

- 2 tablespoons olive oil
- 2/3 cup diced onion, fresh or frozen
- 1 package (about 6 ounces) Israeli or toasted couscous
- 1 can (about 14 ounces) vegetable broth
- 1/2 cup water
- 1 pound large shrimp, shelled and cleaned, thawed if frozen
- 1/2 cup salsa verde
- 3 tablespoons ranch dressing, regular or light
- 2 teaspoons dried dill (optional)

shrimp couscous with creamy salsa verde

This very easy, highly flavored one-pot meal is made with Israeli couscous. Couscous is ground-up pasta. The most familiar type is Moroccan, which has been precooked and dried so that all you have to do is add boiling water to hydrate it. The pearls of Israeli couscous are bigger and rounder, and they are toasted before being cooked in liquid. The result is more textural than fine-ground couscous. Here it is enhanced with sautéed shrimp and a tangy, creamy sauce made from a jar of salsa verde cooled with a bit of ranch salad dressing.

DIRECTIONS

Heat the oil in a large skillet over medium heat. Add the onion and sauté until tender. Add the couscous and cook until lightly toasted, about 3 minutes. Add the broth and water. Heat until boiling, reduce to a simmer, cover, and simmer for 5 minutes. Stir in the shrimp, cover, and simmer until the shrimp are firm and opaque, another 5 minutes. Remove from the heat and stir in the salsa, ranch dressing, and dill (if desired) before serving.

COOKING WITH SALAD DRESSING

Salad dressings are not designed to be heated. Although they can be creamy and rich right out of the fridge, heat them to a simmer and they will disassemble. Most dressings are mixtures of oil, vinegar, and seasoning, modified with the addition of emulsifiers, gums, and in the case of ranch dressing, buttermilk. All of these elements are sensitive to heat, so the trick to cooking with them is to use them as flavoring rather than as a cooking medium. Always add salad dressing near the end of cooking, preferably after the pan has been removed from the fire.

1   container (about 15 ounces)
     ricotta cheese

8   ounces smoked mozzarella
     cheese, coarsely shredded

     Salt and ground black pepper
     to taste

1   jar (about 26 ounces) fire-roasted
     tomato sauce

12   sheets (about 12 ounces) no-boil
     lasagna noodles

8   ounces (about 2 cups) cooked
     chicken, shredded, rotisserie or
     homemade

¼   cup shredded imported
     Romano cheese

1   tablespoon extra-virgin olive oil

rotisserie chicken lasagna with smoked mozzarella

If you think of lasagna as a dish of slow-simmered sauces, meat, and cheese, think again. This one is all about fire and smoke. The flavor of the open fire invades its structure without a match ever being struck, by layering smoked mozzarella, rotisserie-roasted chicken, and fire-roasted tomato sauce. Your mother's lasagna was never like this.

DIRECTIONS

Heat the oven to 375°F. In a medium bowl, mix the ricotta cheese, smoked mozzarella, salt, and pepper.

Spread ½ cup of the tomato sauce over the bottom of a 9-by-13-inch baking dish. Top with a layer of 3 noodles; spread 1 cup sauce over the noodles, and top with one third of the ricotta mixture and one third of the chicken. Top with another layer of noodles, another 1 cup sauce, half of the remaining ricotta mixture, and half of the remaining chicken. Make another layer of noodles, another cup of sauce, and the remaining ricotta mixture and chicken. Cover with the remaining noodles. Add ½ cup water to the remaining pasta sauce in the jar, seal with the lid, and shake to combine. Pour over the top of the lasagna and cover tightly with foil. Bake for 45 minutes.

Uncover, top with the Romano cheese, and bake for another 15 minutes. Top with the olive oil and let rest for at least 15 minutes before serving. Cut into 6 portions. Lasagna slices better after it has been refrigerated or frozen and reheated.

RESTING LASAGNA (OR ANY CASSEROLE)

By the time lasagna is removed from the oven, it is roiling with steam inside. When you cut it, the trapped steam either billows into the air or precipitates into water, leaving a puddle in the bottom of the dish. The solution—rest it for 15 minutes before serving. This gives the steam time to be absorbed into the pasta layers, causing the pasta to plump and soften more. Since there is less free water, the center is drier and less likely to ooze and fall apart. If you bake lasagna a day ahead, the solidifying benefits will be even greater.

1   pound medium shell-shaped pasta

¼   cup extra-virgin olive oil

8   cloves garlic, thinly sliced

2   tablespoons chopped basil
    leaves, or 1 tablespoon basil
    pesto, jarred or homemade
    (page 339)

    Salt and ground black pepper
    to taste

⅓   cup grated imported Parmesan
    or Romano cheese, or a blend

conchiglie with garlic chips and cheese

This simple rendition of aglio e olio (garlic in oil), the most basic of pasta sauces, takes on a novel character by changing the nature of the garlic. Instead of simply flavoring oil with minced garlic, you shave the garlic into paper-thin slices that are crisped in hot olive oil, as if they were potato chips. The crunch of these garlic slivers becomes a dynamic textural counterpoint to the oil-slicked pasta.

DIRECTIONS

Bring a large pot of salted water to a boil. Add the pasta, stirring a few times to ensure that it does not stick to itself. Boil vigorously for the time recommended on the package or until tender. Drain.

Heat 2 tablespoons of the oil in a skillet over medium-high heat. Add the garlic and cook until browned, stirring often. Remove from the heat. Toss with the pasta, basil, salt, pepper, cheese, and remaining olive oil before serving.

1 package (about 16 ounces) potato gnocchi

¼ cup extra-virgin olive oil

1 teaspoon chopped garlic, preferably fresh

1 can (about 14 ounces) diced tomatoes, drained

3 anchovy fillets, finely chopped

Juice of ½ lemon

2 tablespoons chopped Italian (flat-leaf) parsley

Salt and ground black pepper to taste

gnocchi with tomatoes, lemon, and anchovy

For a long time, prepared gnocchi was only available frozen, but now good-quality gnocchi is sold on the shelf right beside the dry pastas. In this recipe the gnocchi are prepared in classic style; they are boiled for a few minutes and then sautéed to crisp their edges. Without the browning step, gnocchi can be doughy and unpleasant.

DIRECTIONS

Bring a large pot of lightly salted water to a boil. Add the gnocchi and boil until they rise to the surface, about 5 minutes; drain.

Heat half of the oil in a large skillet over high heat. Add the gnocchi and sauté until they are dry and browned on their edges; transfer to a serving bowl. Add the garlic to the pan and cook for about 30 seconds. Add the tomatoes and heat through. Add the remaining ingredients, including the remaining olive oil. Season to taste with salt and pepper and pour the sauce over the gnocchi before serving.

- 1 tablespoon olive oil
- 1 box (about 6 ounces) Israeli or toasted couscous
- 1 teaspoon ground cumin
- ½ teaspoon ground coriander
- 1⅓ cups chicken broth
- 1 box (about 10 ounces) frozen winter squash puree, thawed
- Salt and ground black pepper to taste
- 1 tablespoon chopped parsley or cilantro

israeli couscous with winter squash and cumin

This extremely creamy couscous seems more like a long-simmered risotto than an instant pasta. Part of the difference is Israeli couscous, which has large and meaty pearl-sized grains, but much of the credit goes to the addition of frozen winter squash, which cooks into a gorgeous autumnal orange puree that ties everything together.

DIRECTIONS

Heat the oil in a large skillet over medium-high heat. Add the couscous and toast lightly, about 3 minutes. Add the cumin and coriander; stir briefly. Add the broth, squash, salt, and pepper and stir to combine. Reduce the heat to medium-low, cover, and simmer until the couscous is tender and the mixture is creamy, stirring occasionally, about 10 minutes. Be careful to keep the heat low so that the bottom doesn't scorch. Stir in the parsley or cilantro just before serving.

COUSCOUS

Couscous looks like grain, cooks like grain, and tastes like grain, but it is pasta. Traditionally made by peasant women in Morocco, couscous is a semolina pasta that is crumbled into a coarse meal and steamed in a special pot, called a couscoussière, over a stew called couscous. It is a laborious process that requires three separate steamings, but in the end the pasta is puffed and fluffy, and it makes a delicate bed to catch the drippings from the stew.

When you buy a box of couscous, it contains pasta that has already been steamed and dried, so that all you have to do is add boiling water to heat and hydrate it. Now couscous comes in a variety of flavors. Usually the seasoning is in a separate packet so that you can choose to use it or not, but sometimes spices are mixed in with the pasta, in which case the variety will be much less versatile as an ingredient.

Israeli couscous (also known as toasted couscous) has an interesting story behind it. When Moroccan Jews immigrated to Israel, they missed having couscous. An enterprising immigrant attempted to manufacture it, and when the machines tried to duplicate what the couscous makers in Morocco were doing, the pasta came out bigger and rounder, looking more like BBs than grain. Because of its size, Israeli couscous is not instant. It must be cooked briefly in simmering broth, and it must also be toasted to give it a texture; if not, the grains will take on an unpleasant mushy consistency.

⑪ cooking in a rush

In a world where speed equals better, perfection must equal instantaneous. Since I won't waste my time worrying about being perfect, I have drawn my bottom line at 10 minutes for making dinner. Anything faster probably shouldn't qualify as cooking. After all, it takes 3 minutes to toast a slice of bread.

Although almost all of the recipes in this book are relatively quick, the selections in this chapter have speed as their raison d'être. I guarantee that none of them will take you longer than 10 minutes to cook (15 if you're feeling sluggish).

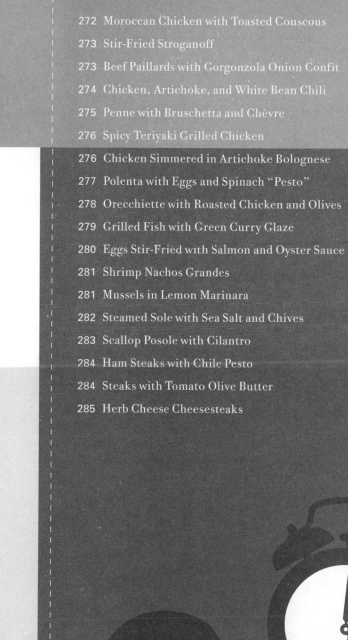

- 2 tablespoons olive oil
- 1 cup chopped onion, frozen or fresh
- 1½ cups Israeli or toasted couscous
- ½ teaspoon minced garlic, fresh or jarred organic
- ½ teaspoon ground coriander
- ½ teaspoon ground cumin
- ¼ teaspoon crushed red pepper flakes
- 1 pound (about 4 cups) cooked meat from a rotisserie or oven-roasted chicken, in bite-size pieces
- 1 bag (about 8 ounces) shredded carrot
- 1 cup golden raisins
- 2 cups vegetable broth

moroccan chicken with toasted couscous

Couscous is the perfect accompaniment for turning leftover chicken into a meal. Because both ingredients are precooked, all you have to do is warm them, which means everything can be cooked together in one pot.

DIRECTIONS

Heat the oil in a large skillet over medium-high heat. Add the onion and cook until tender. Add the couscous and stir until lightly toasted. Stir in the garlic, coriander, cumin, and red pepper flakes. Add the chicken, carrot, raisins, and broth; cover and simmer until the broth has been absorbed and the couscous is tender, about 8 minutes; serve.

1   pound beef stir-fry strips

    Salt and ground black pepper
    to taste

2   tablespoons vegetable oil

2   cups (about 6 ounces) sliced
    mushrooms

1   package (about 10 ounces) refrig-
    erated or frozen bell pepper strips

1/2   teaspoon dried thyme

1   jar (about 12 ounces) beef gravy

1/4   cup sour cream, regular or light

    Rice or noodles for serving
    (optional)

stir-fried stroganoff

Stroganoff is passé. It's a shame, for the simple sauté of beef and mushrooms in a sour cream–enriched gravy is as satisfying as anything that comes out of a skillet. There's nothing unusual in this recipe, except that it has been sped up by sautéing in a wok.

DIRECTIONS

Season the beef with salt and pepper. Heat the oil in a large wok over high heat; add the beef and stir-fry until browned. Add the mushrooms and stir-fry for 30 seconds. Add the bell peppers, thyme, gravy, and salt and pepper; heat to boiling and cook for 1 to 2 minutes. Stir in the sour cream. Serve with rice or noodles, if desired.

1   pound thin-cut beef round steak
    for sandwiches

    Kosher salt and coarsely ground
    black pepper

    No-stick spray olive oil

1/3   cup roasted caramelized onions
    (page 336)

2   tablespoons crumbled
    Gorgonzola cheese

beef paillards with gorgonzola onion confit

A paillard is a piece of meat that is sliced and pounded to paper thinness, so that it sautés instantaneously. When you use thinly sliced sandwich steaks, the work is done for you.

DIRECTIONS

Season the steak slices on both sides with salt and pepper. Heat a large skillet over high heat for several minutes, and spray the bottom with olive oil. Cook the steaks until browned on both sides, about 1 minute per side. Do not crowd the pan; cook in batches if needed, spraying the pan with more oil between batches. Heat the onions in the pan until they are warmed through; stir in the cheese. Top each steak with a portion of the onion mixture before serving.

1	tablespoon olive oil
1½	pounds chicken tenders, each cut into quarters
2	teaspoons chopped garlic, fresh or jarred organic
2	teaspoons ground cumin
1	tablespoon chili powder
1	jar (about 16 ounces) chunky salsa, any heat level, drained
1	can (about 14 ounces) chicken broth
1	can (about 13 ounces) artichoke hearts, drained
1	can (about 15 ounces) white beans (any size), drained and rinsed
2	tablespoons instant powdered hummus or falafel
1	tablespoon chopped cilantro, or 1 teaspoon cilantro pesto

chicken, artichoke, and white bean chili

Chili isn't simple. Although the stew is easy to prepare and as unpretentious as anything one can ladle into a bowl, the balance of flavors is overwhelmingly complex. In this easy 10-minute recipe, the complexity is instantaneous, growing from the bright burn of jalapeño in a jar of salsa, the garlic and coriander in a spoonful of powdered hummus, and the classic Mediterranean combination of artichokes, tomatoes, chicken, and white beans.

DIRECTIONS

Heat the olive oil in a deep skillet over medium heat. Add the chicken and sauté until lightly browned. Stir in the garlic, cumin, chili powder, salsa, and broth; heat to boiling. Add the artichoke hearts and beans and simmer for 5 minutes. Stir in the powdered hummus and cilantro and simmer for 1 minute more before serving.

WHITE BEANS

White beans come in a variety of sizes: pea, navy, Great Northern, and cannellini. Pea beans (small and round) are the classic choice for baked beans; navy beans (a little bigger and oval) are commonly used in soups; Great Northern beans (about the size of pinto beans or small kidney beans) are the ones in a classic cassoulet and in many stews, and cannellini beans (large, meaty, and kidney bean shaped) are often braised with meats, poultry, or fish. Dried white beans are medium-hard and require about an hour of simmering to become tender. All sizes of white beans are available precooked in cans; all they need is to be rinsed, drained, and heated through.

1 pound twisty pasta, such rotelle
   or shells

1 small log (about 5 ounces) fresh
   goat cheese (chèvre)

1 jar (about 17 ounces) tomato
   bruschetta

½ teaspoon crushed red
   pepper flakes

¼ cup coarsely chopped Italian
   (flat-leaf) parsley

¼ cup extra-virgin olive oil

   Salt and ground black pepper
   to taste

penne with bruschetta and chèvre

In Italy many pasta "sauces" are not sauces at all. Rather, they are flavorful ingredients chopped finely enough to disperse evenly and heat through from the residual warmth of a bowl of freshly boiled noodles. It is helpful when tossing pasta with a non-liquid sauce to leave it fairly wet, which will help to lubricate the dry ingredients.

DIRECTIONS

Bring a large pot of salted water to a boil. Add the pasta, stirring a few times to ensure that it does not stick to itself. Boil vigorously for the time recommended on the package or until the pasta is tender. Drain, but leave wet.

Meanwhile, cut the goat cheese into small pieces and toss with the bruschetta, red pepper flakes, parsley, oil, salt, and pepper in a serving bowl. Add the pasta and toss to coat before serving.

spicy teriyaki grilled chicken

MAKES 4 SERVINGS

Oil for coating the grill rack

1/3 cup teriyaki sauce

1 teaspoon Chinese chili paste

1 tablespoon toasted sesame oil

4 boneless, skinless chicken breast halves

1 orange, cut into 8 wedges

I find the flavor of most bottled teriyaki sauces too sweet. In this recipe that sugar is balanced with a spike of spice and a balm of fragrant sesame oil.

DIRECTIONS

Heat a grill set up for direct grilling to high; brush the rack with oil. Meanwhile, mix the teriyaki sauce, chili paste, and sesame oil in a large bowl. Marinate the chicken breasts in the mixture while the grill is heating. Grill until browned and cooked through, 4 to 5 minutes per side. Serve each chicken breast half with 2 orange wedges.

chicken simmered in artichoke bolognese

MAKES 4 SERVINGS

1 jar (about 12 ounces) marinated artichoke hearts

6 boneless, skinless chicken breast halves, trimmed

Salt and ground black pepper to taste

1 tablespoon vegetable oil

1/3 cup milk, low-fat or whole

1 jar (about 24 ounces) marinara sauce, preferably thin

Bolognese is the sauce associated with the cooking of Bologna, where tomato sauces always contain a little milk or cream to sweeten them. In this recipe, chicken is simmered in a prepared marinara sauce that is enhanced by milk and minced artichoke hearts. Because artichoke contains enzymes that make the palate perceive sweetness, they perform the same function that dairy does in a classic Bolognese.

DIRECTIONS

Drain the artichoke hearts, and reserve 1/3 cup of the marinade. Chop the artichoke hearts finely.

Season the chicken with salt and pepper. Heat the oil in a large skillet over medium-high heat. Brown the chicken on both sides; remove. Reduce the heat to medium, add the milk, and scrape up any bits of chicken sticking to the bottom of the pan. Add the marinara sauce, artichoke hearts, and reserved marinade. Return the chicken to the pan and simmer until cooked through, about 5 minutes. Serve the chicken with the sauce.

8   eggs, large or extra-large

Salt and ground black pepper
to taste

2   tablespoons olive oil

1   roll (about 1 pound) polenta, cut
into 8 slices

1   micro-ready bag (about 9 ounces)
baby spinach

2   tablespoons garlic-flavored oil

1/2   cup grated imported
Parmesan cheese

2   tablespoons toasted pine nuts,
pretoasted or homemade
(page 340; optional)

1/4   cup tomato bruschetta, jarred
or refrigerated

polenta with eggs and spinach "pesto"

I am a great fan of eggs for dinner, and this recipe is one of my favorites. Scrambled eggs are served on polenta with sautéed spinach that has been seasoned with the typical ingredients used in pesto: garlic, pine nuts, oil, and cheese.

DIRECTIONS

Mix the eggs, salt, and pepper in a medium bowl. Heat 1 tablespoon of the oil in a large, nonstick skillet over medium-high heat. Brown the polenta slices in the hot oil. Arrange on a serving platter and keep warm.

Meanwhile, place the bag of spinach in a microwave and cook at full power for 3 minutes. Remove the spinach from the bag and toss in a medium bowl, with the garlic oil, Parmesan, pine nuts (if desired), salt, and pepper. Spoon the spinach over the polenta.

Heat the remaining tablespoon of oil in the same skillet over medium heat. Add the eggs and scramble until set but still soft. Spoon over the spinach; top with the bruschetta before serving.

orecchiette with roasted chicken and olives

1 pound orecchiette pasta

½ cup extra-virgin olive oil

1 pound (about 4 cups) cooked meat from a rotisserie or oven-roasted chicken, in bite-size pieces

¼ cup tomato pesto or double tomato paste

⅓ cup muffaletta olive mixture, olive salad, or chopped mixed olives, jarred or homemade (page 339)

1 tablespoon chopped fresh sage

It is always good to have a few recipes in your arsenal that use up leftover roast chicken. White meat and dark meat are equally good, and poached or steamed chicken could be substituted if you want to save calories, although the richness developed during roasting is a delicious element of the sauce.

DIRECTIONS

Bring a large pot of salted water to a boil. Add the pasta, stirring a few times to ensure that it does not stick to itself. Boil vigorously for the time recommended on the package or until the pasta is tender, 8 to 10 minutes.

Meanwhile, heat the oil in a large, nonstick skillet over medium heat. Add the chicken and heat through. Stir in the tomato pesto and olive mixture. Transfer the pasta to the skillet, using a large slotted spoon; allow some of the cooking water to get into the sauce to help loosen it. Add the sage and toss to combine before serving.

CURRY PASTE

In curry-eating cuisines spice is king, and the cooking of spices has great importance. The need to toast whole spices, grind, and simmer them in order to bring out their perfume is taken for granted, and the artful blending of spices to create layers of sensation is considered the essence of fine cooking. Americans don't cook that way. We value hunks of food, and though we might season them to make them taste better, spicing is not what our cooking is about. Is it any wonder that curry has never entered into the mainstream of American home cooking?

Curry paste and jarred curry sauce are standard ingredients in Southeast Asia, and they may be the shortcut that brings real curries into American kitchens. These products are made by blending, toasting, and simmering spices so that you don't have to. All you do is add a bit of paste to the cooking liquid, or use a jar of sauce for the liquid, and you get authentic, long-simmered curry flavor instantly.

These products, especially if they are not made for the U.S. market, can be incendiary and should be used with caution and in combination with other ingredients that provide a balance to the dish.

¹/₄ cup honey

1 teaspoon green curry paste

1 tablespoon vegetable oil

1¹/₂ pounds thick fish fillets, such as halibut, salmon, or sea bass, preferably with skin

Salt and ground black pepper to taste

No-stick spray oil

Oil for brushing grill rack

¹/₂ lime, cut into 4 wedges

grilled fish with green curry glaze

Fish fillets are not meant for grilling, because when they stick they will fall apart. Here's a trick: always grill fish with its skin on. Oil the flesh side of the fillet liberally and grill that side first, just until it is browned the way you want it; don't worry about how deeply it has cooked through. Flip the fillet over and finish cooking it; don't worry if the skin side burns or sticks to the grill rack. In fact, you want it to stick. When the fish is done, slip a long spatula (if the fillet is large you may need two) between the flesh and the skin and transfer the fish to a platter, leaving the skin stuck to the grill. It is easy to scrape off once the grill has cooled.

DIRECTIONS

Heat a grill set up for direct grilling to high. To make the glaze, mix the honey, curry paste, and vegetable oil in a small bowl; set aside.

Season the fish with salt and pepper and coat on both sides with spray oil. Brush the grill rack with oil. Grill the fillets, covered, flesh-side down, until browned, about 4 minutes. Turn over with a large spatula. Brush the flesh side of the fish with half of the glaze, and continue grilling until the flesh flakes to gentle pressure, about 4 minutes more.

Lift the fish from its skin onto a platter. The skin will stick to the grill and can be cleaned off later. Drizzle the fish with the remaining glaze and serve with lime wedges.

6   eggs, large or extra-large

    Salt and ground black pepper
    to taste

1/4 teaspoon hot pepper sauce

6   ounces skinless salmon fillet,
    cut into bite-size pieces

    Juice of 1/2 lime

1   tablespoon vegetable oil

2   scallions, trimmed and
    thinly sliced

1/4 cup Chinese oyster sauce

eggs stir-fried with salmon and oyster sauce

I love the flavor of eggs scrambled in a wok. The whiff of char that glazes anything that touches a hot wok is a wonder with eggs, and this combination of salmon, eggs, and salty-sweet Chinese oyster sauce is an awesome example.

DIRECTIONS

In a medium bowl, mix the eggs, salt, pepper, and hot sauce. Toss the salmon with the lime juice in a separate bowl.

Heat the oil in a large wok over medium-high heat until smoking. Add the salmon and stir-fry until browned and almost cooked through, about 2 minutes. Remove from the wok.

Reduce the heat to low. Add the eggs to the wok and scramble until half set. Add the scallion and salmon pieces and continue to cook until the eggs are fully set but still creamy. Spoon onto a platter and drizzle with oyster sauce to serve.

shrimp nachos grandes

MAKES 4 SERVINGS

1   bag (about 9 ounces) yellow or white corn tortilla chips

1   container (about 8 ounces) hummus

12 ounces cleaned and cooked shrimp, medium or large, thawed if frozen

3/4 cup (about 3 ounces) crumbled feta cheese

1½ cups chunky salsa, any heat level

1   pouch (about 1 cup) refrigerated guacamole, such as Avo Classic

Nacho's not a flavor, it's an architecture—chips, some mashed beans, a protein, something spicy, and cheese. Once you've got the structure, everything else is just filling in the gaps. In this easy dinner I've used hummus, shrimp, salsa, and feta, but it could have been edamame, grilled tuna, chili oil, and tofu; or black beans, grilled chicken, mango salsa, and pepper Jack. Get the picture?

DIRECTIONS

Place half of the chips on a large, microwave-safe platter. Top with half of the hummus in spoonfuls, half of the shrimp, and half of the feta (try to arrange the ingredients evenly so that there is some of each in each bite). Repeat with the remaining chips, hummus, shrimp, and cheese. Cook in a microwave at full power until heated through, about 2 minutes. Spoon the salsa over the top, and serve the guacamole on the side.

mussels in lemon marinara

MAKES 4 SERVINGS

1   jar (24 to 25 ounces) tomato marinara sauce

    Finely grated zest of 1 lemon

    Juice of 2 lemons

½   cup white wine

1   tablespoon extra-virgin olive oil

4   pounds fresh, cleaned live mussels

    Pasta or crusty bread, for serving

No dinner is more delicious than beautifully fresh shellfish steamed in a fragrant marinara sauce. It takes no time, no particular skill, and very few ingredients. Serve it with a lot of crusty bread for sopping up the sauce.

DIRECTIONS

Heat the sauce, lemon zest, lemon juice, wine, and oil in a large, covered, deep skillet over medium-high heat until boiling. Add the mussels, stir to distribute, cover, and simmer until the mussels are open and plump, about 5 minutes. Discard any unopened mussels. Serve with pasta or crusty bread.

1   tablespoon extra-virgin olive oil

4   sole fillets, about 4 ounces each,
    about ¼ inch thick

½   teaspoon coarse sea salt

¼   teaspoon ground black pepper

8   fresh chives, cut into
    1-inch lengths

    Juice of ½ lemon

steamed sole with sea salt and chives

Steaming dinner right on a plate is a form of home cooking in most of Europe that is reserved for the infirm or those with delicate digestion. It is low-fat and ultimately convenient, for the plate can be set up anytime and cooked as needed. In the past it required perching the plate atop a simmering pot of steam, but now all you have to do is slip it into a microwave.

DIRECTIONS

Coat a large dinner plate with half of the olive oil. Arrange the fish in a single layer; season with the salt and pepper, and scatter the chives over the top. Cover with plastic wrap or another plate inverted over the top. Steam in the microwave just until the fish is cooked through, 2 to 3 minutes. Remove the cover and sprinkle with the remaining olive oil and the lemon juice. Serve immediately.

MICROWAVE STEAMING

Microwaves are only slightly stronger than TV waves, much weaker than the energy of a flame. All they can do is make water boil, which is why the microwave oven is nothing more or less than a speedy steamer. Microwaves work by bombarding the water molecules in an ingredient with enough energy to make them move back and forth with incredible speed. Because molecular movement is synonymous with heat, it is not long before the water in microwave-cooked food begins to steam.

1   tablespoon olive oil

1   cup chopped onion, fresh
    or frozen

2   teaspoons chopped garlic,
    fresh or jarred organic

½   cup white wine

½   cup salsa verde

2   cups fish or seafood broth,
    or 1 fish bouillon cube and
    2 cups water

1   can (about 15 ounces) white
    posole (hominy), drained
    and rinsed

    Chopped zest and juice of 1 lime

1   pound unsoaked sea scallops,
    cleaned of tough fibers, halved
    if large

1   tablespoon chopped cilantro,
    or 1 teaspoon cilantro pesto

scallop posole with cilantro

Posole is a Mexican stew made with whole hominy, lime, and cilantro. This recipe takes the flavors of posole and concentrates them into a fragrant, fresh-tasting poaching broth for scallops.

DIRECTIONS

Heat the oil in a large saucepan over medium-high heat. Add the onion and sauté until tender. Add the garlic and cook until aromatic, about 1 minute more. Add the wine, salsa, fish broth, posole, and lime zest. Simmer for 5 minutes.

Shortly before serving, add the lime juice, scallops, and cilantro to the simmering broth; stir to disperse the scallops. Simmer until the scallops are just firm on their surface but soft inside, about 3 minutes. Serve the scallops and hominy in shallow bowls, moistened with some of the broth.

Oil for brushing the grill rack

1 lime, cut in half

2 tablespoons basil pesto, jarred or homemade (page 339)

2 teaspoons Chinese chili paste with garlic

1 tablespoon orange marmalade

1 pound ham steaks, ¼ inch thick (about 2 steaks)

ham steaks with chile pesto

This heat 'n' eat entrée is flavored with an unconventional pesto. I'm calling it a pesto in the literal sense, meaning paste. Other than that, its hot, sweet, tart, herbal essence owes nothing whatsoever to traditional basil pesto.

DIRECTIONS

Heat a grill to high or a ridged griddle over high heat. Brush with oil. Meanwhile, squeeze the juice from half of the lime and combine with the pesto, chili paste, and marmalade; brush on both sides of the ham steaks.

Sear the ham on both sides on the heated grill, about 1 minute per side. Cut into serving-size portions. Cut the other lime half in half and serve with the ham.

2 tablespoons butter, salted or unsalted, softened

2 tablespoons tapenade, jarred or homemade (page 347)

1 teaspoon tomato paste

1½ pounds beef steaks, sirloin, rib steak, tenderloin, T-bone, or porterhouse

Kosher salt and coarsely ground black pepper to taste

steaks with tomato olive butter

Flavoring butter with spices and herbs is a classic composition for adding a finishing glaze to grilled or roasted meat. Although composed butters lend a gourmet panache to whatever they touch, making them involves nothing more than mixing a few prepared ingredients together.

DIRECTIONS

Heat a grill to high or a ridged griddle over high heat. Stir together the butter, tapenade, and tomato paste in a bowl. Divide the mixture into 4 portions and chill. Season the steaks with salt and pepper, and grill to the desired doneness, about 4 minutes per side for medium-rare. Top each serving of steak with a portion of the flavored butter.

1 tablespoon olive oil

2 medium onions, halved and thinly sliced

Salt and ground black pepper to taste

8–9 ounces thin-cut beef round steak for sandwiches

1/3 cup (about 2 ounces) garlic and herb cream cheese

2 sub rolls, about 8 inches, split and warmed

herb cheese cheesesteaks

For a boy who grew up on Philly cheesesteaks, there's something wonderfully perverse about this dressed-up Francophilic riff.

DIRECTIONS

Heat half of the oil in a large skillet over medium-high heat. Add the onions, cover, and sauté until lightly browned and very tender; season with salt and pepper. Transfer to a plate.

Add the remaining oil to the pan. Add the steaks and cook until browned, chopping the meat as it cooks into coarse shreds; season with salt and pepper. Divide the steak into 2 portions. Top each portion with half of the onions. Turn off the heat and cover the pan.

Meanwhile, spread half the cheese over the insides of the rolls. Place a portion of steak in each roll, and spoon the remaining cheese on top to serve.

12 cooking slow & easy

Slow food simmers and spits lazily on a back burner while we play. It rests in a slow cooker while we rest in the next room. It steams gently over a fragrant broth while we run errands, finish up work, or just relax. And the best part is that while we're occupied elsewhere, ingredients are being transformed in ways that no quick-cooking kitchen gadget could duplicate. Flavors are blending, blossoming, and balancing in ways that no amount of expertise could master. Sometimes the best thing a cook can do is sit back and take it easy.

The proliferation of slow-cookers and slow-cooker recipes has helped many home cooks realize that convenience is not always a question of speed. Though I use a slow cooker frequently, I recognize that it has its limits, and I encourage you to embrace the other tools you have in your kitchen (a low oven or a simmering burner come to mind) that can help you make delicious food with a minimum of effort.

fire-roasted tomato gravy

MAKES ABOUT 8 CUPS,
OR 8 SERVINGS

2   cans (about 28 ounces each) fire-roasted whole tomatoes

1   can (about 28 ounces) fire-roasted crushed tomatoes

1   cup V8 vegetable juice

1   package (about ½ ounce) dried mushrooms, chopped

    Salt and ground black pepper to taste

2   tablespoons extra-virgin olive oil

This intense, hearty tomato sauce cooks all day while you are occupied elsewhere. The robust flavor comes from the smokiness of canned fire-roasted tomatoes, which give the sauce a mahogany hue, flecked with bits of charred tomato skin. The addition of V8 is important; it delivers a rounded vegetable flavor that balances the smokiness of the tomatoes, and the dried mushrooms plump as the sauce simmers, lending a texture similar to that of meat sauce.

DIRECTIONS

Crush the whole tomatoes and add to a large slow cooker. Add the crushed tomatoes, V8, dried mushrooms, salt, and pepper. Cover and cook on low for 8 hours. Add the olive oil and use as a pasta sauce, or for cooking meats, poultry, or seafood.

turkey poêle with sage and garlic

MAKES ABOUT 10 SERVINGS

1   turkey, about 10 pounds, giblets and wing tips removed

    Salt and ground black pepper to taste

12 cloves garlic, sliced

⅓   cup (about 3 grams) fresh sage leaves, coarsely chopped

½   cup extra-virgin olive oil

You cannot roast in a slow cooker, but you can get succulent results with a classic method of cooking fish and poultry called *poêle*, poaching in oil (or butter). As the meat warms in the oil, it is continually basted so that it cannot dry out. And because the oil stays on the surface the food absorbs very little fat, making it similar to roasted meat nutritionally.

DIRECTIONS

Wash the turkey, pat dry, and season inside and out with salt and pepper. Place the turkey in a 6- or 8-quart slow-cooker, and scatter the garlic and sage over and around it. Pour the oil over the top, cover, and cook on low for 6 to 8 hours, until a thermometer inserted in a thick part of the thigh registers 165°F. Cut into pieces before serving.

1½ pounds skinned and boned salmon fillet, cut into 4 pieces

Salt and ground black pepper to taste

3 tablespoons extra-virgin olive oil

1 medium onion, peeled, halved from top to bottom, and thinly sliced

½ teaspoon chopped garlic

1 package (about 8 ounces) organic quick wild rice, such as Lundberg

2¼ cups water

2 ounces smoked salmon, diced

2 tablespoons chopped Italian (flat-leaf) parsley

smoky salmon braised with wild rice

Wild rice is a hearty, meaty grain that takes forever to get tender. Recently a strain of organic quick-cooking wild rice has been developed by Lundberg Family Farms that can be simmered to tenderness in about 30 minutes, just about the same amount of time it takes to braise a thick piece of salmon.

DIRECTIONS

Season the salmon with salt and pepper. Heat 1 tablespoon of the oil in a large skillet over medium-high heat and sear the salmon on both sides; remove to a plate.

Reduce the heat to medium, add another tablespoon of oil and the onion, and cook until tender; add the garlic and cook for a few more seconds. Stir in the rice and water and season with salt and pepper. Heat to simmering, stirring once. Cover and simmer for 20 minutes.

Scatter the smoked salmon and parsley over the rice. Nestle the salmon pieces into the rice, drizzle the remaining tablespoon of oil over the salmon, cover, and simmer until the fish flakes to gentle pressure and the rice is puffed and tender, about 5 more minutes. Serve a portion of salmon with a portion of rice.

1   chicken, about 4 pounds, cut
    into 8 pieces

    Salt and ground black pepper
    to taste

2   tablespoons olive oil

1   medium onion, halved lengthwise
    and sliced

2   teaspoons minced garlic

3   tablespoons chopped Italian
    (flat-leaf) parsley

2   cups chicken broth

2   preserved lemons, cut into chunks

chicken braised with preserved lemon

Preserved lemons are a staple of the Arab kitchen, made by salting lemons until they release their juices to form a salty, tart brine. Once preserved, the lemon rind softens, allowing you to use the whole lemon chopped up in a sauce or stew. The flavor is a unique combination of lemon perfume, natural tartness, and bright pickling, and it is so intense that little else is needed. Preserved lemons are sold in Mediterranean markets and high-end food stores.

DIRECTIONS

Season the chicken pieces with salt and pepper. Heat the oil in a large skillet over medium-high heat, and brown the chicken on all sides. Add the onion and cook until it loses its raw look, a few minutes. Add the garlic, parsley, broth, and lemon and heat to boiling. Reduce the heat to medium-low so that the liquid simmers gently. Cover and simmer until the chicken is tender, about 50 minutes.

Remove the lemon pieces and puree them in a food processor. Stir back into the liquid in the pan and simmer for a minute or two before serving.

1   pound dried white beans, such
    as navy beans or Great Northern

1   cup chopped onion, fresh
    or frozen

1   teaspoon ground coriander

1   teaspoon ground cumin

1   cinnamon stick

1/4   cup honey

4   carrots, peeled, trimmed, and
    cut into chunks

1   container (about 32 ounces)
    vegetable broth

2   tablespoons fresh lemon juice

    Salt and ground black pepper
    to taste

slow-cooked moroccan baked beans

One of the advantages of cooking dried beans in a slow-cooker is that they don't require presoaking. They do take a long time to cook, though, about 10 hours, but I have often found that one of the disadvantages of other slow-cooker recipes is that if you put them on early in the morning they overcook by the time you get home for dinner. These baked beans are flavored with an exotic Arab palate.

DIRECTIONS

Combine the white beans, onion, coriander, cumin, cinnamon stick, honey, carrots, and broth in a large slow-cooker and cook on low until the beans are tender and most of the liquid has been absorbed, about 10 hours. Season with lemon juice, salt, and pepper. Remove the cinnamon stick before serving.

HOW DOES A SLOW-COOKER WORK?

The first slow-cooker was introduced in the early 1970s by Rival, under the trademarked name Crock-Pot. It was composed of a ceramic crockery insert set in a metal housing unit that heated from the sides, which is still the basic design of all slow-cookers. The unit generates moderate heat so that the outside of the housing never gets dangerously hot but, because ceramic is a steady conductor of heat, the insert keeps a constant temperature of about 200°F when the unit is set on low, and 300°F when set on high.

Because a slow-cooker is a closed environment, there is far less evaporation than when cooking on a stove-top or in an oven, causing the contents to tend to get watered down. For that reason you should reduce the amount of liquid when adapting recipes to a slow-cooker. Sauces will need extra thickening, and the level of seasoning will need to be increased.

Because browning doesn't begin until 300°F and boiling liquid is only 212°F, the tendency of a slow-cooker to retain moisture inhibits ingredients from browning. If you want a browned flavor or color, it is necessary to sear the ingredients beforehand.

4   turkey thighs, about 2 pounds
    total, skin removed

    Salt and ground black pepper
    to taste

2   tablespoons extra-virgin olive oil

2   medium onions, peeled and
    quartered

1   tablespoon finely chopped
    garlic, preferably fresh

    Juice of 2 lemons (about 1/3 cup)

1   can (about 4 ounces) chopped
    green chiles

1   cinnamon stick

1   can (about 14 ounces)
    chicken broth

1   cup (about 4 ounces) dried
    apricot halves

1   cup couscous, preferably
    whole wheat

turkey tagine with apricots

A tagine is a North African stew cooked in a conical ceramic pot (called a tagine). And although the pot does help to concentrate flavors, for all but purists, it is not essential. There is plenty going on in the fragrant combination of olive oil, onion, garlic, lemon, chiles, cinnamon, and apricots to seduce an adventurous palate.

DIRECTIONS

Season the turkey thighs with salt and pepper. Heat the oil in a large skillet over medium-high heat, and brown the turkey on both sides. Add the onion, cover, and cook until it loses its raw look, a few minutes. Add the garlic, lemon juice, chiles, cinnamon stick, broth, and apricots and heat to boiling. Reduce the heat to medium-low so that the liquid simmers gently. Cover and simmer until the turkey is tender, about 50 minutes.

Remove the turkey to a platter. Remove the cinnamon stick, heat the liquid in the pan to boiling, and stir in the couscous. If using whole wheat couscous, simmer for 5 minutes. If using regular couscous, remove from the heat, cover, and set aside for 5 minutes. Serve the turkey on a bed of couscous.

1½ pounds cubed lamb

Salt and ground black pepper to taste

2 tablespoons olive oil

1 medium onion, coarsely chopped

2 carrots, peeled and cut into chunks

2 ribs celery, peeled and cut into chunks

12 ounces red or gold potatoes, unpeeled, cut into chunks

1 cup V8 vegetable juice

3 cups beef broth

½ teaspoon dried thyme

2 bay leaves

⅓ cup steel-cut (Irish) oats

lamb stewed with cut oats

Steel-cut oats, also sold as Scottish or Irish oatmeal, is a hearty grain that deserves an honored place outside of the cereal bowl. In this recipe it takes the place of barley or noodles in a full-flavored lamb stew. To increase the vegetable flavors, which give a stew most of its depth, I have used V8 juice for part of the liquid.

DIRECTIONS

Season the lamb with salt and pepper. Heat the oil in a large skillet or Dutch oven over medium-high heat. Add the lamb and brown on all sides; transfer to a plate.

Add the onion, carrots, and celery and cook until lightly browned. Stir in the potatoes. Add the juice, broth, thyme, and bay leaves, and heat to boiling. Return the lamb to the pot, cover, and simmer until the lamb is tender, about 1 hour. Remove the bay leaves.

Add the oats and stir to disperse; simmer until the oats are tender, about 30 minutes. Adjust the seasoning before serving.

1 turkey, about 12 pounds, washed inside and out and dried

2 tablespoons kosher salt

1 teaspoon coarsely ground black pepper

2 teaspoons dried poultry seasoning

slow-roasted turkey

This fail-safe way of roasting meat gives the moistest results possible. It is the method used in most restaurants for roasting prime rib, and it works great for turkey. The only caveats are that you must *never* stuff the turkey, and your oven must be calibrated correctly; a discrepancy as small as 10°F can mean disaster.

DIRECTIONS

Heat the oven to 450°F. Season the turkey inside and out with the salt, pepper, and poultry seasoning. Place on a rack in a roasting pan. Roast for 45 minutes. Reduce the oven temperature to 170°F and roast for at least 12 hours more. (Longer will not cause overcooking.) There is no need to let the turkey rest before carving.

THE THEORY BEHIND SLOW-ROASTING

To slow-roast, place a turkey in a very hot oven (at least 400°F) to brown the skin and kill any bacteria on the surface (where bacterial counts are highest). Then reduce the temperature to 170°F, which is the internal temperature of turkey at full doneness. Because the oven is no hotter than you want the roast to be when it is done, it is impossible for the turkey to overcook.

In traditional roasting, the outside of the meat must get hotter than the desired temperature for doneness, in order to get the interior up to the proper degree, with the inevitable results that some parts of the roast dry out before the rest is done. But in slow-roasting the meat literally warms to doneness. No section ever gets overdone. No part ever breaks down and becomes dry, even when held in the oven for extended periods. The results are stupendous.

However, I must include a note of concern. The U.S. Department of Agriculture does not recommend slow-roasting, believing that it has the potential of producing undesirable bacteria levels. Their concern is based on the precept that the longer a meat stays between 40°F and 140°F the greater the opportunity for pathogenic bacteria to grow.

Slow-roasting does take longer to get the interior of the meat above 140°F, but once the temperature passes the danger zone any bacteria present are destroyed. And since this technique requires that the surface be cooked to 400°F and that roasting take place for at least an hour per pound, all sections of the roast are guaranteed to reach full doneness.

I have used this technique for nearly thirty years, with excellent results every time. I have told countless friends and students about it and have received only appreciation in return. If slow-roasted meat was not so succulent, and if I had any reason to believe that the technique was risky, I would not buck the system. But the results are good, and in my experience the technique has always proven to be safe.

1   game hen, about 1½ pounds,
    quartered

2   pieces veal shank, about
    8 ounces each, cut for
    osso buco

4   pieces beef short ribs, about
    7 ounces each

    Salt and ground black pepper
    to taste

1   ham steak, about 8 ounces,
    cut into quarters

1   bag (about 1 pound) soup greens
    (includes 1 turnip, 1 carrot,
    1 parsnip, 1 onion, 1 rib celery,
    and parsley and dill sprigs)

1   cup white wine

1   cup chicken broth

1   bay leaf

    Mustard and/or horseradish,
    for serving (optional)

crock-pot au feu

Pot au feu, bollito misto, corned beef and cabbage—almost every culinary culture has a boiled dinner in its repertoire. What's the difference between a boiled meal and a stew? For one thing, browning. Boiled meals are just boiled; they never get the browned, roasted quality that gives meat cookery its succulence. But what they miss in browning they make up for in variety. Boiled meals tend to be chock-full of meat. It is not unusual for them to have three or four different types of meat in the same pot. And that is the case here. Serve a small portion of each meat with some mustard or horseradish. The vegetables are there to add flavor; serve them if you like, but it is not essential.

DIRECTIONS

Season the game hen, veal, and beef with salt and pepper. Place in a 6- or 8-quart slow-cooker. Nestle the ham among the pieces. Peel the vegetables and cut into bite-size pieces, and chop the herbs finely. Add to the cooker, along with the wine, broth, and bay leaf. Cover and cook on low for 8 hours; discard the bay leaf. Serve a portion of each meat, moistened with some of the cooking liquid. Accompany with mustard and/or horseradish, if desired.

1   duck, about 5 pounds, quartered

2   tablespoons five-spice powder

2   tablespoons soy sauce

1   teaspoon Chinese chili paste

1   orange

1   cup olive oil

five-spice duck confit

Confit is an ingenious way the ancients developed for preserving meat, in which meat is cooked in a large amount of fat until it is tender. As the dish cools, the fat solidifies around the meat, forming an airtight seal that guards against the possibility of bacterial contamination. Confit could be kept in a cool cellar all winter, providing meat as needed. Although it is no longer necessary to preserve meat in this way, the flavor and texture are wonderfully rich. The only problem is that the technique takes time. Fortunately, a slow-cooker makes it effortless.

DIRECTIONS

Trim any visible excess fat from the duck. Mix the five-spice powder, soy sauce, and chili paste, and rub it into the meat (not the skin). Place the duck, skin-side down, in a single layer across the bottom of a slow-cooker.

Remove the zest from the orange in strips with a vegetable peeler, and tuck the strips between the duck pieces. Squeeze the juice from the orange over the top. Add the oil, cover the cooker, and cook on low for 6 hours.

To serve, remove the duck from its liquid and spoon some of the juices over the top. You can also refrigerate the duck in its juices for later use. Once chilled, the oil in the liquid will solidify, which will keep the meat fresh for 4 to 6 weeks in the refrigerator.

1½   pounds cubed lamb

     Salt and ground black pepper
     to taste

2   tablespoons extra-virgin olive oil

2   tablespoons chopped garlic

1   teaspoon dried oregano

     Pinch of crushed red pepper
     flakes

1   can (about 14 ounces)
     chicken broth

1   can or frozen package (about
     10 ounces) artichoke hearts,
     drained or thawed

1   can (about 16 ounces) cannellini
     beans, drained and rinsed

     Juice of ½ lemon

2   scallions, trimmed and sliced

lamb braised with artichokes and beans

Lamb, artichoke, and white kidney beans are a triumphant Mediterranean triumvirate. In this recipe, half of the beans are reserved and mashed with lemon juice into a thickening paste that is added just before serving, thereby eliminating any need for a starchy thickener like flour.

DIRECTIONS

Season the lamb with salt and pepper. Heat the oil in a large skillet or Dutch oven over medium-high heat. Add the lamb and brown on all sides. Add the garlic, oregano, pepper flakes, and broth. Heat to boiling, and reduce the heat until the liquid simmers. Simmer for 1 hour.

Add the artichokes and half the beans; simmer for 30 minutes. Mash the remaining beans with the lemon juice. Add to the stew and simmer until thickened, another 5 minutes. Stir in the scallions, and serve.

PERFECT CHEESECAKE

Like a custard, cheesecake sets at 180°F (any hotter and it gets grainy). The traditional defense is baking in a water bath. Because the water in the bath can reach only 212°F regardless of how hot the oven gets, it ensures that the temperature at the edge of the cake will never get too hot. But I've got a better idea: lowering the oven temperature to 200°F makes a water bath redundant. Because the oven is barely hotter than the finished temperature of the cake, overcooking is impossible, and because it bakes so slowly, it never cracks, never dries out, and is as creamy at its edge as it is at its heart.

No-stick spray oil

1/2 cup grated imported Parmesan cheese

2 pounds cream cheese (can be reduced fat), at room temperature

1 tablespoon extra-virgin olive oil

Salt and ground black pepper to taste

Pinch of cayenne

1 teaspoon minced garlic, fresh or jarred organic

1/3 cup chopped fresh dill

3 tablespoons wine vinegar

1/4 cup whiskey

5 eggs, large or extra-large

8 ounces smoked salmon, chopped

1 cup (4 ounces) shredded Gruyère or Swiss cheese

overnight savory cheesecake

A cheesecake can be savory or sweet. Replacing sugar, vanilla, and fruit with Parmesan, dill, and smoked salmon transports a cheesecake from the end of the meal into a sophisticated hors d'oeuvre. Serve it with thinly sliced toasted black bread or bagel rounds.

DIRECTIONS

Heat the oven to 200°F. Coat the interior of a 9-inch cheesecake pan or a 2-quart soufflé dish with spray oil and dust with 3 tablespoons of the Parmesan cheese.

Beat the cream cheese until soft in a large bowl. Add the oil, salt, pepper, cayenne, garlic, dill, vinegar, and whiskey and beat until smooth. Beat in the eggs just until incorporated. Stir in the salmon and Gruyère until evenly dispersed.

Pour into the prepared pan and bake for 6 to 8 hours or overnight. There is no need for a water bath (see box). Allow to cool in the pan.

To remove from the pan, hold the cake on its side, allowing gravity to help the cake separate from the side of the pan. Rotate the pan until the sides of the cake have been released all the way around. Cover with a sheet of wax paper and a plate. Turn over, remove the pan, and chill the cake, upside down, for at least 4 hours or as long as several days. Cover with plastic wrap when firm.

To serve, unwrap, cover with a serving plate, and invert. Remove the top plate and wax paper. Slice into thin wedges with a long, thin knife dipped in water.

BBQ short ribs and lentils

4   pieces beef short ribs,
    about 7 ounces each

    Salt and ground black pepper
    to taste

    No-stick flour and oil
    baking spray

1   jar (about 16 ounces)
    barbecue sauce

1   cup water

1½ cups lentils

1   medium onion, peeled
    and quartered

Although it is always tempting to prepare slow-cooker recipes completely in one vessel, the inability to brown meat can be unacceptable when cooking red meat, which is why I have added a browning step to this recipe.

DIRECTIONS

Heat a large skillet or Dutch oven over high heat. Season the short ribs on all sides with salt and pepper and coat with baking spray. Brown on all sides in the hot skillet. Transfer to a slow-cooker, add the remaining ingredients, and cook on low until the lentils are soft and the beef is tender, about 8 hours. Serve the short ribs on a bed of lentils.

corned beef choucroute

1   corned beef brisket,
    about 2½ pounds

2   medium onions, peeled and
    quartered

1   bag (about 32 ounces)
    refrigerated sauerkraut,
    drained and rinsed

1   can (about 12 ounces) beer

2   pounds small round potatoes,
    red or yellow, left whole

    Ground black pepper to taste

1   bay leaf

¼   teaspoon ground allspice

Corned beef and cabbage is the perfect recipe for a sojourn in a slow-cooker. Here I have used the flavors of an Alsatian choucroute, which is simply corned beef and cabbage Rhine-style.

DIRECTIONS

Place the corned beef fat side down in a slow-cooker. Add the remaining ingredients in even layers, cover, and cook on low for 8 hours. Remove the corned beef to a cutting board; rest for about 5 minutes, then slice. Serve garnished with the sauerkraut, onions and potatoes.

4   pieces beef short ribs, about
    7 ounces each

    Salt and ground black pepper
    to taste

    No-stick flour and oil baking spray

1   medium sweet potato (about
    10 ounces), peeled and cut
    into chunks

12 baby-cut carrots

1   cup chopped onion, fresh
    or frozen

1   teaspoon pumpkin pie spice

¼   cup dark brown sugar

1   cup beef broth

½   cup (about 3 ounces)
    chopped dried figs

¼   cup (about 1½ ounces)
    jumbo raisins

easy beef tzimmes

Tzimmes, the sweet and sour Jewish stew, is the inspiration for
this slow-cooked collaboration of beef short ribs, sweet root
vegetables, and dried fruit. Tzimmes is designed to cook in a slow
oven overnight, to abide by the proscription against cooking on
the Sabbath. This stew doesn't take quite that long. It will need
2 hours, but if it stays in the oven for an hour longer no harm will
be done.

DIRECTIONS

Heat the oven to 250°F; heat a large skillet or Dutch oven over
high heat. Meanwhile, season the short ribs on all sides with salt
and pepper and coat with baking spray. Brown on all sides in the
hot skillet. Add the remaining ingredients, stirring to combine
and lifting the browned ribs to allow the liquid to flow all around
them. Cover and heat to boiling; place in the oven and bake for
2 hours. Serve the short ribs with the vegetables.

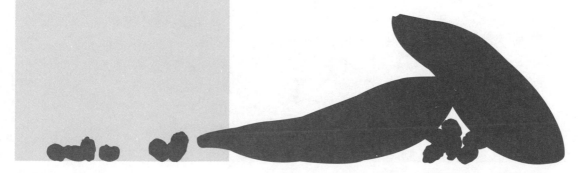

13 desserts & treats

Dessert is a food set apart, complete with its own basic food groups (ice cream, pastry, pudding, and cake) and a nutritional system that's best described as mental health food.

Though you may love dessert, the prospect of making it (particularly baking from scratch) can be a big deal. Home cooks bake for special occasions, but for an everyday dessert—no way! Not only does it require advanced planning to soften butter, but it means hauling out and cleaning up an arsenal of strainers, spatulas, beaters, and bowls. One of the great advantages of using prepared ingredients is that all of the mess takes place in a factory rather than in your kitchen. Besides, like any skill, baking takes practice, and if you're not practiced, Pepperidge Farm probably makes better pastry than you do.

1   refrigerated pie crust

1   jar (about 12 ounces) dulce de leche dessert topping

1   egg, large or extra-large

3/4 cup heavy cream

1   teaspoon baking soda

2   ripe bananas, finely chopped

1   cup almond meal

1/2 cup brown sugar, dark or light

2   tablespoons unsalted butter, melted

dulce de leche banana pie

Hold on to your taste buds. This combination of caramelized milk, bananas, and ground almonds is palate shattering. Although it tastes as though it took massive amounts of time and innate pastry skills, the ready availability of dulce de leche dessert sauce and high-quality prepared pie crusts turns this restaurant-quality dessert into a dump-and-bake classic.

DIRECTIONS

Heat the oven to 350°F. The prepared pie crust will measure about 11 inches in diameter; using a rolling pin or your hands, press it to a diameter of about 13 inches. Line a 9½- or 10-inch glass pie pan with the pastry and crimp the edges.

Mix the dulce de leche, egg, cream, and baking soda in a bowl until smooth. Stir in the bananas and pour into the crust. Mix the almond meal, sugar, and butter until crumbly. Cover the top of the pie with the crumbs and bake until browned and bubbly, about 30 minutes. Cool on a rack for at least 20 minutes before cutting into wedges.

1½ cups confectioners' sugar

¼ cup flour

½ teaspoon ground cinnamon

1 canned chipotle pepper en adobo, seeds removed, finely chopped

1 tablespoon adobo sauce from the chipotle peppers (optional)

1 teaspoon balsamic vinegar

¼ teaspoon almond extract

3 pounds frozen sweet dark cherries, thawed and drained

1 box (about 15 ounces) pastry crust for a double-crust 9-inch pie

chipotle cherry pie

Most of the time, the magical effect of sugar on peppers is employed in savory foods, but another more novel approach is gaining popularity for desserts. Heat and sweet have entered the pastry realm, with jalapeño jelly, chocolate truffles aglow with chiles, and black pepper spice cake, but to my palate nothing surpasses the inspired pairing of chipotle (smoked jalapeños) and cherries. This intoxicating pie has a slow burn that is quenched deliciously with a scoop of Basil Ricotta Ice Cream (page 322).

DIRECTIONS

Heat the oven to 400°F.

Mix the confectioners' sugar, flour, and cinnamon in a large mixing bowl. Stir in the chipotle pepper, adobo sauce (if you want the pie to be extra spicy), vinegar, almond extract, and cherries until all of the dry ingredients have been moistened.

Line a 9-inch pie pan with one of the pastry crusts, fill with the cherry mixture, and top with the second crust. Fold the edges over and crimp to seal. Cut a few slits in the top crust and bake until the crusts are crisp and golden brown, and the juices inside the pie are bubbling, about 50 minutes. Let cool for 15 to 20 minutes before serving.

No-stick flour and oil baking spray

1   prepared 8- or 9-inch pecan pie, thawed if frozen

1   box (about 1 pound 4 ounces) fudge brownie mix, makes a 9-by-13-inch pan

1/4 cup brewed coffee or water

2   tablespoons bourbon or other whiskey

1/2 cup vegetable oil

2   eggs, large or extra-large

chocolate pecan torte

I don't know what is better: the divine decadence of this super-rich ultra-gooey chocolate confection or the unbridled delight I get whenever I get to smash a pie into the bottom of a cake pan.

DIRECTIONS

Heat the oven to 325°F. Spray the interior of a 9-inch springform pan with baking spray.

Cover the surface of the pie with plastic wrap and top with a plate. Invert the pie onto the plate, and remove the pie tin. Invert the prepared springform pan over the pie and then invert the whole, so that the pie slides into the pan. Remove the plate and, using the plastic wrap to keep your hands clean, smash the pie so that it fills the bottom of the pan.

Mix the brownie mix, coffee, bourbon, oil, and eggs in a medium mixing bowl until smooth and the texture of wet mud. Pour over the pie and smooth the top. Bake until the sides are firm and the top is crusty but the center is still soft, about 50 minutes. Cool until the pan is comfortable to the touch; remove the sides of the pan and cool completely. Cut into wedges to serve.

No-stick flour and oil baking spray

¼ pound (1 stick) unsalted butter, melted

1 jar (about 16 ounces) dark chocolate fudge sauce

⅔ cup sugar

3 eggs, large or extra-large

¼ teaspoon almond extract

1⅔ cups (about 5½ ounces) almond meal or finely ground almonds

hot fudge nut torte

This rendition of a French almond torte is as dense and dark as the classic but much easier to prepare. Using fudge sauce in place of solid chocolate eliminates the need for melting, which can be problematic for novice bakers.

DIRECTIONS

Heat the oven to 375°F. Spray an 8- or 9-inch round layer cake pan with baking spray.

Mix the butter, ⅔ cup fudge sauce, sugar, eggs, and almond extract in a bowl until smooth. Fold in the almonds until evenly dispersed, and pour the mixture into the pan; bake until the top is crusty and the edges are set but the center is still soft, about 35 minutes. Cool in the pan on a rack until comfortable to touch. Run a knife around the edge and invert onto a serving plate. Warm the remaining fudge sauce until flowing, and drizzle over the top before serving.

MAKES 12 SERVINGS

- 1 refrigerated 9-inch pie crust
- 1/3 cup dark brown sugar
- 1 jar (about 18 ounces) butterscotch or caramel dessert topping
- 6 tablespoons instant cappuccino coffee mix
- 1/4 teaspoon ground cinnamon
- 3 eggs, large or extra-large
- 2 cups (about 7 ounces) pecan halves

cappuccino pecan pie

If you find the typical pecan pie a wee bit too sweet, and you like your cappuccino dusty with cinnamon, and you believe that caramel deserves to be classified as its own food group, then this dessert is your destiny.

DIRECTIONS

Heat the oven to 350°F. Line a 9-inch pie plate with the crust. Turn under the edges and crimp, if desired. Scatter the brown sugar in an even layer across the bottom of the crust.

Combine the butterscotch topping, cappuccino mix, cinnamon, and eggs in a bowl until blended. Stir in the pecans and pour into the crust. Bake until the top is set and browned and the filling is still soft in its center, about 35 minutes. Let cool on a rack for at least 30 minutes before slicing. Serve warm or at room temperature.

PREPARED PIE CRUST

Although mixing up pastry dough is simple, it is not easy. Doing it well takes practice, and those who don't practice probably should purchase. If you are someone who makes beautiful pastry with little effort, there is no reason for you ever to buy a prepared pie crust, but for the rest of the known universe there are some high-quality options, over which no one need hang her head in shame. There are frozen pie shells in pans, both baked and unbaked; refrigerated pie dough rolled into rounds; paper-thin layers of phyllo; boxes of pie crust mix; and frozen puff pastry sheets that are of such high quality and so easy to use that only a culinary masochist would choose to make it from scratch. For a standard round 8- or 9-inch pie shell, I suggest refrigerated pastry rounds. They are a step up from frozen pie crust in the pan, which tends to be chipped and freezer burnt. If you don't mind doing a little more work for a little better quality, try a box of pie crust mix (all you add is water), which requires rolling but is surprisingly flaky, very tender, and completely foolproof.

No-stick flour and oil baking spray

1   box (about 16 ounces)
    brownie mix

2   eggs, large or extra-large

⅓   cup brandy

¼   cup canola oil

2   pounds fruit and nut trail mix,
    with large pieces like apricots or
    bananas cut into small pieces

chocolate brandy fruitcake

I am not a fan of commercial fruitcakes—you know, the kind leaden with candied fruit and stale Brazil nuts. This dark, dense chocolate pâté is nothing like those mass-produced confectionery doorstops. It is made simply by adding brandy to a brownie mix and folding in a few packs of your favorite trail mix (I suggest the type with lots of dried fruit and nuts, avoiding those with weird extruded date bits and sugar-coated raisins).

DIRECTIONS

Heat the oven to 350°F. Coat a 10-inch tube pan with baking spray.

Mix all of the remaining ingredients in a large bowl until well blended; the mixture will be thick. Scrape into the prepared pan and bake until a tester inserted into the crest comes out with a moist crumb clinging to it, about 1 hour. Cool on a rack until the pan is comfortable to the touch. Run a knife around the edges of the cake (don't forget the tube), cover the top loosely with plastic wrap, and invert onto a plate. When you feel the cake drop onto the plate, remove the pan and invert onto a cooling rack to cool the rest of the way. Cut into thin slices and serve.

pineapple and blueberry cornbread

MAKES 8 SERVINGS

No-stick spray oil

1 box (about 15 ounces) cornbread mix

1 egg, large or extra-large

½ cup vegetable oil

¾ cup pineapple juice

1 can (about 14 ounces) blueberries in water, well drained, or 1 pound frozen blueberries, thawed and drained

The more you know about baking, the more interesting this simple breakfast bread becomes. Most of us are accustomed to blueberries in corn muffins, and we know that buttermilk makes baked goods more tender. The science behind the magic of baking with buttermilk has to do with the power of acids to break down the proteins in a batter that would otherwise make the resulting product tough. In this recipe the buttermilk is replaced with pineapple juice. The tenderizing effect is the same, and the flavor interplay between the blueberries and pineapple is delightful.

DIRECTIONS

Heat the oven to 375°F. Spray a 10-inch skillet with a metal handle with oil and place in the oven while you prepare the batter.

Beat the cornbread mix, egg, oil, and pineapple juice in a large bowl with a whisk until smooth and the consistency of unbeaten cream. Fold in the blueberries. Carefully remove the hot skillet from the oven, using a thick pot holder, and place it on a scorch-proof surface. Scrape the batter into the pan and smooth the surface. Bake until the top is golden and the center springs back to gentle pressure, about 30 minutes.

Cool on a wire rack in the skillet for 5 minutes before cutting into wedges and serving.

For the cake:

No-stick flour and oil baking spray

1 box (about 18 ounces) devil's food cake mix

2 tablespoons unsweetened cocoa powder

½ cup vegetable oil

2 cups unsweetened applesauce

3 large eggs, or ¾ cup liquid eggs

For the frosting:

2 containers (16 ounces each) marshmallow cream, such as Marshmallow Fluff

¼ cup ground cinnamon, preferably Saigon or Vietnamese

Pinch of cayenne pepper

applesauce chocolate layer cake with cinnamon frosting

This easy all-American cake has a lot going on behind the scenes. You won't taste the applesauce. So why is it there? It's the moisture, which is the same reason that carrots are in carrot cake and zucchini inhabits vegetable bread. As the cake sits, the sugar in the batter continuously draws moisture out of the fruit or vegetable, with the result that the cake will stay moist until the produce is desiccated.

DIRECTIONS

Heat the oven to 350ºF. Coat two 8- or 9-inch round layer cake pans with baking spray.

To make the cake, combine the cake mix and cocoa in a large mixing bowl, add the oil, applesauce, and eggs, and beat with a mixer on high or by hand for 2 minutes, until the batter is smooth and the consistency of lightly beaten cream. Divide between the prepared pans, and bake for 25 minutes for 9-inch layers, 30 minutes for 8-inch layers. The layers are done when they are springy in their centers. Let cool in the pans on racks for 15 minutes, then remove from the pans and cool completely on racks.

To make the frosting, place the marshmallow cream, cinnamon, and cayenne in a microwave-safe mixing bowl. Cover with plastic wrap and microwave at full power for 1 minute, until the mixture is warm and creamy. Stir to combine thoroughly.

When the cake layers are completely cool, spread a layer of frosting on top of one layer and top with the second layer. Frost the sides of the cake and then the top. (If the frosting becomes too stiff, warm in a microwave at full power for 20 seconds.) Transfer to a serving plate, cut into wedges, and serve.

MAKES 12 SERVINGS

1 jar (8 ounces) fig spread or preserves, preferably Adriatic Fig Spread

4 cups milk, any fat content

1 cup sugar

¼ teaspoon almond extract

½ teaspoon vanilla extract

2 tablespoons port wine

4 extra-large eggs, or 1 cup egg substitute

Croatia (formerly part of Yugoslavia) hugs the eastern shore of the Adriatic directly across from Italy. Its climate and agriculture are similar to those of northern Italy, but its gastronomic roots are more Slavic, Turkish, and Greek, influences that are deliciously embodied in the Adriatic Fig Spread that becomes the sauce for this elegant flan. Made from hand-picked Dalmatian figs, it is a natural preserve with just enough sugar to caramelize as the flan bakes, forming a glaze that plays magically with the perfume of port wine in the custard.

DIRECTIONS

Heat the oven to 350°F. Spread the fig spread over the bottom of a 10-inch shallow baking dish. Place in the oven for 5 to 8 minutes while you prepare the custard for the flan.

Combine the milk and sugar in a microwave-safe bowl, cover with plastic wrap, and microwave at full power for 4 minutes. Remove from the microwave and whisk in the extracts, wine, and eggs. Remove the prepared pan from the oven and ladle the custard into the pan; place in a larger pan and add enough water to the larger pan to come at least 1 inch up the side of the flan pan. Bake until a knife inserted in the center comes out clean, about 50 minutes.

Remove the baking dish from the pan of water and let cool to room temperature. Refrigerate until chilled before serving. To serve, run a knife around the edge of the custard, cover with a platter, and invert. As soon as you hear the flan drop into place, remove the pan. Serve cut into wedges.

1   can (about 15 ounces) apricot
    halves in syrup, heavy or light

1   cup frozen raspberries

1   spray can (about 8 ounces)
    sweetened whipped cream or
    nondairy topping

¼   cup toasted shelled pistachio
    nuts, coarsely chopped

apricot raspberry fool with toasted pistachios

"Fool" is an Old World name for an uncooked spur-of-the-moment pudding. This beautiful coral-colored fool is made with canned apricots, frozen raspberries, and prepared whipped cream. If you need a sophisticated dessert sometime within the next 10 minutes, this is the recipe for you.

DIRECTIONS

Drain about half of the syrup from the apricots. Combine the remaining contents of the can of apricots and the raspberries in a blender or food processor. Process until smooth and transfer to a bowl. Shake the can of whipped cream vigorously and squirt its contents into the bowl. Fold the fruit and whipped topping together until thoroughly blended, taking care to deflate the mixture as little as possible. Serve immediately in dessert bowls or wineglasses. Top liberally with pistachios. Or cover and chill for up to 24 hours and top with pistachios just before serving.

½   lemon

1   container (32 ounces) whole-milk
    ricotta cheese, drained

    Pinch of salt

1   cup confectioners' sugar

½   teaspoon vanilla extract

lemon ricotta mousse

Ricotta cheese is one of the most versatile ingredients you can have on hand. It is a pasta sauce and an instant light lunch, or in this case it is a mousse waiting to happen.

DIRECTIONS

Grate the zest (the colored skin) from the lemon with a fine grater. Squeeze the juice; you should have about 1 tablespoon. Combine the ricotta cheese, salt, sugar, and vanilla in a food processor and puree until smooth. Stir in the lemon zest and juice. Scrape into a serving dish or individual dessert dishes, cover, and chill for at least an hour. Serve within 48 hours.

No-stick spray oil

1   package (about 16 ounces) gingerbread mix

1   teaspoon ground black pepper

1/2   teaspoon ground chipotle pepper

1/8   teaspoon ground cayenne red pepper

2   teaspoons spicy brown mustard

1   egg, large or extra-large

1 1/4   cups apple juice

multi-pepper gingerbread

I grew up enamored with gingerbread. To my peewee palate it was mind-blowing compared to tamer, sweeter cakes. As I have matured, either gingerbread has gotten meeker or my taste buds have coarsened, because my childhood thrill goes unrealized with every gingerbread I try. All this has brought me to this version, which spikes a traditional gingerbread with black pepper and chiles. At last, nostalgia and innovation meet.

DIRECTIONS

Heat the oven to 350°F. Coat the interior of an 8-by-8-inch baking pan with oil.

Mix all of the remaining ingredients in a large bowl until well blended and the consistency of lightly beaten cream. Scrape into the prepared pan and bake until a tester inserted into the center comes out with a moist crumb clinging to it, about 35 minutes. Cool on a rack until the pan is comfortable to the touch. Remove from the pan and set on a cooling rack to cool the rest of the way before serving.

No-stick flour and oil baking spray

1   box (about 18 ounces) spice cake mix

1½ cups chai tea latte concentrate, such as Oregon Chai

⅓   cup nut oil, such as walnut oil

3   eggs, large or extra-large

8   slices crystallized ginger, finely diced (about ½ cup; optional)

1   cup prepared whipped cream cheese icing

spiced chai tea cake

Chai is black tea infused with spice cake spices—cinnamon, ginger, cardamom, clove, allspice, and mace. So it seemed a logical experiment to introduce it into a spice cake recipe. The results were surprising. The cake didn't get spicier. Instead, it became more complex in flavor, subtler and wonderfully floral.

DIRECTIONS

Heat the oven to 350°F. Spray the interior of a nonstick Bundt pan with baking spray.

Combine the cake mix, 1⅓ cups chai concentrate, oil, and eggs in a large bowl and beat until smooth and fluffy, about 2 minutes. Stir in the candied ginger, if desired. Spoon into the Bundt pan and bake until a tester inserted in the crest of the cake comes out clean, about 40 minutes. Cool in the pan for at least 20 minutes. Invert the cake onto a serving plate and cool to room temperature.

Mix the icing with the remaining chai concentrate and drizzle over the top of the cake, allowing the glaze to run down the sides in rivulets. Slice and serve.

CHAI CONCENTRATE

Chai is brewed from a blend of black tea, honey, sugar, and various spices, usually cardamom, ginger, cinnamon, cloves, and sometimes pepper. It is served mixed with warm milk throughout Southeast Asia. About 10 years ago, chai started to be manufactured commercially in the United States. Now it is available in tea bags, as liquid tea, instant tea, and most commonly as a tea concentrate. Chai concentrate can be used full strength in cooking or mixed with an equal amount of milk and drunk as a beverage. Although it is frequently made with organic ingredients and marketed under a healthful halo, don't be deceived. Chai is a sweetened beverage like any other, and its calorie content is nearly twice that of commercial soda pop.

No-stick spray oil

3 meyer lemons, or regular lemons or limes

1 box (16 ounces) pound cake mix

2 tablespoons poppy seeds

2 eggs, large or extra-large

Fruited dulce de leche (page 332), for serving (optional)

meyer lemon poppy seed cake

Meyer lemons don't taste like lemons. Their flavor is closer to tangerine, with a lot of the same brightness as lime about them. This cake is similar to a lemon poppy seed cake, but more subtle and perfumed. Feel free to substitute another citrus juice if you can't find Meyer lemons.

DIRECTIONS

Heat the oven to 350°F. Coat the interior of an 8-by-4-by-2½-inch loaf pan with cooking spray.

Grate the zest (the colored skin) from the lemons with a fine grater. Squeeze the juice from the lemons and add enough water to make ¾ cup.

Combine the cake mix, lemon zest, lemon juice, poppy seeds, and eggs in a large bowl, and beat by hand for about 4 minutes or with an electric mixer for 3 minutes, until the batter is silky, thick, and smooth. Pour into the prepared pan and bake until a tester inserted in the crack comes out clean, 45 to 50 minutes. Cool in the pan for at least 10 minutes; remove from the pan and cool on a rack to room temperature. Slice and serve with Fruited Dulce de Leche, if desired.

1   tablespoon unsalted butter

1   large package (about 1 pound)
    refrigerated cinnamon rolls with
    icing (not cream cheese icing)

2   cans (about 14 ounces each)
    sliced peaches in heavy
    syrup, drained

½   teaspoon ground cinnamon

cinnamon peach upside-down coffee cake

I learned about making a variety of coffee cakes using refrigerated cinnamon rolls from Melanie Barnard (she's explored the subject intensely in her book *Ready, Set, Dough*). While working out the possibilities, I noticed that some products came with a separate packet of icing, and it dawned on me that I might be able to make a streamlined version of an upside-down cake by caramelizing the icing in the bottom of a skillet and topping it with fruit and the cut-up rolls. It's spectacular.

DIRECTIONS

Heat the oven to 375°F.

Melt the butter over medium heat in a 10-inch nonstick skillet with an oven-safe handle. Spoon the icing from the cinnamon roll package into the skillet and melt over the bottom of the pan; continue cooking until the edges are browned and the center has turned a medium beige color. Remove from the heat.

Arrange the peach slices radiating from the center of the pan in concentric circles. Scatter any pieces that don't fit neatly in the pattern over the top. Sprinkle with the cinnamon. Cut each cinnamon roll into 6 wedges and arrange evenly over the surface of the peaches, leaving no more than ½ inch between pieces. Place in the oven and bake until browned and bubbling at the edges, 25 to 30 minutes; let rest for 5 minutes.

Cover with a platter and invert. Rap the top with the butt end of a knife to help loosen any slices of peach that might be clinging to the pan. Remove the pan; if any peach slices are still in the pan, lift them out with a spatula and replace on the top of the cake. Cool for 5 minutes before serving.

No-stick oil spray

1 box (about 14 ounces) banana bread mix

½ cup chai tea latte concentrate, such as Oregon Chai

¼ cup honey

3 tablespoons canola oil

2 eggs, large or extra-large

½ cup raisins

½ cup walnut pieces

honey banana cake

The difference between a sweet bread and a plain cake is one of semantics. Serve this moist, honeyed, perfumed banana cake-bread as an elaboration on breakfast, a simplification of dessert, or an exotic snack.

DIRECTIONS

Heat the oven to 350°F. Coat the interior of an 8-by-4-by-2½-inch loaf pan with cooking spray.

Mix all of the remaining ingredients in a large bowl until well blended; the batter will be the consistency of lightly beaten cream. Scrape into the prepared pan and bake until a tester inserted into the crest comes out with a moist crumb clinging to it, about 30 minutes. Cool on a rack until the pan is comfortable to the touch. Remove from the pan and set on a cooling rack to cool the rest of the way. Transfer to a serving plate; slice and serve.

BUYING AND STORING HONEY

Honey is sold in four forms:

• **Comb honey** is a piece of honey-filled beeswax comb that is completely unprocessed. Because of that, it has more flavor than a processed honey but is prone to the activity of sugar-fermenting yeasts, which are always present in honey.

• **Liquid honey** is centrifugally extracted from the comb, heated to around 160°F to destroy any yeasts, strained to remove pieces of wax and other debris, and finally filtered to remove pollen grains and small air bubbles, which could cause the honey to cloud. Honeys that are filtered and heated are better at resisting crystallization during storage, but any enzymes that were in the honey are destroyed by such processing.

• **Crystallized (creamy) honey** is a mixture of liquid honey and a small amount of finely crystallized honey that is cooled until it solidifies into a spreadable paste.

• **Chunk honey** is a piece of honeycomb in a jar with liquid honey poured around it.

All sugars liquefy as their temperature rises and solidify as they cool; honey is no exception. Creamy honey will become liquid when heated, and liquid honey will crystallize when refrigerated or stored at room temperature for a long time. If honey should become cloudy or crystallized, heating it briefly in a microwave will clarify and liquefy it. Be careful to make sure it doesn't boil; honey burns easily.

No-stick flour and oil baking spray

2   sticks (1/2 pound) cold unsalted butter, cut into tablespoon-size chunks

2   cups sugar

2   tablespoons finely grated orange zest, or 1/4 teaspoon orange extract

2   tablespoons vanilla extract

8   eggs, large or extra-large

2   boxes (8 ounces each) corn-muffin mix

1/3 cup orange juice

1/2 cup bourbon

bourbon-soaked orange cornmeal cake

If you haven't guessed it already, I am a cornmeal zealot. I love the textural shift it provides in a sweet cake. We have become so used to aerated fluff when it comes to cake that getting a bite of cake with grit is downright spiritually cleansing. This one is moistened with orange-flavored bourbon syrup after it comes out of the oven.

DIRECTIONS

Heat the oven to 350°F. Spray the interior of a nonstick Bundt pan with baking spray.

Place the butter in a large microwave-safe bowl and microwave for 15 seconds. Beat until creamy. Add 1½ cups of the sugar and the orange zest and beat until the sugar and butter are well combined. Mix in the vanilla and eggs until homogenous; don't worry if the batter looks slightly split. Beat in the corn-muffin mix (the batter will have the consistency of wet mud) and pour into the prepared pan. Bake until springy in the center, about 45 minutes. Cool in the pan for 5 minutes before inverting onto a rimmed platter.

While the cake is cooling, combine the remaining ½ cup sugar, the orange juice, and half of the bourbon in a skillet. Heat to boiling and boil until the surface is filled with big, bursting bubbles, 2 to 3 minutes. Remove from the heat and add the remaining bourbon. Poke holes all over the cake with a toothpick or a skewer. Spoon the bourbon syrup over the cake while it is still warm. Transfer to a serving plate; slice and serve.

No-stick flour and oil baking spray

1   box (about 1 pound) brownie mix

2   cups (about 8 ounces) shelled
    nuts, such as whole almonds,
    walnut haves, pecan halves,
    or hazelnuts

3   extra-large eggs

¼   teaspoon almond extract

brownie biscotti

No one will guess that these intense chocolate crisps were made from a mix. A word of warning about brownie mixes. It used to be that they all came in a 16-ounce box and made a square pan of brownies (the size was so universal that a square baking pan became known as a brownie pan). Now, however, they've been super-sized. A family-size box of brownie mix makes a larger pan and is too much for this recipe. If that is the brownie mix you bought, you can increase the nuts to 2½ cups, the almond extract by a drop, and the eggs by about half an egg (I know this sounds ridiculous, but it's the only way it works). Bake it in a 9-by-13-inch pan; the baking time will be the same.

DIRECTIONS

Heat the oven to 350°F. Spray a 9-by-9-inch baking dish with baking spray.

Toss the brownie mix and nuts together in a large mixing bowl. If the brownie mix contains a package of chocolate syrup, reserve it for another use. Mix in the eggs and almond extract until all of the dry ingredients have been moistened and a stiff batter forms. Scrape into the pan and pack into an even layer. Bake until the cake is firm in the center, about 35 minutes. Remove from the oven and let cool for 15 minutes.

Cover with a cutting board, invert, and remove the pan. Cool for another 5 minutes. Cut the cake into 3 strips, scoring the surface with a serrated knife and finishing cutting through with a large chopping knife; then cut each strip into 10 or 11 rectangular strips, using the same method. Return the strips to the pan, setting each on one of its narrow sides, like dominoes, leaving about ¼ inch between cookies. To fit them all in the pan you will have to make two layers. Just rest the top layer across the bottom layer. Return to the oven and bake until the cookies are crisp on all sides, about 25 minutes more. Cool on a rack before serving.

No-stick flour and oil baking spray

1   egg white or 3 tablespoons liquid
    egg substitute

1/4   teaspoon almond extract

1   package (18 ounces/20 cookies)
    refrigerated sugar cookie dough

1   package (8 ounces) pine nuts

pignoli biscuits

These pine nut–laden plain cookies are *molto Italiano*–delicately crisp and inundated with the heady, piney scent of pignoli. No one will guess they are made with refrigerated dough. They are very attractive when dusted with confectioners' sugar while they are still slightly warm.

DIRECTIONS

Heat the oven to 325°F. Coat a cookie sheet with baking spray, or line it with a sheet of parchment or a silicone baking sheet, such a Silpat sheet.

Combine the egg white and almond extract in a small bowl. Form the cookie dough into 40 balls. Coat the balls one at a time with egg white and dredge in the pine nuts until each cookie is completely coated with nuts. Fill in any bald spots with nuts by hand, and place the cookie on the cookie sheet. Continue making cookies with the rest of the dough, placing the balls about 1½ inches apart. You will have enough dough to make about 3 batches. Bake until the cookies are golden brown and the nuts have just begun to color, about 15 minutes. Cool on the pan for a few minutes before removing to a cooling rack with a small spatula. Keep tightly covered.

MAKES 6 SERVINGS

2 cups half-and-half or cream

1 cup sugar

1 cup basil leaves, finely chopped

Pinch of salt

1 teaspoon vanilla extract

1 container (15 ounces) whole-milk ricotta cheese

basil ricotta ice cream

It has become chic to infuse herbal flavors into traditional sweet preparations. Often the effect is awkward and forced, but basil shows promise. There are hundreds of varieties of edible basils, and many of them lend themselves to being used in sweets. Common European basil (the most prolific variety in the States) has an anise flavor that is wonderful in this ice cream. But equally good are lemon, lime, or cinnamon basil. Whatever type you use, you will be able to enjoy the lovely pale green pastel of this remarkable ice cream. (It is unbelievable with the Chipotle Cherry Pie on page 305.)

DIRECTIONS

Heat the half-and-half, sugar, basil, and salt in a saucepan until the sugar is dissolved and the mixture is simmering. Set aside for 5 minutes and pass through a strainer to remove the basil. Puree the basil-infused cream with the vanilla and ricotta cheese in a food processor until smooth and creamy. Pour into a shallow baking pan and freeze until solid, at least 4 hours.

Cut the frozen mixture into small squares; puree in a food processor in 2 batches until the mixture comes together into a ball. Store in a tightly closed container and serve with an ice cream scoop. If the mixture should become too solid to scoop, thaw for a few seconds in a microwave.

1   large can (about 30 ounces) apricot halves in heavy syrup

½   teaspoon sweet vinegar, such as maple, vanilla, or aged balsamic

apricot sorbet

This easy method of making sorbet can be done with any canned fruit in syrup. Try pears with a little vanilla, peaches with raspberry vinegar, litchis with pickled ginger, or pineapple with a touch of sherry vinegar.

DIRECTIONS

Place the can of apricots in the freezer and freeze until solid, at least overnight. No more than 2 hours before serving, run the frozen can under warm water to thaw the edges. Remove the top and bottom of the can and slide the contents into a large bowl. Chop into coarse chunks and puree in a food processor with the vinegar until chopped finely enough to form a smooth ball. Store in a tightly closed container in the freezer for up to 24 hours. If the mixture should freeze solid, puree it again to refresh it.

1   can (about 15 ounces) pears in heavy syrup

1   can (about 16 ounces) jellied cranberry sauce

1   teaspoon lime juice, fresh or organic bottled

pear and cranberry sorbet

This not-too-sweet crimson-hued sorbet is less intense than cranberry sauce and not as timid as poached pears. It is great for dessert but could also be served as a fanciful palate cleanser after the Thanksgiving meal.

DIRECTIONS

Puree the pears with their syrup, the cranberry sauce, and the lime juice in a food processor or blender until completely smooth. Pour into a shallow pan and freeze until solid, about 4 hours or longer. Cut into cubes, and puree in a food processor until creamy. Store in a tightly closed container in the freezer for up to 1 week. If the mixture should become solid, puree it again before serving.

- -

1   package (18 ounces) refrigerated
    sugar cookie dough

1   jar (8 ounces) red pepper puree
    or spread

1   cup confectioners' sugar

    Pinch of grated nutmeg

1   teaspoon lemon juice, fresh or
    bottled organic

½   cup (2 ounces) chopped
    pistachio nuts

sweet red pepper tart

Recently in Rome I was taken to a very small trattoria that is known for its desserts. The owner recommended a flat cake glazed with red jam on the dessert cart and challenged me to identify the fruit in the glaze. I couldn't, and his answer, "peperoni," which of course I heard as "pepperoni," made no sense. But after the third bite I caught on. It was red bell pepper, sweetened with enough sugar to obscure its vegetable identity and reveal its true botanical roots. Like a tomato, or an eggplant, or an apple, a bell pepper is a fruit, and in the context of this cake, it was a revelation. Needless to say, I started experimenting as soon as I returned home, and this recipe is one of the results. Streamlined by the use of jarred red pepper spread and refrigerated cookie dough, it is effortless to prepare, and one of the most sophisticated desserts you may ever encounter.

DIRECTIONS

Heat the oven to 375°F. The cookie dough will be divided into 20 squares; press 14 of those squares into an even layer in the bottom of a 9-inch tart or pie pan. Bake until the dough is just beginning to brown at the edge, about 12 minutes.

- -

Meanwhile, mix the remaining cookie dough, the red pepper puree, sugar, nutmeg, and lemon juice in a bowl. Spread over the baked dough, leaving ¼ inch exposed at the perimeter, and bake until the edge of the pepper spread has formed a skin, about 12 minutes more. Sprinkle the pistachios over the top and bake for 10 more minutes. Cool completely. You can dust the tart with more confectioners' sugar before serving, if you want.

THE SWEET SIDE OF PEPPER SPREAD

Red pepper puree, red pepper spread, red pepper pesto, and red pepper paste are all very similar products. Some may include the addition of garlic, hot pepper, eggplant, or herbs, and although such additions don't make a lot of difference in most recipes, they will in the Sweet Red Pepper Tart (facing page), so avoid spreads with a lot of herbs or garlic. A small amount won't matter and can even make the finished tart more interesting (for instance, a bit of hot pepper gives a tantalizing bite), but if herbs or garlic are high up in the ingredient list, you would do better to try a brand that is more or less pure red pepper (surprisingly, the presence of eggplant in the puree has very little effect on the flavor of the finished product). Remember, the addition of sugar enhances the fruitiness of the pepper puree and also obscures its savory qualities, so feel free to adjust the amount of sugar in the filling to taste.

2 tablespoons nut oil or melted unsalted butter

2 pounds frozen sliced peaches, thawed

3/4 cup granulated sugar

1/4 cup cornstarch

2 teaspoons balsamic vinegar

1 1/2 pounds frozen raspberries

8 ounces prepared cornbread, crumbled (2 cups crumbs)

1 1/4 cups candied or glazed nuts, pecans or walnuts, broken

1/3 cup light brown sugar

1/2 teaspoon ground cinnamon

peach and raspberry cornbread crumble

Regardless of what you call them—cobblers, crumbles, pandowdies, or brown betties—whenever you bake fruit topped with a crust it is helpful to get the fruit cooked a little before the crust goes on. Otherwise the interior remains wet and the topping gets soggy.

DIRECTIONS

Heat the oven to 400°F. Grease a 9-by-13-inch baking dish with 1 teaspoon of the oil or butter.

Combine the peaches, granulated sugar, cornstarch, and vinegar in a bowl until the dry ingredients are dissolved and the peaches are evenly coated. Add the raspberries and toss gently to combine. Pack the fruit into the baking dish, and bake until the edges are bubbling and the top looks dry, about 40 minutes.

Meanwhile, spread the cornbread crumbs on a sheet pan and bake in the oven until slightly toasted, about 5 minutes. Mix the toasted crumbs with the nuts, brown sugar, cinnamon, and remaining oil or butter. Top the baked fruit with the crumb mixture in an even layer that covers the entire surface. Bake until the top is browned and the juices are bubbling vigorously, 10 to 15 minutes more. Let cool for at least 15 minutes before serving.

1   container (about 15 ounces)
    ricotta cheese, whole milk or
    part-skim

1/3 cup honey

3/4 teaspoon vanilla extract

1/2 cup (about 2 ounces)
    sliced almonds

1   cup (about 6 ounces) semisweet
    chocolate mini-morsels

12 cinnamon graham crackers,
    broken in half

1   box (3.4 ounces) instant banana
    cream pudding mix

1/8 teaspoon ground cinnamon

1   large bottle (about 14 ounces)
    creamy coffee-flavored drink,
    such as Starbucks Frappuccino

1/4 cup molasses

1   cup strong coffee

cannoli ice cream sandwiches

Because ricotta cheese is naturally creamy and thick, it can be
turned into an ice cream just by sweetening it and smoothing its
grainy texture in a food processor. The result is something like
frozen cannoli filling. To enhance the cannoli association, the
ricotta ice cream is loaded up with chocolate chips and almonds
and sandwiched between cookies.

DIRECTIONS

Combine the ricotta, honey, and vanilla, and pour into a shallow
container. Freeze until solid, about 4 hours or longer, cut into cubes,
and puree in a food processor until creamy. Mix in the almonds
and the chocolate morsels and make sandwiches by layering
2 tablespoons of the ice cream mixture between 2 graham cracker
squares. Freeze until ready to serve.

banoffee ice cream

The combination of banana and coffee seems idiosyncratic, but it
has caught on in restaurants under the name "banoffee." Dessert
menus are riddled with banoffee pies, and mousses, and layer
cakes. Here's an easy banoffee ice cream made with banana pudding and a bottle of creamy coffee-flavored drink.

DIRECTIONS

Mix the pudding, cinnamon, and coffee drink with a mixing whisk
until blended and thick, about 2 minutes. Stir in the molasses
and coffee, and pour into a wide, shallow pan, such as a layer cake
pan. Cover and freeze until solid, at least 8 hours. Puree in 2
batches in a food processor until smooth. Store in the freezer for
up to 6 hours before serving.

No-stick spray oil

3 tablespoons unsalted butter

1 package (about 10 ounces) mini-marshmallows

½ teaspoon apple cider vinegar

6 cups raisin bran cereal, crumbled

1 cup (about 6 ounces) semisweet chocolate mini-morsels

raisin bran brownies

These are a hearty rendition of the familiar squares made from crispy rice cereal. The only difference between these and the recipe on the cereal box is the choice of cereal and the addition of cider vinegar, which cuts the sweetness and enhances the flavor of raisins.

DIRECTIONS

Coat a 9-by-13-inch baking pan with spray oil.

Melt the butter in a large pot over medium-high heat. Add the marshmallows and stir until melted. Stir in the vinegar and remove from the heat. Stir in the cereal and chocolate chips until completely coated with the marshmallow mixture. Pack into the prepared baking pan and let cool until set, at least 30 minutes. Cut into 36 squares (a 6-by-6 grid) and serve.

No-stick flour and oil baking spray

1   box (about 15 ounces) cornbread mix (*not* corn-muffin mix)

3/4 cup light brown sugar

1   pound (about 3 1/2 cups) pecan halves

5   large eggs, or 1 cup liquid egg substitute

1   teaspoon vanilla extract

praline cornbread biscotti

These caramel-nuanced whole-grain dipping cookies are filled with pecans. The combination of brown sugar and pecans gives the impression of praline (caramelized sugar and nuts), without the trouble of making the candy.

DIRECTIONS

Heat the oven to 350ºF. Coat the interior of a 9-by-13-inch glass baking dish with baking spray.

Combine the cornbread mix, sugar, and pecans in a large bowl. Add the eggs and vanilla, and mix with a large fork until the dry ingredients have been moistened (if the batter is crumbly, add a little more egg or a teaspoon of milk). Scrape the batter into the dish and flatten into an even layer, using a spatula or the back of a wide wooden spoon. Bake until a tester inserted in the center comes out clean, about 30 minutes.

Remove the pan from the oven. Cover with a cutting board, invert, and remove the pan. Let cool for 15 minutes. Cut the cake in half lengthwise, scoring the surface with a serrated knife and then cutting through with a straight-edge knife. Cut each half into 15 to 16 rectangular strips. Return the strips to the pan, setting each on one of its narrow sides, like dominoes. You might have to make a second layer to fit all of the biscotti in the pan. Return to the oven to bake until golden brown and crisp, about 25 minutes more.

CORNBREAD MIXES

You will notice that this recipe specifies cornbread mix rather than corn-muffin mix. The reason is subtle and affects only hard, crisp baked goods, like biscotti. Cornbreads are baked in wide pans and need the strength of protein-rich flour to maintain their structure as they rise. Muffins, on the other hand, are small, and don't need much structure to maintain their shape, so muffin mix contains flour that is high in starch to ensure fluffy results. Since soft and fluffy are the antithesis of biscotti, most corn-muffin mixes won't work in this recipe.

No-stick flour and oil baking spray

1/4 cup vegetable oil

2 eggs, large or extra-large

1 cup light brown sugar

1 teaspoon vanilla extract

1 tablespoon instant espresso powder

Pinch of salt

1/2 teaspoon baking powder

1 cup toasted wheat germ

1 cup chopped walnuts

espresso wheat germ brownies

These flourless brownies are held together by one of the most fibrous of grain products, wheat germ. Wheat germ has a pronounced roasted flavor that is enhanced by other caramelized and browned elements. So the additions of dark coffee and brown sugar are natural. The brownies are exceptionally chewy and will stay moist for at least a week, kept tightly wrapped.

DIRECTIONS

Heat the oven to 350°F. Coat an 8-by-8-inch baking pan with baking spray.

Mix the oil, eggs, sugar, vanilla, espresso powder, salt, and baking powder in a bowl until blended. Stir in the wheat germ and walnuts and scrape into the prepared baking pan. Bake until the surface is dry and a tester inserted in the center comes out clean, about 35 minutes. Cool for at least 20 minutes before cutting into 2-inch squares and serving.

chocolate coconut ice cream

This easy homemade ice cream is dairy-free (great for lactose-intolerant baby boomers). I keep a can of cream of coconut in my freezer so that I can whip up this exotic and delicious frozen confection whenever the mood strikes.

MAKES 4 SERVINGS

1 can (about 14 ounces) cream of coconut

2 ounces semisweet chocolate, melted and cooled

⅓ cup strong coffee or prepared instant coffee

1 tablespoon fresh lime juice

DIRECTIONS

Place the cream of coconut in the freezer until frozen solid, about 24 hours. It is fine to leave the can in the freezer for weeks so that you can make this dessert anytime.

Run the can under warm water for a minute. Open the can at both ends and push the contents onto a cutting board. Cut into pieces and place in the work bowl of a food processor. Add the remaining ingredients and process until smooth. Scrape into a plastic container, cover tightly, and freeze for up to 24 hours. Serve in scoops. If the ice cream should freeze hard, process it again to make it scoopable.

cinnamon caramel baked apples

These burnished baked apples are infused with cinnamon-scented caramel. The caramel is baked into the apples until they tinge with brown, and then a thin glaze is gilded over the top.

MAKES 6 SERVINGS

⅔ cup butterscotch caramel dessert topping

1 tablespoon ground cinnamon

Pinch of salt

1 tablespoon brandy, or 1 teaspoon apple cider vinegar

6 large Rome apples, cored through their stem ends, bottoms left intact

½ cup raisins

DIRECTIONS

Heat the oven to 375°F. Mix the caramel topping, cinnamon, salt, and brandy in a bowl. Set the apples, cored-side up, in a large pie plate or other flat baking dish. Fill the cavity of each apple with raisins. Spoon about half of the caramel mixture over the apples and bake for 30 minutes. Baste with half of the remaining sauce and bake until the caramel is lightly browned and the apples are tender, about 20 minutes more. Cool for at least 10 minutes and top with the remaining sauce. Serve warm.

1   can (14 ounces) sweetened condensed milk, regular, low-fat, or fat free

2/3 cup tart juice like pomegranate, cranberry, or citrus juice

fruited dulce de leche

Dulce de leche is caramelized sweetened milk that is used as flavoring or as a sauce. This recipe is of the sauce variety. It is almost effortless to make at home: just heat an opened can of condensed milk in the oven until it browns. This one is flavored with fruit juice, which cuts the sweetness and gives it an added flavor dimension. It is wonderful to pour over a plain cake, such as the Meyer Lemon Poppy Seed Cake on page 316.

DIRECTIONS

Heat the oven to 425°F.

Pour the condensed milk into a pie pan and cover with foil, crimping any overlap tightly around the edges of the pan, and place in a larger pan of water. Bake until the milk turns a golden brown, about 1 hour. Remove the pie pan from its water bath and mix the milk with a whisk until smooth. Add the juice and stir until fully incorporated. Serve warm or at room temperature. Store in the refrigerator for up to 1 week.

CANNED DAIRY

Concentrated milk was one of the first industrially processed food products. In 1853, Gail Borden started manufacturing boiled concentrated milk mixed with large amounts of sugar to keep it from spoiling. It was used to help feed the military during the Civil War and is an important source of dairy in areas of the world where refrigeration is uncommon. Unsweetened sterilized evaporated milk came about in 1884 in Switzerland.

Both unsweetened and sweetened canned milk are made by heating raw milk under a partial vacuum so that it boils at about 120°F, causing it to lose about half its water content without overcoagulating its protein. The concentration of lactose and protein causes the milk to darken slightly, giving evaporated milk a light tan cast. Sweetened condensed milk is made by adding sugar to evaporated milk until the contents are about 55 percent sugar. Since microbes can't grow in such an environment, sterilization is not necessary. This is why sweetened milk is whiter than evaporated milk and has a less cooked flavor.

no-bake lemon strawberry pie

1 box (about 3 ounces) lemon-flavored gelatin

¾ cup boiling water

3 containers (6 ounces each, 2¼ cups total) vanilla yogurt, preferably low-fat

¼ teaspoon mint extract

1 prepared 9-inch graham cracker or other cookie crust, about 6 ounces

12 large strawberries, greens trimmed, halved lengthwise

Although I do not usually contaminate dessert with diet concerns, this easy yogurt cream pie tempts me to do so. It has a thimbleful of fat (less than 3 grams) and less sugar than a lollipop; plus it packs 5 grams of protein in every slice. But that's not why you should try it; make it for the bright lemon flavor and the lighter-than-air texture.

DIRECTIONS

Dissolve the gelatin in the boiling water in a bowl, stirring until the mixture is completely clear. Add ½ cup to the yogurt and mint extract, stirring until completely combined. Pour into the crust, cover with plastic wrap, and chill until firm, at least 2 hours.

Arrange the strawberry halves, cut-sides down, over the top of the pie. Warm the remaining gelatin in a microwave until fluid and brush over the strawberries. Refrigerate until ready to serve.

appendix
homemade convenience

I know how frustrating it is when your local market doesn't carry one of the ingredients in a recipe, and that is why this appendix is here. All of these ingredients (except for the caramelized onions) are available in packaged form. But for the rare occasion when you have to make one of them from scratch, here's how to do it.

2   pounds large yellow onions

2   tablespoons olive oil

1/2 teaspoon kosher salt

1/4 teaspoon ground black pepper

2   tablespoons water

roasted caramelized onions

Although roasted garlic products abound, no one, as yet, has manufactured and marketed a roasted onion. One day a savvy produce packager will figure this out and reap the rewards, but until then we will have to make our own. Fortunately, the process is easy, and the finished onions will keep well in a closed container in the refrigerator for about 2 weeks.

DIRECTIONS

Heat the oven to 400°F. Cut the onions in half. Lay them on their cut sides and cut off the pointed ends; remove the dry layers. Trim the root end so that all the roots and dirt are gone but the core holding the layers of onion together is still attached. Cut each onion half into 6 to 8 thin wedges.

Toss the onions, olive oil, salt, and pepper on a large, rimmed sheet pan and spread out in an even layer. Roast for 30 minutes, tossing the onions halfway through to help them caramelize evenly. When they are done they will be browned on their edges.

Remove from the oven and sprinkle the water over the top. Toss to combine, using the moisture to scrape any brown bits stuck to the bottom of the pan into the onions. Refrigerate in a tightly closed container for up to 2 weeks. Use in any preparation calling for caramelized or roasted onions.

1   large bell pepper, any color

roasted peppers

Although this recipe is written for a single pepper, it's just as easy to roast a bunch as it is one. If roasting them on a gas burner, you should be able to fit two per burner.

DIRECTIONS

Place the pepper directly onto the grate of a gas burner set on high, at the highest setting of a broiler, or over a hot grill. As the skin on one side of the pepper burns, turn it over until the skin is uniformly burnt. Be careful to keep it moving so that the flesh under the skin doesn't char. Place the pepper in a paper bag or a bowl, close the bag or cover the bowl, and set aside until cool.

When the pepper is cool enough to handle, peel off the burnt skin. Bits of skin will stick to your hands; rinse them under cold water as you peel, but try not to run the pepper under water, because some of its flavor will get washed away. Remove the stems and seeds and cut the flesh of the pepper however you want.

Store roasted peppers in the refrigerator for up to 1 week. This recipe can be multiplied for as many peppers as you want to roast.

3   whole heads garlic

1   tablespoon olive oil

roasted caramelized garlic

Roasted garlic is sold in whole cloves, chopped, and minced. But if you don't have any, it's fairly easy to make yourself. It can be refrigerated or frozen.

DIRECTIONS

Heat the oven to 400°F. Cut the pointed ends off the garlic heads, exposing most of the cloves. Place each garlic head cut-side up on a 6-inch square of aluminum foil, drizzle each with 1 teaspoon of the oil, and wrap the foil around the garlic so that it is completely enclosed. Place near the middle of the oven and roast for 30 minutes.

Unwrap and let cool for 10 minutes. Peel the papery skin from the roasted garlic cloves. Refrigerate in a tightly closed container for up to 2 weeks. Use in any recipe calling for roasted garlic.

basil pesto

Jarred pesto is widely available and of good quality, but if you want to make your own here is how to do it.

MAKES ¾ CUP,
about 12 servings

4   ounces fresh basil, stems removed

4   cloves garlic, coarsely chopped

2   tablespoons toasted pine nuts, pretoasted or homemade (page 340)

½   cup extra-virgin olive oil

⅓   cup freshly grated imported Parmesan cheese

Salt and ground black pepper to taste

DIRECTIONS

Chop the basil and garlic finely in a food processor. Add the pine nuts, olive oil, Parmesan, salt, and pepper and process in pulses until well blended. Use immediately or store in the refrigerator for up to 1 week.

muffaletta or olive salad

Jarred muffaletta is a great way to deliver instant pizzazz to a salad, pizza, or pasta. If you can't find it on your grocer's shelves, here is how to make it. It will keep in the refrigerator for longer than you would.

MAKES 2 CUPS

1   medium onion, finely chopped

3   tablespoons olive oil

3   cloves garlic, minced

1   can (about 15 ounces) diced tomatoes, drained

½   cup chopped pitted oil-cured black olives (about 20)

½   cup chopped pitted Spanish olives (about 14)

2   tablespoons chopped fresh basil leaves

Salt and ground black pepper to taste

DIRECTIONS

Cook the onion in 1 tablespoon of the oil in a large skillet over medium heat until it is tender, about 4 minutes. Add the garlic and tomatoes and cook over high heat until the tomatoes release their juice but still remain in visible pieces, 2 to 3 minutes. Remove from the heat; add the olives, basil, remaining 2 tablespoons oil, salt, and pepper. Use immediately or store in the refrigerator for up to 2 weeks.

1   cup whole almonds, hazelnuts, cashews, walnut halves, pine nuts, or pecan halves

toasted nuts

The microwave will not brown anything, except nuts. It's easy, it's fast, and it's foolproof.

DIRECTIONS

Place the nuts in a shallow glass pie pan or other microwave-safe dish that will hold them in a single layer. Cook at full power for 4 to 5 minutes, stirring twice, until the nuts are a shade darker and smell toasted.

1   cup hulled sesame seeds

toasted sesame seeds

It's easy to tell when sesame seeds are done toasting–just listen for the popping.

DIRECTIONS

Place the sesame seeds in a shallow glass pie pan or other microwave-safe dish that will hold them in a layer no thicker than ¼ inch. Cook at full power for 2 to 3 minutes, stirring once, until the seeds start popping, are a shade darker, and smell toasted.

½ cup sweetened shredded coconut

¼ teaspoon coarse sea salt or
    kosher salt

toasted coconut

Because shredded coconut is infused with sugar, it browns faster than most nuts do. Keep a close watch. It won't seem to be doing anything, and then all at once it will start to brown. As soon as that happens, give it a stir and you will have beautifully speckled toasted coconut.

DIRECTIONS

Spread the coconut on a microwave-safe plate large enough to hold it in a layer no thicker than ¼ inch. Cook at full power for 45 seconds. Toss with a fork and microwave in 20-second intervals until the coconut is spotted with brown, stirring occasionally. Toss with the salt.

3 ounces nuts (about ⅔ cup
   almonds or hazelnuts, or ¾ cup
   pecan or walnut halves)

nut meal

Nut meal (also called nut flour) is now sold in many markets in the baking aisle, housed either with the shelled nuts or with other flours. If you can't find it, making your own in a food processor couldn't be easier.

DIRECTIONS

Place the nuts in the work bowl of a food processor. Process in pulses until finely ground. Scrape the sides and bottom of the work bowl with a small spatula once during the process to ensure an even grind.

roasted winter vegetables

MAKES 6 SERVINGS

1 large red onion, halved and cut into ½-inch-thick wedges

1 large sweet potato, peeled, halved, and cut into wedges

2 carrots, peeled and cut into 1-inch chunks

1 package (8 ounces) sliced mushrooms

1 turnip, peeled and cut into bite-size chunks

2 tablespoons olive oil

Salt and ground black pepper to taste

1 teaspoon chopped garlic, fresh or jarred organic

Having a container of roasted vegetables in your refrigerator will do more to improve the way you cook than almost anything else I can think of. They are an elegant spur-of-the-moment side dish, but more importantly they will add instant flavor to soups, stews, and pan sauces.

DIRECTIONS

Heat the oven to 425ºF.

Toss the onion, sweet potato, carrots, mushrooms, and turnips together on a rimmed sheet pan. Add the oil and toss to coat; season liberally with salt and pepper. Roast for 30 minutes, add the garlic, and continue roasting for 5 minutes more, until the edges of most of the vegetables have browned and they are uniformly tender but not mushy. Serve at once as a side dish, or in any recipe calling for roasted vegetables. Store in a tightly covered container in the refrigerator for up to 1 week.

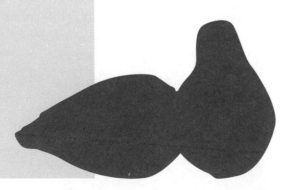

1 medium zucchini, cut into
½-inch slices

1 medium eggplant, cut into
1-inch chunks

1 red bell pepper, stemmed,
seeded, and cut into strips

1 package (8 ounces) sliced
mushrooms

1 cup chopped onion, frozen
or fresh

6 large plum tomatoes, each cut
into 6 wedges

2 tablespoons olive oil

Salt and ground black pepper
to taste

1 teaspoon chopped garlic,
fresh or jarred organic

roasted summer vegetables

Here is another roasted vegetable recipe for warm-weather vegetables. Toss them with vinaigrette for an instant salad.

DIRECTIONS

Heat the oven to 425ºF.

Toss the zucchini, eggplant, bell pepper, mushrooms, onion, and tomatoes together on a rimmed sheet pan. Add the oil and toss to coat; season liberally with salt and pepper. Roast for 15 minutes, add the garlic, and continue roasting for 5 minutes more, until the edges of most of the vegetables have browned and they are uniformly tender but not mushy. Serve at once as a side dish, or in any recipe calling for roasted vegetables. Store in a tightly covered container in the refrigerator for up to 1 week.

flavored oils

Here is an easy way to make any flavored oil. It is best stored in a cool, dark place, where it will stay fresh for several months. If you use a rich oil, like olive oil, it may turn opaque during storage; just warm it to clear it.

MAKES ABOUT 2 CUPS

2 cups oil, any type

1–2 cups flavorful stuff, such as dry herbs, chiles, sun-dried tomatoes, dried mushrooms, garlic, etc.

DIRECTIONS

Heat the oil until warm. Place the flavorful stuff in a sealable container. Pour the oil over the top, cover, and steep for at least 24 hours; strain. Store, tightly covered, at room temperature in a cool, dark place for up to 2 months.

flavored vinegars

Flavored vinegars are helpful for adding an aromatic tang to salads, soups, or sauces. They are also an instantaneous way to dress a grilled fish or chicken breast.

MAKES ABOUT 2 CUPS

2 cups vinegar, any type

1 cup flavorful stuff, such as herbs, chiles, fresh fruit, vanilla, maple sugar, etc.

DIRECTIONS

Heat the vinegar until warm. Place the flavorful stuff in a sealable container. Pour the vinegar over the top, cover, and steep for at least 24 hours; strain. Store, tightly covered, at room temperature for up to 2 months.

1 lemon, 1 lime, or 1 orange

citrus zest

Citrus zest is used frequently in baking, but it is also a brilliant way to deliver a bright citrus flavor to any sauce, stew, or soup without adding acid.

DIRECTIONS

Method 1: Rub the fruit against the finest teeth of a grater, turning the fruit so that you remove only the thin, colored skin. Try to avoid removing any of the white rind underneath.

Method 2: Peel the colored skin from the outside of the fruit, using a vegetable peeler, trying to avoid removing any of the white rind underneath. Chop the rind with a sharp knife into thin strips, or mince it, as desired.

Method 3: Remove the colored skin from the outside of the fruit, using a citrus zester, trying to avoid removing any of the white rind underneath. The zest will come off in thin strips; chop if desired.

1 pound fresh beets

Salt and ground black pepper
to taste

microwaved beets

If you think that beets taste like bitter dirt, chances are you have
only had them boiled, a technique that robs them of their sweetness. Roasting is a much better way to cook them, but it takes
hours. This method gives you the sweetness of roasting in a fraction of the time.

DIRECTIONS

Cut the leaves and stems from the beets, leaving about an inch
of stems. Wash the beets to remove any loose surface dirt; leave
wet. Snap off the "tail." Place in a microwave-safe bowl, season
with salt and pepper, cover with plastic wrap, and microwave at
full power until the beets are tender, 12 to 15 minutes.

When the beets are cooked, run them under cold water just until
they are cool enough to handle. Cut the stem end from each beet,
slip off the skin, and cut as desired. Serve at once as a side dish,
or in any recipe calling for roasted beets. Store in a tightly covered
container in the refrigerator for up to 1 week.

8   ounces (about 2 cups) wrinkly
    pitted black olives (preferably
    oil-cured)

3   cloves garlic, coarsely chopped

2   teaspoons finely chopped
    anchovy fillet or anchovy paste

¼   cup extra-virgin olive oil

    Salt and ground black pepper
    to taste

tapenade

Tapenade, the lush olive pesto of Provence, is widely available
in shelf-stable jars and refrigerated containers. If you must make
your own, here is a recipe.

DIRECTIONS

Combine the olives and garlic in a food processor and pulse until
coarsely chopped. Add the remaining ingredients and continue to
process in pulses until the mixture is blended but still has some
texture. Use immediately or store in the refrigerator for up to 2 months.

1   tablespoon vegetable oil, any type

¼   cup chopped onion, fresh
    or frozen

1   teaspoon minced garlic, fresh
    or jarred organic

1   teaspoon Chinese chili paste

1   tablespoon soy sauce

1   tablespoon minced ginger,
    fresh or jarred

½   teaspoon ground cumin

½   teaspoon ground coriander

½   cup creamy peanut butter

1   cup vegetable or chicken broth

2   scallions, trimmed and thinly sliced

thai peanut sauce

Peanut sauce, also called satay, has a long list of ingredients
but mixes up in minutes. You can also buy it jarred and in dehydrated packets.

DIRECTIONS

Heat the oil in a large skillet over medium heat. Add the onion
and cook until tender, about 3 minutes. Add the garlic and cook
for another minute. Add the remaining ingredients and stir until
the peanut butter is dissolved. Simmer until the sauce reaches a
creamy consistency, 2 or 3 minutes. Use immediately or store in
the refrigerator for up to 2 weeks.

hummus

MAKES ABOUT 2 CUPS

- 1 can (about 15 ounces) garbanzo beans (chickpeas)
- 2 tablespoons tahini (sesame paste)
- 2 cloves garlic, coarsely chopped
- 3 tablespoons fresh lemon juice
- 1 teaspoon kosher salt
- 1 tablespoon olive oil

Although tahini is essential to an authentic hummus, some people don't like its flavor. If that describes you, or you just don't have any tahini, you can omit it from the recipe, but if you do, use a little less of the bean liquid when pureeing the garbanzos.

DIRECTIONS

Drain the beans, retaining the liquid. Combine the beans, half the reserved bean liquid, the tahini, garlic, lemon juice, and salt in a food processor. Puree until smooth. If you want the hummus thinner, add more of the bean liquid. Transfer to a container, stir in the oil, and store in the refrigerator until needed, up to 2 weeks.

baba ghanouj

MAKES ABOUT 3 CUPS

- 1 large eggplant
- 1 teaspoon minced fresh garlic
- ½ cup olive oil
- 2 tablespoons fresh lemon juice
- 2 tomatoes, chopped
- 3 tablespoons chopped Italian (flat-leaf) parsley
- Salt and ground black pepper to taste

I use this smoky eggplant dip for thickening sauces and flavoring soups as well as using it as an easy appetizer and sandwich spread.

DIRECTIONS

Heat the oven to 400°F.

Pierce the eggplant all over with a fork; place on an oven rack and roast until soft, about 45 minutes. Let cool; cut off the stem and peel the skin. Mash the eggplant with a large fork in a large bowl, working the garlic, oil, and lemon juice into the mixture as you mash. Stir in the tomatoes and parsley. Season with salt and pepper. Use immediately or store in the refrigerator for up to 2 weeks.

2 tablespoons vegetable oil

2 cups finely chopped onion, fresh or frozen

1 tablespoon minced garlic, fresh or jarred organic

2 tablespoons minced ginger, fresh or jarred

1 cinnamon stick

4 cardamom pods

1½ teaspoons whole cumin seed

2 teaspoons ground turmeric

½ teaspoon crushed red pepper flakes

1 can (about 15 ounces) crushed tomatoes

1½ cups hot water

Kosher salt to taste

curry simmer sauce

This all-purpose curry sauce takes a lot of ingredients and considerable work. I think you should just go buy a jar, but if you can't find it in your local market, and you can't mail order it, or the raj has not yet come to your town, here's an opportunity to roll up your sleeves and get to work.

DIRECTIONS

Heat half the oil in a large, nonstick skillet over medium heat. Add the onion and cook until light brown, stirring often to prevent burning. Add the garlic and ginger and cook until the mixture is fragrant, another minute or two.

Add the remaining tablespoon of oil and the cinnamon, cardamom, and cumin. Cook until the spices puff slightly and begin to brown, about 2 minutes, stirring often. Add the turmeric and red pepper flakes, and stir rapidly for a few seconds. Add the tomatoes, water, and salt and simmer until the sauce is lightly thickened, about 20 minutes. You may need to add more water as the mixture simmers to keep it from getting too thick. Strain out the spices.

Use immediately or store in the refrigerator for up to 2 weeks.

index